IGNITION: BEETHOVEN

Reception Documents from the Paul Sacher Foundation

Edited by
Felix Meyer and Simon Obert

The Boydell Press
2020

IMPRINT

A Publication of the Paul Sacher Foundation

Catalogue of the Exhibition *Ignition: Beethoven – Reception Documents from the Paul Sacher Foundation*
13 November 2020 – 2 March 2021
in the Beethoven-Haus Bonn
An exhibition by the Paul Sacher Foundation,
curated by Felix Meyer and Simon Obert
Exhibition design: Andrea Gruber, Basel

Translations from German: J. Bradford Robinson
(texts by Hermann Danuser, Simone Hohmaier, Matthias Kassel, Felix Meyer, Simon Obert, Wolfgang Rathert, Matthias Schmidt, Michelle Ziegler, and Heidy Zimmermann)
Translations from Italian: John O'Donnell
(texts by Giovanni Cestino and Angela Ida De Benedictis)

Copy editing: Kathryn Puffett
Index: Liisa Lanzrein and Heidy Zimmermann

English language edition published by the Boydell Press
German language edition published by Schott Music, Mainz

Design and typesetting:
Büro für Buchgestaltung Sibylle Ryser, Basel
Reproduction: Bildpunkt AG, Münchenstein/Basel
Setting of musical notation: Notengrafik Berlin
Fonts: FF Scala (Martin Majoor, 1990),
LL Brown (Aurèle Sack, 2011)
Paper: Profimatt 150 gm^2, Algro Design 300 gm^2
Printed by Gremper AG, Basel/Pratteln
Bound by Grollimund AG, Reinach/Basel
Printed in Switzerland

First published 2020
The Boydell Press, Woodbridge, UK
ISBN 978 1 78327 590 8

The Boydell Press is an imprint of Boydell & Brewer Ltd
PO Box 9, Woodbridge, Suffolk IP12 3DF, UK
and of Boydell & Brewer Inc.
668 Mt Hope Avenue, Rochester, NY 14620-2731, USA
www.boydellandbrewer.com

Art responds to art.

Wolfgang Rihm

Preface

The present publication was designed to accompany an exhibition mounted by the Paul Sacher Foundation at the invitation of the Beethoven-Haus in Bonn. As the Foundation's research archive centers on music of the twentieth and twenty-first centuries, and as its holdings largely comprise collections and posthumous estates from composers (plus a few performer collections), it was logical to focus on the reception of Beethoven among composers of the last one-hundred-twenty years. The book thus deals with the manner in which artists have engaged creatively with Beethoven – with his music, his ideas, and everything his name has stood and continues to stand for. In contrast, the other two principal modes of musical reception – analysis and performance – are touched on only peripherally, the first in the form of a few verbal documents from composers, the latter in the form of sources for a Beethoven adaptation by Cathy Berberian. Although both these areas are represented in the Foundation's holdings by quite interesting manuscripts and recordings, they do scant justice to the wide-ranging spectrum of recent Beethoven interpretations and performance traditions. Another reason for limiting ourselves to the reception of Beethoven by composers was that the spatial restrictions at the Beethoven-Haus made it clear from the outset that ours would be a small-scale showcase exhibition.

Even within these limitations, however, the subject still remains vast. Although Beethoven's impact was most immediate in the nineteenth century, countless composers of the twentieth and twenty-first centuries have grappled with him in a great many ways. It is all the more striking, then, that the subject is not nearly as well-researched as one might expect. True, much has been written about the verbal and imaginative ties to Beethoven, our changing image of Beethoven, and the various ways in which he has been politically and ideologically co-opted. We need only mention three earlier "classics": Arno Schmitz's monograph on the Romantic image of Beethoven, Leo Schrade's study of Beethoven in France, and Hans Heinrich Eggebrecht's exhaustive investigation of writings on Beethoven.[1] But to the present day, only halting attempts have been made to produce a broad-based study of Beethoven's reception among twentieth- and twenty-first-century composers that goes beyond isolated figures or pieces.[2]

Nor does our book, being limited to the archival holdings of the Paul Sacher Foundation, seek to create such a larger picture. Nevertheless, to convey an impression of how rich and multifaceted this subject can be, we have attempted within these confines to make our coverage as broad as possible, that is, to display a maximum variety of documents. In our book, these documents – music manuscripts, text manuscripts, photographs, and similar items – are largely presented in full-page reproductions and accompanied by detailed commentaries provided by members of the Foundation's scholarly staff or board of trustees. They are grouped into four chapters, each of which focuses on a particular aspect of Beethoven's reception and is introduced by a longer exploratory essay from a guest author. Chapter 1 is devoted to "Learning and Teaching through Beethoven"; here the focus falls on Beethoven in the

1 Arnold Schmitz, *Das romantische Beethovenbild: Darstellung und Kritik* (Berlin: Dümmler, 1927); Leo Schrade, *Beethoven in France: The Growth of an Idea* (New Haven: Yale University Press, 1942); and Hans Heinrich Eggebrecht, *Zur Geschichte der Beethoven-Rezeption* (Mainz: Akademie der Wissenschaften und der Literatur, 1972); enlarged edn. (Laaber: Laaber, 1994).

2 See especially Reinhold Brinkmann, "Wirkungen Beethovens in der Kammermusik," in *Beiträge zu Beethovens Kammermusik: Symposion Bonn 1984*, ed. Sieghard Brandenburg and Helmut Loos (Munich: Henle, 1987), 79–110; reprinted in idem, *Vom Pfeifen und von alten Dampfmaschinen: Aufsätze zur Musik von Beethoven bis Rihm* (Vienna: Zsolnay, 2006), 32–72; Margaret Notley, "'With a Beethoven-like sublimity': Beethoven in the Works of Other Composers," in *The Cambridge Companion to Beethoven*, ed. Glenn Stanley (Cambridge: Cambridge University Press, 2000), 239–54; Jörn Peter Hiekel, "Der 'moderne' Beethoven: Reflexe auf sein Komponieren in der Neuen Musik," *Neue Zeitschrift für Musik* 175, no. 4 (2014): 34–41, expanded as "Jenseits von Pathos und Banalität: Beethoven-Reflexe in der Neuen Musik," in *Zwischen Bearbeitung und Recycling: Zur Situation der neuen Musik, im Kontext der postmodernen Diskussion über Kunst und Ästhetik der Kunst*, ed. Dieter Torkewitz (Vienna: Praesens, 2016), 67–80; and Rainer Nonnenmann, "Der ewige Revolutionär? Ludwig van Beethoven im gegenwärtigen Komponieren – Teil 1: Orchesterwerke," *MusikTexte* 166 (August 2020): 71–79.

context of teaching and, in some cases, music theory, whether this means the use of his works as models for orchestration exercises or their elevation to stylistic paradigms or embodiments of an exemplary kind of musical logic. In contrast, Chapter 2, entitled "Idealizations," directs the reader's attention to the ideational attributions or excesses to which Beethoven's music has always been prone, whether because of its omnipresence and trenchancy or because of its spiritual content. Chapter 3 then shows several "Strategies of Reference" for making Beethoven our contemporary; here the spectrum ranges from brief quotations and allusions to the "over-painting" of longer stretches of music. Finally, Chapter 4 is devoted to the thematic complex of "Distortion – Dismantlement": the twentieth century in particular has increasingly witnessed the emergence of "Beethoven-critical" works, especially in the context of his commemorative anniversaries, although the critique tends to be aimed at the exaggerated cult of Beethoven rather than his music.

We hope that our book *Iginition: Beethoven* will not only fulfill its function as an exhibition catalogue, but will prove interesting beyond the occasion that gave rise to it. We also hope that it will offer useful stimuli – and perhaps even a pinch of explosives – to spark further study of this virtually inexhaustible subject.

We wish to extend our gratitude to all those persons and institutions that contributed to the success of the exhibition and the present publication. Pride of place must go to the Bonn Beethoven-Haus, especially the former curator of its collection, Michael Ladenburger, and his successor Julia Ronge. It was over two years ago that they approached us with the idea of mounting an exhibition in Bonn during the Beethoven Jubilee – an idea that we gladly accepted. We also wish to thank all the other staff members of the Beethoven-Haus, in particular its director Malte Boecker, who welcomed and decisively supported the project, as well as Nicole Kämpken, Julia Ronge, Christine Siegert, and Ursula Timmer-Fontani, all of whom assisted us in word and deed in a great many ways. We are also indebted to our colleagues at the Paul Sacher Foundation, without whose assistance and ideas it would not have been possible to realize the project in its present form; Liisa Lanzrein, who actively supported us in various matters; Thomas Fichter of Musikfabrik Köln, who took an early interest in the project and joined us in planning the exhibition's musical events; and all those who offered helpful suggestions, advice, and information (here Paul Griffiths deserves special mention). Finally, we are grateful to the authors of the texts and their translators, to Fredi Zumkehr (Bildpunkt), and especially scenographer Andrea Gruber and book designer Sibylle Ryser, who both impressed us once again with their commitment, professionalism, and creativity.

Felix Meyer and Simon Obert

Throughout this book, all archival holdings from the Paul Sacher Foundation are referred to by the collection and the abbreviation "PSS" (e.g. "Igor Stravinsky Collection, PSS").

1

LEARNING AND TEACHING THROUGH BEETHOVEN

Matthias Schmidt

"As Eurydice was seen"
Beethoven and the Teaching of Composition after 1900

The music of Ludwig van Beethoven is considered to have been a driving force behind a fundamental change in listening expectations between the late eighteenth and the nineteenth centuries. In this period, we have been told again and again, the listeners' attention was increasingly directed toward teleological progress and the seamless unifying development of musical processes in accordance with "unalterable rational laws."[1] Until well into the twentieth century Beethoven's music was a major field of activity for music historians and educators. Accordingly, the ideas ascribed to it were also transferred from the world of aesthetics to everyday existence: no other music, it was argued, was better suited to give cultural credence to the guiding economic principles of the modern era, such as labor and rationalization, development and growth.[2] Whether this view can be accounted for primarily by the quality of Beethoven's music, the ease with which it can be taught, or simply by the ideology of "aggressive nationalism"[3] eludes an easy answer. But there can be no doubt that it resulted in the establishment of a long-lasting "Beethoven paradigm"[4] for the whole of Western musical thought, a paradigm with a powerful impact on compositional technique and aesthetics.

Traces of this epochal breech around 1800, between a seemingly natural "sense of tradition" and a newly fertile "awareness of the past," were already evident during Beethoven's lifetime.[5] The associated loss of a "self-evident bidirectional gaze" at past and present[6] already appeared in the way contemporaries dealt with the unique phenomenon of Beethoven. At an early date disconcerted critics spoke of the "dark artificiality or [...] artificial darkness" of Beethoven's piano sonatas, uncomfortably accentuating their artistry and deliberateness.[7] A few decades later, on the other

1 Adolph Bernhard Marx, *Die Lehre von der musikalischen Komposition, praktisch theoretisch*, vol. 3, 3rd edn. (Leipzig: Breitkopf & Härtel, 1857), 604. See also Karl H. Wörner, *Das Zeitalter der thematischen Prozesse in der Geschichte der Musik* (Regensburg: Bosse, 1969), xiii–xxiii.

2 See Anselm Gerhard, "Die 'Vorherrschaft der deutschen Musik' nach 1945 – eine Ironie der Geschichte," in *Deutsche Leitkultur Musik? Zur Musikgeschichte nach dem Holocaust*, ed. Albrecht Riethmüller (Stuttgart: Steiner, 2006), 13–27, esp. 24.

3 Anselm Gerhard, "'Kanon' in der Musikgeschichtsschreibung: Nationalistische Gewohnheiten nach dem Ende der nationalistischen Epoche," *Archiv für Musikwissenschaft* 57 (2000): 18–30, at 25.

4 Lydia Goehr, *The Imaginary Museum of Musical Works: An Essay in the Philosophy of Music* (Oxford: Clarendon Press, 1992), 205–42.

5 Carl Dahlhaus, "Traditionszerfall im 19. und 20. Jahrhundert," in idem, *Gesammelte Schriften*, vol. 1, ed. Hermann Danuser, Hans-Joachim Hinrichsen and Tobias Plebuch (Laaber: Laaber, 2001), 180–95, at 185–95. See also Wolfgang Kaempfer, "Die zerbrochene Zeit: Zum Ausfall des Zeitgetriebes in der europäischen Moderne," in *Entzauberte Zeit: Der melancholische Geist der Moderne*, ed. Ludger Heidbrink (Munich: Hanser, 1997), 120–43, esp. 126.

6 Kaempfer, "Die zerbrochene Zeit" (see note 5), 142.

7 Anonymous review of the three op. 10 piano sonatas in *Allgemeine Musikalische Zeitung* 2, no. 2 (1799): cols. 25–27, at 25.

hand, criticism had turned positive and established the "paradigm": all composition textbooks that touched on Beethoven now praised the deliberate balance he struck between uniqueness and convention, originality and accessibility.

One of the foundational documents of the "Beethoven paradigm" is the well-known adage that Count Ferdinand von Waldstein entered in the young composer's album: "With the help of unceasing diligence you will receive the spirit of Mozart from the hands of Haydn."[8] Its binding character led not only to a far-reaching battle for Beethoven's legacy between the New German School and the circles associated with Johannes Brahms and Joseph Joachim, but also to profound changes in the field of music theory. Waldstein's observation might have served primarily as evidence of facts in the craft of composition. Instead, it was made to carry a metaphysical burden, as when Wagner spoke of the redemption of the "human spirit" through Beethoven's "German spirit."[9] Beethoven's music was thereby perceived at once as a hypertrophic musico-political message and a technically perfect instantiation of structural consistency.

The essential point to note is that the longstanding impact on musical thought and the teaching of composition resulted from the combination of both of these things. The relevant textbooks, from Adolph Bernhard Marx to Hugo Riemann, all of which are fully beholden to Beethoven, thus perpetrated a training method marked by cultural ideology until well into the twentieth century. From the very outset, any claim to rank as art was, for this doctrine, inseparable from the idea of a weighty "earnestness of the creative urge,"[10] both in the handling of themes and motifs (as pure structural elements) and in harmony (in its consistent expansion of late eighteenth-century achievements). Marx, writing in the mid-nineteenth century, already focused the definition of fundamentally new principles of construction exclusively on Beethoven, namely, on the "rational unfolding of the organism," "organism" being the term he and others applied to the work of art.[11] Such "teleological" ideas were in tune with the spirit of the times,[12] and they in turn lent weight to a compositional impact that the whole of nineteenth-century Western musical thought was prepared to define as standard.

Legitimation of the Idea

In many respects, the academic teaching of composition in the early 1990s drew directly on the convictions of the previous century. It can be viewed as an attempt to systematize the above definitions of processuality and developmental logic in Beethoven's music. Beethoven was considered to be the composer who uniquely united the backward glance at classical harmony and counterpoint and the forward glance at its romantic counterparts. His music therefore appeared to be an artistic paragon for the demonstration of coherence, for it engendered trust in the straightforwardness and explicability of a world marked in equal measure by multilayered and sublime inscrutability. In this way, it ideally linked the demands of theorists, who set their sights on systematic thought, and artists, who strove for individual innovations.[13] Consequently, the institutionalized teaching of composition in this period sought to codify and classify just such a view of Beethoven's music, a view widespread in the nineteenth century and still present in Riemann's attempt toward

8 "Durch ununterbrochenen Fleiß erhalten Sie: Mozart's Geist aus Haydens Händen." *Ludwig van Beethovens Stammbuch*, ed. Hans Gerstinger (Bielefeld: Velhagen & Klasing, 1927), n.p. The English translation is taken from Lewis Lockwood, *Beethoven: The Music and the Life* (New York: W.W. Norton, 2005), 50.

9 *Richard Wagner's* Beethoven *(1870)*, trans. Roger Allen (Woodbridge: Boydell, 2014), 91.

10 Jörn Peter Hiekel, "Der 'moderne' Beethoven: Reflexe auf sein Komponieren in der Neuen Musik," *Neue Zeitschrift für Musik* 175, no. 4 (2014): 34–41, at 35.

11 Adolph Bernhard Marx, *Die Lehre von der musikalischen Komposition, praktisch theoretisch*, vol. 1, 5th edn. (Leipzig: Breitkopf & Härtel, 1858), 513.

12 See Wörner, *Das Zeitalter der thematischen Prozesse* (see note 1), xiii.

13 See Scott Burnham's "Posthumous influence and reception" section of "Beethoven, Ludwig van" in *The New Grove Dictionary of Music and Musicians*, ed. Stanley Sadie (London: Macmillan, 2001), vol. 3, 110–14.

PLATE 1
Arnold Schoenberg, teaching at the University of California in Los Angeles; taken from the leaflet "Spring Homecoming" of the UCLA, 1940
(ARNOLD SCHÖNBERG CENTER, VIENNA)

a fully ramified doctrine of music. That Beethoven's oeuvre had risen into the canon of the German musical tradition was initially viewed by educators as an injunction to preserve his achievement.

For good reasons, composers associated with the post-1900 avant-garde, such as Max Reger and Richard Strauss, therefore gave the academic teaching of their era a wide berth, or retreated to a staunchly academic form of music theory remote from their own composing (as did Franz Schreker). In contrast, the young Arnold Schoenberg viewed teaching as a sort of life mission: even at that time he was considered a creator of highly controversial music which, not least from a compulsory need for justification, shaped his theoretical writings and was in turn permeated by them. Nonetheless, before the First World War he was unable to find a position at a larger academic educational institution. He generally taught privately, conveying a blend of compositional rules based on the Viennese classics and free conversation aligned on the individual level of his pupils. A self-taught composer who honed his craft on Beethoven, he noted in his *Harmonielehre* of 1911, not without bitterness, that "the evolution of no other art is so greatly encumbered by its teachers as is that of music." The theorist, he continued, knows that "the pupil learns most of all through the example shown him by the masters in their masterworks"; to secure his own relevance, the theorist therefore "seeks to create a substitute by replacing the living example with theory, with the system."[14] Schoenberg parted ways with Marx and Riemann by envisaging a music theory whose historical awareness is focused on sonic "phenomena," not on "laws we believe we have found."[15]

To the end of his days, Schoenberg tried to find solutions to problems of modern music by analytically studying the music of his forebears.[16] A prime example of this is his use of didactic examples for beginners in his late *Fundamentals of Musical Composition,* which arose from his teaching activities in America (SEE PLATE 1).

14 Arnold Schoenberg, *Theory of Harmony,* trans. Roy E. Carter (London: Faber & Faber, 1978), 7–8. See also Wolfgang Rathert, "Konzeptionen des akademischen Kompositionsunterrichts in der Weimarer Republik," in *Musikkultur in der Weimarer Republik,* ed. idem and Giselher Schubert (Mainz: Schott, 2001), 101–13, esp. 102–03.

15 Schoenberg, *Theory of Harmony* (see note 14), 8.

16 See Neil Boynton, "'And two times two equals four in every climate': Die Formenlehre der Wiener Schule als internationales Projekt," in *Musiktheoretisches Denken und kultureller Kontext,* ed. Dörte Schmidt (Schliengen: Argus, 2005), 203–29.

Of Beethoven's music, he preferred to use the chamber music up to the beginning of the "middle period," i.e. the piano sonatas from opp. 2 to 31 or the op. 18 string quartets. He turned less often to works postdating 1803, and rarely to those from the final period (the first volume of the piano sonatas is even proclaimed, in the *Fundamentals,* to be a "required supplement" to the textbook).[17] Perhaps Schoenberg considered that aspect of Beethoven's late music impractical for teaching that Wagner once called the "abrupt contrastment, the hasty intersection."[18] To Schoenberg, the special suitability of Beethoven's earlier works for teaching beginners resided in their readily intelligible deployment and violation of the traditional canon of rules, and therefore their especially clear definitions of the relation between norm and individuation: "This is Beethoven's principle," he once wrote, "it should come as a surprise, but not unexpected."[19] Even so, in advising his students to draw on the set of rules, he was not pleading on behalf of a "mechanically copied" model; rather, students were meant to assimilate exemplary music via its "mental essence."[20]

Teachability

Just what constituted that "essence" was virtually impossible to grasp in terms of craftsmanship, and as a result composition, for Schoenberg, ultimately remained a "secret science."[21] He constantly stressed the limits of such communicability: teaching composition, he wrote, should "restrict itself to that which is really its task: to help the pupil attain such skills as will enable him to produce something of *established effectiveness,*" and to ensure that "the pupil can produce something which in its materials and techniques resembles older compositions – that is, up to the point where, even in the technical, mechanical aspects, the creative mind forsakes every [conventional] control."[22] In this way Schoenberg's notion of teaching, even with regard to Beethoven, was aimed at the borderline area that appeared still teachable without denying music's fundamental non-teachability. It was in this sense that Erwin Ratz recalled Schoenberg's teaching, which employed Beethoven's sonatas and string quartets, not as formal blueprints, but as a means of "developing the student's individual sense of form."[23]

Schoenberg shared this basic idea of limited teachability with Ferruccio Busoni. Busoni was the first composer in a prominent teaching position (he headed a master class in composition at the Berlin Academy of Arts from 1920 on) to maintain a style of teaching that stood opposed to formalistic doctrines in the artistic spirit of the traditional aesthetic of genius. Moreover, his teaching took place within an educational coterie that, not coincidentally, studied much the same music as Schoenberg (between Bach and Beethoven). To Busoni, the "essence of music" was a *noumenon,* an ideational universe filled with "all forms, motives, and combinations of past and future music."[24] With the initial appointments of Busoni and Pfitzner, and later Schoenberg, Schreker, and Hindemith (an exemplary attempt to establish Berlin "master schools" at the Academy of Arts and the Academic Hochschule),[25] the avant-garde of the 1920s achieved a sort of return to teaching, less in a preliminary sense than with an artistic emphasis.[26] The focus now fell on restoring control over the previously formalized content of composition teaching to its actual creators: the composers themselves.[27]

17 Arnold Schoenberg, *Fundamentals of Musical Composition,* ed. Gerald Strang and Leonard Stein (London: Faber & Faber, 1985), xiv.

18 Richard Wagner, *Opera and Drama,* trans. William Ashton Ellis (Lincoln: University of Nebraska Press, 1995), 73.

19 Warren Langlie, [Interview with Arnold Schoenberg], typescript, 1948–50, p. 248 (Arnold Schönberg Center, Vienna, Satellite Collection L26).

20 Arnold Schoenberg, "Program Notes for the Juilliard String Quartet Performance of the Four String Quartets, end of December 1949 or early January," in idem, *Schoenberg's Program Notes and Musical Analyses,* Schoenberg in Words, vol. 3, ed. J. Daniel Jenkins (New York: Oxford University Press, 2016), 354–96, at 359.

21 Arnold Schoenberg, "On the Question of Modern Composition Teaching," in idem, *Style and Idea: Selected Writings of Arnold Schoenberg,* ed. Leonard Stein (London: Faber & Faber, 1975), 373–76, at 375.

22 Schoenberg, *Theory of Harmony* (see note 14), 11.

23 Walter Szmolyan, "Die Geburtsstätte der Zwölftontechnik: Schönbergs Mödlinger Haus in Gefahr," *Österreichische Musikzeitschrift* 26 (1971): 113–24, at 118 and 120.

24 Ferruccio Busoni, "The Essence of Music: A Paving of the Way to an Understanding of the Everlasting Calendar," in idem, *The Essence of Music and Other Papers,* trans. Rosamond Ley (New York: Dover, 1965), 193–200, at 197.

25 See Wolfgang Rathert, "Die Meisterschulen für Komposition der Akademie der Künste," in *"Die Kunst hat nie ein Mensch allein besessen": 1696–1996, Dreihundert Jahre Akademie der Künste / Hochschule der Künste,* ed. Akademie der Künste and Hochschule der Künste (Berlin: Henschel, 1996), 481–90.

26 See Rathert, "Konzeptionen des akademischen Kompositionsunterrichts" (see note 14), 104.

27 See ibid. and Dörte Schmidt and Franziska Stoff, "Meisterausbildung *und* institutionalisierte 'höhere Bildung'? Die Akademisierung der Kompositionsausbildung in Berlin und ihre kulturpolitische Dynamik," in *Von Arosa nach Leipzig: Hans Schaeuble und sein Kompositionsstudium am Leipziger Konservatorium,* ed. Hans-Joachim Hinrichsen and Urs Fischer (Kassel: Bärenreiter, 2016), 63–113, esp. 82–89.

However, this reattainment of aesthetic liberty harbored the danger of introducing an ideological bias into compositional technique. After all, in addition to the exemplary qualities of norm and violation in Beethoven's music – qualities with advantages for teaching – Schoenberg was unquestionably intent on "constructing a legitimation narrative based on the progress of musical material,"[28] a narrative that made a connection between Beethoven's manner of thematic-motivic composition and his own dodecaphonic method. Schoenberg's pupils Erwin Stein and Josef Rufer likewise evinced such strategic rationales, according to which Schoenberg's technique of developmental variation, in its "thematic homogeneity," harkened back to Beethoven.[29] It was in this spirit that Schoenberg later advised his pupil Anton Webern, in a course on the "Path to Composition with Twelve Tones," to employ examples from Beethoven in order to demonstrate historically the "development" of musical coherence.[30] In consequence, between 1934 and 1938 Webern offered four series of lectures "On Musical Forms," attended by amateurs and members of his own circle of pupils. Here, too, Beethoven's early piano sonatas formed the essential foundation of analysis. In a second part of the learning process, the pupil's compositional exercises were discussed in private individual lessons – a plan fully in keeping with Schoenberg's line of thought.[31]

Webern's image of Beethoven was decisively marked by Schoenberg's doctrine of the "musical idea," and secondarily by the historiology of his academic teacher Guido Adler (he attended the latter's relevant lectures and analysis courses at Vienna University).[32] Schoenberg reclaimed the "ideational" reception of traditions by exploiting their inherent potential for change, pronouncing "I conserve the progress!"[33] The awareness of being firmly grounded in the evolutionary history of music, and thus ineluctably beholden to musical tradition, also nourished Webern's conviction as to how a contemporary music should be conceived: "Beethoven concludes the development of these forms in which ideas were presented. What happened then [...] all makes use of these forms, just as our music does, the music of our day."[34] In this respect, the educational strategies Webern employed in his course on forms reveal a close rapport with Schoenberg's *Fundamentals*. Their goal was to inculcate the underlying formal principles and themes of tradition using structural analyses of musical periods and sentences, with Beethoven's piano sonatas providing the examples:[35] The "period and the eight-bar sentence," he argued, "found their purest expression in Beethoven."[36] For this reason he often used the same examples as Schoenberg, e.g. from Beethoven's early piano sonatas, especially opp. 2, 7, and 10. Schoenberg's and Webern's analyses of the 1930s resemble each other to a tee, and were presumably rooted in the lessons Webern had had with Schoenberg decades earlier.[37]

The things we clearly notice in the development of the teaching of Schoenberg and his pupils from the 1920s on apply to Beethoven historiography as a whole during the same period: it was marked by an anti-Romantic objectivity centered on form, an objectivity that nevertheless claimed to descry a moral force in the powerful creative impetus and superior balance of Beethoven's music.[38] For composers of a younger generation, however, such a "late-classical ideology of humanity" in Beethoven's music was "barely alive nowadays." But this need not imply that interest in the technical side of his music had fundamentally vanished – or

28 Nikolaus Urbanek, "'Man kann nicht mehr wie Beethoven komponieren, aber man muß so *denken* wie er komponierte': Beethoven in der Kompositionslehre der Wiener Schule," in *Mozart und Schönberg: Wiener Klassik und Wiener Schule*, ed. Hartmut Krones and Christian Meyer (Vienna: Böhlau, 2012), 261–88, at 269 and 272.

29 Erwin Stein, "Musical Thought: Beethoven and Schoenberg" [1927], in idem, *Orpheus in New Guises* (London: Rockliff, 1953), 90–95, at 93.

30 Arnold Schoenberg, letter to Anton Webern (carbon copy), 20 January 1931, Arnold Schoenberg Collection, Library of Congress, Washington, DC; quoted from a scan in the letter database of the Arnold Schoenberg Center, Vienna, www.schoenberg.at/scans/DVD033/2016_1.jpg (accessed 9 June 2020). An English translation can be found in Arnold Schoenberg, *Letters*, ed. Erwin Stein, trans. Eithne Wilkins and Ernst Kaiser (London: Faber & Faber, 1964), 146–47.

31 Larger discussion in Neil Boynton, "Einleitung," in Anton Webern, *Über musikalische Formen: Aus den Vortragsmitschriften von Ludwig Zenk, Siegfried Oehlgiesser, Rudolf Schopf und Erna Apostel*, ed. idem (Mainz: Schott, 2002), 11–205.

32 See Gareth Cox, *Anton Weberns Studienzeit: Seine Entwicklung im Lichte der Sätze und Fragmente für Klavier* (Frankfurt am Main: Lang, 1992), 41–43 and 65.

33 Quoted from Dika Newlin, *Schoenberg Remembered: Diaries and Recollections (1938–76)* (New York: Pendragon, 1980), 208 (diary entry of 10 April 1940).

34 Anton Webern, *The Path to the New Music*, ed. Willi Reich, trans. Leo Black (Bryn Mawr: Theodore Presser, 1963), 33.

35 See Else Cross, "Anton von Webern as I knew him," *Royal Academy of Music Magazine* 197 (1969): 11–15, esp. 11–12.

36 Webern, *The Path to the New Music* (see note 34), 33.

37 See Boynton, "And two times two equals four in every climate" (see note 16), 225.

38 See August Halm, *Beethoven* (Berlin: Hesse, 1927), 64–65. See also Scott Burnham, "The four ages of Beethoven: critical reception and the canonic composer," in *The Cambridge Companion to Beethoven*, ed. Glenn Stanley (Cambridge University Press, 2000), 272–91, esp. 282–87.

so claimed Ernst Krenek, a composer thoroughly trained in his craft by Schreker, and the newly fledged creator of a "jazz" opera (*Jonny spielt auf*).[39] Artists such as Krenek, Hindemith, or even Ernst Toch (as is evident in the *Melodielehre* of this Mannheim-trained pupil of Bernhard Sekles)[40] continued to analyze Beethoven in those days and to exploit him for their music. Hindemith, however, who became professor of composition at the Berlin Musikhochschule in 1927, did not espouse the "law" in Schoenberg's sense, much less Webern's nomothetics or the predominance of a "musical idea," which for him was merely a point of departure for traversing the path "from the divine to the earth" during the actual labor of composition.[41] Instead, his teaching was a matter of prosaic craftsmanship, and consequently had the object of conveying a broad range of practical skills to his students, from writing to performance.

In this context, the archaizing modern terminology of Hindemith's *Unterweisung im Tonsatz* (The Craft of Musical Composition) was deliberately chosen: it corresponded to his unemotional, utilitarian view of the teaching of composition, a view directed against the nineteenth-century concept of the "work."[42] Nevertheless, the search for a universal and objective order formed a common bond between Hindemith and Schoenberg in the academic training of composers, a training that has been described as "a synthesis of modernity and classicism."[43] A few years later, however, this fragile unity of academicism and modernity in contemporary music fell asunder: Schoenberg and Hindemith sought separate paths in American exile, and before long Theodor W. Adorno had irreconcilably divided the composing of these two "degenerate" artists into legitimate (progressive) and illegitimate (regressive).[44] At the same time, the ideological appropriation of Beethoven was blithely proceeding under the cultural policies of the Third Reich.

Ban on Regression

The appropriation of the "heroic" Beethoven as "the Nazi musical icon par excellence"[45] left his works amazingly unscathed. One reason for this was that the post-1933 cultural "brain drain" of exiled music intellectuals took with it, as it were, the tradition of definitive Beethoven performance and analysis. (From a sociological standpoint, it is interesting to note that the more markedly European culture unraveled politically, the more staunchly figures such as Schoenberg or his admirer Rudolph Réti, both of whom had been wrenched from their native environment, clung in their textbooks to the notion that Beethoven's works revealed unity in music.[46]) As a result, Beethoven could be used both as a political symbol of resistance to Germany's barbaric treatment of its own culture and as a vehicle for overcoming that very treatment.

Conversely, in the postwar years the cultural climate was filled with the task of liberating music from any taint of political co-optation. A material-based "ban on regression" advanced to become the "basis of aesthetic morality" in the 1950s:[47] the aim was to radically redefine music as a system of communication, together with all the methods and objectives of music theory. Instead of counterpoint, harmony, and form, which were still obligatory in the teaching of Schoenberg or Heinrich Schenker, the principal subject of music theory became the analysis and

39 Ernst Krenek's reply to Felix Joachimson, "Beethoven in der Meinung der jungen Musiker: Eine Rundfrage," *Die literarische Welt* 3, no. 12 (25 March 1927): 3. See also Dominik Hartmann, "Beethovens Ruhm: Versuch einer Entmythologisierung," in *Beethovenjubiläum, 100 Jahre Musikverein, Schauspielfestival: Almanach der Wiener Festwochen 1970*, ed. Kurt Blaukopf (Vienna: Jugend und Volk, 1970), 10–19, esp. 19.

40 Ernst Toch, *Melodielehre: Ein Beitrag zur Musiktheorie* (Berlin: Hesse, 1923). See also Luitgard Schader, "Das Verhältnis von Ernst Tochs *Melodielehre* zu Ernst Kurths *Grundlagen des linearen Kontrapunkts*," *Musiktheorie* 18 (2003): 51–64.

41 Paul Hindemith, "Komposition und Kompositionsunterricht," in idem, *Aufsätze, Vorträge, Reden*, ed. Giselher Schubert (Zurich: Atlantis, 1994), 47–115, at 51.

42 Paul Hindemith, *Unterweisung im Tonsatz*, 3 vols. (Mainz: Schott, 1937, 1939 and 1970). Vols. 1 and 2 published in English as *The Craft of Musical Composition*. Book 1: *Theoretical Part*, trans. Arthur Mendel (New York: Associated Music Publishers, 1942), book 2: *Exercises in Two-part Writing*, trans. Otto Ortmann (New York: Associated Music Publishers, 1941). See also Ludwig Holtmeier, "Von der Musiktheorie zum Tonsatz: Zur Geschichte eines geschichtslosen Faches," *Zeitschrift der Gesellschaft für Musiktheorie* 1, no. 1 (2003): 11–34, esp. 13–15.

43 Rathert, "Konzeptionen des akademischen Kompositionsunterrichts" (see note 14), 104.

44 Ibid., 113.

45 Michael H. Kater, "Introduction," in *Music and Nazis: Art under Tyranny, 1933–1945*, ed. idem and Albrecht Riethmüller (Laaber: Laaber, 2003), 9–14, at 9.

46 See e.g. Rudolph Réti, *The Thematic Process in Music* (New York: Macmillan, 1951), and idem, *Thematic Patterns in Sonatas of Beethoven*, ed. Deryck Cooke (London: Faber & Faber, 1967). Much the same applies to the exiled pupils of Heinrich Schenker, who spread their teacher's Beethoven analyses (e.g. his monographs on the Fifth and Ninth Symphonies) throughout the world.

47 Helmut Lachenmann, "Paradiese auf Zeit: Gespräch mit Peter Szendy," in idem, *Musik als existentielle Erfahrung: Schriften 1966–1995*, ed. Josef Häusler, 2nd edn. (Wiesbaden: Breitkopf & Härtel, 2004), 205–12, at 206.

synthesis of the components of sounds.[48] Once again, as in the early twentieth century, music theory thus found itself uncomfortably "straddling the fence" between academic scholarship and craft apprenticeship.[49] To be sure, the concept of music was radically expanded in avant-garde circles; but at the same time the concept of *Tonsatz* or musical craftsmanship – a concept already ennobled by Hindemith and established during the Third Reich (as opposed to the earlier "music theory") – developed into a politically anodyne, pragmatically aligned technical term in the teaching of composition at institutes of higher learning in the German-speaking regions.[50]

Adorno, a key figure in the debates on the musical avant-garde after 1945, soon clarified how the mentality of postwar composers was to leave its mark on teaching: "One can no longer compose like Beethoven, but one must *think* as he composed."[51] On the one hand, composers who remained in Germany, such as Wolfgang Fortner (one of his pupils was Hans Werner Henze) and Johann Nepomuk David (the teacher of, among others, Helmut Lachenmann) continued to propound the classical Beethoven image as an ideal point of reference in music history. Beginning in 1950 Hanns Eisler, having returned from his American exile, cultivated Schoenberg's focus on Beethoven's music in his master class at the East Berlin Academy of Arts. On the other hand, the young postwar avant-garde sought to radically question the relevance of composers like Beethoven as objects for the learning of music.

It seemed difficult to bridge these two conflicting positions, for "a yawning chasm" had arisen between the "infrastructures" of dodecaphonic music and classical forms,[52] even though, in the eyes of the "Viennese School," both were rooted in the Beethoven tradition of motivic-thematic workmanship. But its legacy became increasingly irreconcilable with the musical philosophy of the early serialists. And it was precisely the classical-romantic legacy of the prewar avant-garde that Pierre Boulez, in self-assured consensus with the *zeitgeist* of the early 1950s, criticized as Schoenberg's reactionary posture.

Underground Traditions

Nonetheless, it is no coincidence that Ernst Krenek, in 1956, delivered a two-part lecture expressly on late Beethoven at the Darmstadt Summer Course, and thus at the educational hub of European avant-garde music. Krenek, now returned from exile (temporarily), was a composer embedded in the benevolent yet critical surroundings of the "Viennese School"; not only had he practiced the techniques of twelve-tone music and serialism himself, he also advocated the *espressivo* style in the spirit of Beethoven's classical-romantic tradition. He therefore straddled an ideological and stylistic divide between the prewar and postwar perspectives present in Darmstadt at the time. That music like Beethoven's can be "thought," if no longer "composed," thus became, for Adorno and Krenek alike, an issue in the relation between music theory and the teaching of composition.

As early as 1940, Krenek had pointed out that, although there used to be a firm system of rules, techniques, and devices – in short, a "method of putting tones together" – that preceded any mastery of the composer's craft, this picture was obsolete in times when "originality" ("with which the musician expresses his own

48 See Gianmario Borio, "Komponisten als Theoretiker: Zum Stand der Musiktheorie im Umfeld des seriellen Komponierens," in *Musiktheoretisches Denken und kultureller Kontext* (see note 16), 247–74, esp. 247–48.

49 Ibid., 257, and Carl Dahlhaus, "Die Musiktheorie im 18. und 19. Jahrhundert: Zweiter Teil," in idem, *Gesammelte Schriften* (see note 5), vol. 4, 411–707, at 438.

50 Holtmeier, "Von der Musiktheorie zum Tonsatz" (see note 42), 13–15.

51 Theodor W. Adorno, *Beethoven: The Philosophy of Music: Fragments und Texts*, ed. Rolf Tiedemann, trans. Edmund Jephcott (Cambridge: Polity Press, 2002), 160.

52 Pierre Boulez, "Schoenberg is Dead" [1951], in idem, *Stocktakings from an Apprenticeship*, ed. Paule Thévenin, trans. Stephen Walsh (Oxford: Clarendon Press, 1991), 209–14, at 212.

personality") was elevated to an aesthetic axiom.[53] However, the large amount of technical knowledge, the preliminary intellectual processes, and thus the conditions necessary to "express" oneself continued to proceed via the assimilation of past music. The "shackles and limitations," he claimed, were an important prerequisite en route to "artistic freedom," this being an unresolvable "dialectic paradox."[54] In this sense, Krenek's Darmstadt lecture on Beethoven's op. 132 string quartet and the *Grosse Fuge* took into account the *zeitgeist*'s demand for total organization of the material by identifying the "radical frugality of the thematic material" and a "developmental character from beginning to end" that "bordered on the dodecaphonic universe." But on the other hand, he stressed the expressively charged simultaneity of "contrasting formal ideas" that resisted assimilation into an organic unity.[55]

In technical terms, Krenek argued from the standpoint of serialism. In aesthetic terms, however, he argued against the co-optation of Beethoven in favor of a purported objectivity and straightforward logic. He did this by emphasizing precisely the irreconcilable and unorthodox nature of his subject, not least in order to counteract the compulsion for coherence in serial music, which allegedly stood in the Beethoven tradition but believed it had left that tradition leagues behind in technique. Krenek gave an up-to-date twist to the ideas of the "Viennese School" and the relevance of the Beethovenian model by pointing to the late works, which held out the prospect of a new path between technoid serialism and the polite classicism of Fortner or David. Accordingly, the notion of a simultaneous culmination of freedom and restriction in late Beethoven also attracted such younger composers and teachers as Luigi Nono, Hans Zender (at the Frankfurt Musikhochschule), and Dieter Schnebel (at the Berlin Musikhochschule), even prompting the latter to forge a connection between the "fractured" formal world of late Beethoven and the "approaching disintegration of bourgeois society."[56]

Examples of a sophisticated Beethoven reception far removed from Germany's zone of nationalist conflict can be found in the teaching and education of Béla Bartók, György Ligeti, and György Kurtág in Hungary. Around the turn of the century, Beethoven was an incontestably central figure for music students in the Austro-Hungarian Empire. Bartók commented in retrospect that the "ideal of beauty" in his youth corresponded "not so much to the manner of Bach or Mozart as to that of Beethoven."[57] Accordingly, he amassed a comprehensive knowledge of Beethoven's music.[58] He already performed the opening movement of the "Waldstein" Sonata at the age of eleven, and a piano transcription of the fugal opening movement of the op. 131 quartet (a piece which, he claimed, set him into "transports of rapture") survives in his hand, presumably prepared when he was thirteen. He spent the first money he ever earned on full scores of Beethoven works (including the *Missa Solemnis*). As a student at the Budapest Academy of Music, he studied the solo piano works and the solo parts of the piano concertos with István Thomán and the chamber music with Hans Koessler. The motivic technique of the latter unquestionably left a mark on his own string quartets (Koessler based his instruction on Ludwig Bussler's *Formenlehre,* which draws fundamentally on Beethoven's music).[59] A few years later, after obtaining a professorship at the Academy of Music in 1907, he was commissioned to prepare annotated editions of

53 Ernst Krenek, "Teaching Composition" [1940], in *Ernst Krenek, Zeitgenosse des 20. Jahrhunderts: Zum 100. Geburtstag / Ernst Krenek, Companion of the Twentieth Century: Birthday Centennial*, ed. Matthias Schmidt (Vienna: Wiener Stadt- und Landesbibliothek, 2000), 95–103, at 95.

54 Ibid., 103.

55 Ernst Krenek, "Beethovens späte Streichquartette" [1956], in *Ernst Krenek – nicht nur Komponist*, ed. Gernot Gruber, Claudia Maurer Zenck and Matthias Schmidt (Schliengen: Argus, 2018), 205–24, at 216–18 and 223. See also Maurer Zenck, "Krenek analysiert Beethoven live," in ibid., 159–82.

56 Dieter Schnebel, "Das angegriffene Material: Zur Gestaltung bei Beethoven," in *Beethoven '70* (Frankfurt am Main: Fischer, 1970), 45–55, at 54.

57 Béla Bartók, letter to Edwin van der Nüll (c. 1927), in Béla Bartók, *Briefe*, ed. János Demény (Budapest: Corvina Press, 1973), vol. 2, 70.

58 Larger discussion in László Vikárius, "Von 'Beethoven und die Ungarn' bis zum 'ungarischen Beethoven': Zu Béla Bartóks Beethoven-Rezeption," in *Beethoven-Rezeption in Mittel- und Osteuropa: Bericht über die Internationale Musikwissenschaftliche Konferenz vom 22. bis 26. Oktober 2014 in Leipzig*, ed. Helmut Loos (Leipzig: Schröder, 2015), 82–95.

59 See Wolfgang Rathert, "Adagio ohne Liebe? Hans Koessler, der Lehrer Bartóks," *Musiktheorie* 31 (2016): 293–309.

Beethoven's piano pieces and sonatas (among other things), of which he produced no fewer than twenty-five of the sonatas by 1912 (only sonatas nos. 28 and 32 were left at the preparatory stage). And, as is well known, he quoted a female friend who called the barely twenty-year-old musician, not without a flirtatious undertone, "'the future Beethoven of Hungary' (!)" – an assessment he was doubtless happy to accept.[60]

After the war, in socialist Hungary, Bartók's role as a folksong collector and radical modernist was regarded with ambivalence. Yet his work left a lasting imprint on the generations that followed. Ligeti, on the lee side of the Western avant-garde, yet interested in its developments, received solid training in the composer's craft from two Bartók pupils, Ferenc Farkas and Sándor Veress. Faced with mediocre instruction in counterpoint,[61] he even sought to orient himself directly on Bartók. Accordingly, Ligeti's string quartets demonstrate a sort of "tissue of generic ties" to those of Bartók and Veress. The points in common between the three composers are in turn rooted in Bartók's classical-romantic training, and thus indirectly on ideational trace elements from Beethoven's music, including the notion of motivic textures evolving from a single germ cell, thinking in terms of developmental processes, and a multi-perspective engagement with sonata form.[62] From 1950 Ligeti himself taught Beethoven's music at the Franz Liszt Academy in Budapest, where he held a teaching position in theory.[63] In 1956 he moved to the West, where, as an outsider, he was little burdened by the ideological clashes in contemporary music. Here he sought an "ambivalent connection" to the strange yet familiar heritage of Austro-German music of the eighteenth and nineteenth centuries. On the one hand, he later said, he "negated" it, while on the other it had "always played a subliminal role" for him.[64] For "behind the music," he explained, "there is a music, and behind that yet another music." The potential "infinite regress" that thereby arose, he continued,[65] made all remembered music appear as if "viewed through an inverted telescope."[66]

It was this deliberate assimilation at one remove, so to speak, that also caused Kurtág, Ligeti's fellow student and an avowed adherent of the Austro-German tradition, to call Bartók's music his mother tongue and, in turn, to trace that music back to Beethoven.[67] A commitment of this sort to Beethoven, viewed through the glasses of a specifically Hungarian tradition (which resided, of course, in such well-known elements as rigorous construction and compressed expressivity), also left deep traces on Kurtág's own highly fertile (instrumental) teaching activities. They show with special clarity how Beethoven's music appears in the background as a stylistic factor while remaining alive as an ideational principle, as a cultural idea, and especially as an "aura of Beethovenian dignity" that persisted like an "underground tradition without revealing the slightest direct connection to Beethoven's stylistic elements."[68] This sort of line of tradition continued, for example, during Peter Eötvös's period of study at the Budapest Academy in the early 1960s, when he prepared stylistic exercises and orchestrations after Beethoven under the Kodály pupil János Viski (SEE PLATE 2, P. 24).

60 Béla Bartók, letter to his mother, 18 June 1903, in idem, *Letters*, ed. János Demény, trans. Péter Balabán and István Farkas, rev. Elisabeth West and Colin Mason (Budapest: Corvina Press, 1971), 25.
61 See Simone Hohmaier, "'Veress war ein Vorbild, aber kein guter Lehrer': Zur Frage einer kompositorischen Veress-Rezeption bei Kurtág und Ligeti," in *Sándor Veress: Komponist – Lehrer – Forscher*, ed. Doris Lanz and Anselm Gerhard (Kassel: Bärenreiter, 2008), 142–58, esp. 143.
62 See ibid., 152–55.
63 See the commentary on Ligeti's *System of Classical Harmony* by Heidy Zimmermann in this volume, 43–46.
64 György Ligeti, quoted from Ove Nordwall, *György Ligeti: Eine Monographie* (Mainz: Schott, 1971), 128.
65 Ibid., 133.
66 György Ligeti, "Raumwirkungen in der Musik Gustav Mahlers," in idem, *Gesammelte Schriften*, ed. Monika Lichtenfeld (Mainz: Schott, 2007), vol. 1, 279–84, at 279.
67 See Simone Hohmaier, *"Meine Muttersprache ist Bartók …": Einfluß und Material in György Kurtágs "Quartetto per archi" op. 1 (1959)* (Saarbrücken: Pfau, 1997), 13.
68 György Ligeti, "Laudatio auf György Kurtág," *Gesammelte Schriften*, vol. 1 (see note 66), 458–89, at 488–89.

PLATE 2
Peter Eötvös, Orchestration of Ludwig van Beethoven's Piano Sonata in C minor, op. 13 (*Pathétique*). Full score fair copy, p. 1
(PETER EÖTVÖS COLLECTION, PSS)

Beethoven the Chameleon

Since the 1960s the view of modernism as the history of a teleologically evolving, integral understanding of order has gradually expanded. Where the integral-serial music of the 1950s was still aligned on the most advanced state of the musical material, a "liberated music" no longer had to be exclusively new in order to be seen as standing at the pinnacle of its age.[69] At the same time, in an often candid engagement with common patterns of tradition, it was associated with a reversion to the previously scorned category of "expression." This took place, for example, on the level of historical homage or compositional collage, with which an art now released from the demand for unconditional novelty sought a foothold in the past. Within this framework, Beethoven was numbered among the composers of rapturous "direct musical utterances," to quote Wolfgang Rihm.[70] This sort of backward-looking "replacement of structure with expression as an ideal"[71] drew above all on the historicist musical tradition of the *fin de siècle* and took shape, despite all its insistence on immediacy, primarily in the form of "music about music." Beethoven, who still

69 See Heinz-Klaus Metzger, "John Cage, or Liberated Music" (trans. Ian Pepper), *October* 82 (1997): 48–61; again in *John Cage*, ed. Julia Robinson (Cambridge, MA: MIT Press, 2011), 1–16.

70 Wolfgang Rihm, "Während der Arbeit an *Tutuguri:* Gespräch mit Hartmut Lück" [1982], in idem, *ausgesprochen: Schriften und Gespräche*, ed. Ulrich Mosch (Winterthur: Amadeus, 1994), vol. 2, 69–78, at 73.

71 Hermann Danuser, *Die Musik des 20. Jahrhunderts* (Laaber: Laaber, 1984), 406.

functioned as a role model around 1900, thus became a stimulus to and a legitimizing factor for composition, now mediated sonically via a roundabout path, e.g. via the late-romantic orchestral sound of Gustav Mahler or Richard Strauss, which was frequently adapted in the 1970s, and which in itself was already the result of a highly deliberated engagement with Beethoven.

The attendant detachment and historicization of Beethoven also had consequences for his role in the teaching of composition, now far more clearly subdivided into work areas than was the case fifty years earlier. Instruction in music theory, which continued to include Beethoven as a matter of course, was now augmented with practical instruction that no longer reflected formal procedures or models, but at most individual observations on particular Beethoven works. In this way, however, experiences drawn from historical ideals of musical craftsmanship could be readily combined with those from the students' own composing and its theoretical contemplation. The resulting points of contact could be seen, for example, in the pedagogically motivated thoughts of Nicolaus A. Huber, who always conducted analyses on the basis of his own compositional experiences (and in this way was able to draw a fruitful comparison between, say, the *Eroica* and a piece by John Cage),[72] or in the work of Salvatore Sciarrino, who built up a figural morphology of music from Beethoven to the present day, and thereby saw general figures of thought already rooted in Beethoven (including, for example, "processes of accumulation" from heterogeneous sonic energies, a phenomenon that Sciarrino observed at the opening of the Ninth Symphony).[73]

The goal of this was by no means to supplant unwanted traditionalism: around 1970 the composer Helmut Lachenmann was convinced that there was no longer an intact semiotic and communicative system of "musical language" that made it possible to communicate in a meaningful way. In the struggle against the ingrained habits of a corrupt music industry, he maintained in the early 1970s, art was a "medium of insecurity," and Beethoven's legacy of treating compositional technique in a critical spirit was particularly compelling.[74] Beethoven's works had, he said, delivered their impact "as a latent or overt scandal, as an expressive redefinition of resources startled out of reification,"[75] and his symphonies were "breaches of socialized sonic ceremonies" to which they in turn owed their "irresistible aura" today.[76] It therefore comes as no surprise that Lachenmann never regretted "working with traditional resources" with his teacher Johann Nepomuk David.[77] Even during his studies with Luigi Nono between 1958 and 1960 he analyzed not only current music but "the works of the old masters" (including Beethoven), "always in ever-new aspects."[78] Later he himself taught theory and ear training at the Musikhochschulen in Hanover and Stuttgart. It was "necessary," he said, for composers to become acquainted with "earlier styles" and to "master them to some extent." Learning from earlier composers, he felt, helped one to "practice their kind of freedom, and to become familiar with and assess its level, in order to derive standards and responsibility for oneself." The resultant "unavoidable conflict with tonal habits of listening" must be made "conscious."[79]

As Adorno once remarked in a similar sense, "Beethoven – his language, his substance and tonality in general, that is, the whole system of bourgeois music – is irrecoverably lost to us, and is perceived only as something vanishing

72 Nicolaus A. Huber, "John Cage: *Cheap Imitation*" [1979], in idem, *Durchleuchtungen: Texte zur Musik 1964–1999*, ed. Josef Häusler (Wiesbaden: Breitkopf & Härtel, 2000), 84–94, at 91. See also Norbert Fröhlich, "Gegenwärtige kompositorische Praxis und auf sie bezogene Theorie," in *Musiktheorie und Komposition: XII. Jahreskongress der Gesellschaft für Musiktheorie Essen 2012*, ed. Markus Roth and Matthias Schlothfeld (Hildesheim: Olms, 2015), 17–31, esp. 23–24.

73 Salvatore Sciarrino, *Le figure della musica da Beethoven a oggi* (Milan: Ricordi, 1998), 29–31. See also Sebastian Claren, "Musikalische Figurenlehre: Salvatore Sciarrino als Analytiker und Komponist," *Musik & Ästhetik* 6, no. 22 (2002): 106–11, and Markus Roth, "Sciarrinos analytischer Blick: Kategorien der Wahrnehmung in 'Le figure della Musica da Beethoven a oggi,'" in *Musiktheorie und Komposition* (see note 72), 77–85.

74 Helmut Lachenmann, "Zum Verhältnis Kompositionstechnik – Gesellschaftlicher Standort," in idem, *Musik als existentielle Erfahrung* (see note 47), 93–97, at 95.

75 Helmut Lachenmann, "Zum Problem des musikalisch Schönen heute," ibid., 104–10, at 108–09.

76 Helmut Lachenmann, "Musik als existentielle Erfahrung: Gespräch mit Ulrich Mosch," ibid., 213–26, at 226.

77 Helmut Lachenmann, "Werkstatt-Gespräch mit Ursula Stützbecher," in ibid., 145–52, at 145. In this context see e.g. the Beethoven examples in Peter Hölzl, *Der Lehrer Johann Nepomuk David: Aus dem Unterricht bei J. N. David an der Stuttgarter Musikhochschule* (Vienna: Doblinger, 1992), 29, 37–40 and 42.

78 Lachenmann, "Paradiese auf Zeit" (see note 47), 205.

79 Lachenmann, "Werkstatt-Gespräch" (see note 77), 145.

from sight. As Eurydice was seen. *Everything* must be understood from that perspective."[80] Perhaps the most obvious sign of such a gain in depletion was the growing interest of composers in the history of Beethoven's impact. To reflect the Beethoven myth in a critical spirit, but at the same time to campaign on behalf of his music, was the driving force behind works of the 1970s and 1980s from Kagel's *Ludwig van* and Reiner Bredemeyer's *Bagatellen für B.* to Luc Ferrari's *Strathoven*.[81] The main focus of their treatment of Beethoven resided above all in social and economic questions associated with the formation of the musical canon, nourished on the magnetic attraction of a reception spanning more than two centuries.[82]

Hans Heinrich Eggebrecht once noted that a "Beethoven as he really was" – an "original" awaiting discovery among the accumulated debris of history – never existed. Rather, Eggebrecht continued, he had always been a construct of that history, completely and irreversibly.[83] This awareness found expression in a shift from the analysis of Beethoven as composer to the examination of the manner in which he was, and currently still is, constructed by posterity. In other words, Beethoven, as both an object and a product of cultural ideologies in the age of "music about music," ekes out his existence in critically reflected quotations and stylistic allusions. It seems to fit this form of perception at one remove that the subject of instruction in music theory today is generally nothing more than Beethoven's craftsmanship rehashed in casebook examples.

And yet, this does not preclude the possibility that Beethoven's music itself, and not just the study of its reception, can, in the future, also form part of a compositional theory of "thinking in notes." In more recent musical creations it is hardly possible any more to keep theoretical and compositional thought meaningfully separate, and artistic reflection on one's own actions may still harbor many a surprising challenge in the music of Beethoven the chameleon.[84] Nonetheless, the once tight-knit tension between ideology and technique which, in Beethoven, maintained its impact for such a long time as both scandal and inspiration, seems to have been largely neutralized in its significance for composing today.

80 Adorno, *Beethoven: The Philosophy of Music* (see note 51), 6.

81 See e.g. Hiekel, "Der 'moderne' Beethoven" (see note 10), 35–38.

82 See Margaret Notley, "'With a Beethoven-like sublimity': Beethoven in the Works of Other Composers," in *The Cambridge Companion to Beethoven* (see note 38), 239–54.

83 Hans Heinrich Eggebrecht, *Zur Geschichte der Beethoven-Rezeption*, 2nd edn. (Laaber: Laaber, 1994), 20–23.

84 See Wolfgang Hufschmidt, *Denken in Tönen: Eine Einführung in die Musik als Komposition* (Saarbrücken: Pfau, 2004).

Henry Brant
Arrangement of the "Hammerklavier" Sonata, op. 106 (c. 1935)

To connoisseurs of recent music history, Henry Brant (1913–2008) is known above all as a pioneer of "spatial music," a composer who made a seminal contribution to experimental music in the United States with large-scale works formed from the clash and combination of sub-ensembles. An extremely versatile musician active as a conductor, multi-instrumentalist, theorist, and teacher, Brant was, however, by no means a radical iconoclast: on the contrary, he drew on a deep knowledge of European and American musical traditions. Not the least expression of his ties to the past are his many arrangements of works by other composers, from Josquin Desprez to Charles Ives. Although some of these arrangements were originally written for special occasions, many arose simply from curiosity – that is, from a desire to illuminate certain well-known masterpieces by transcribing them for other instruments. Perhaps the *opus summum* of the latter was his orchestration of Charles Ives's *Concord Sonata*, a project that occupied him for decades until its completion in 1994, producing a brilliant reinterpretation of the original.[1] In contrast, his arrangement for wind quintet of Beethoven's String Quartet in C-sharp minor (op. 131) – to choose only one example – was written for a particular occasion: it was commissioned by the Dorian Woodwind Quintet, which gave his "translation" its première in New York on 10 February 1971.

But even as a young man Brant, with his arrangements, made a particular study of Beethoven's late works. Evidence of this is provided by several pieces from the early 1930s preserved among his posthumous papers, including the two transcriptions here on display: a two-piano arrangement of the *Grosse Fuge* in B-flat major, op. 133 (SEE PLATES 1 AND 2, PP. 28–29), and a string quartet arrangement of the great "Hammerklavier" Sonata in B-flat major, op. 106. The son of a professional violinist, Brant grew up in Montreal and studied in New York at the Institute of Musical Art and the Juilliard Graduate School, where his teachers included Leopold Mannes and Rubin Goldmark (composition) and James Friskin (piano). At the same time, somewhat as a counterweight to the traditional alignment of the curriculum at these institutions, he took informal lessons from such modernist figures as Henry Cowell, Aaron Copland, Wallingford Riegger, and Goerge Antheil. (He once said, in retrospect, that during these years he led a sort of musical double life: "[T]he way to exist was to write one kind of music for the Juilliard School, for my conservative instructors, and another kind for downtown where they really composed music."[2]) The suspicion arises that both of these Beethoven arrangements originated as assignments during his studies at the Institute of Musical Art or the Juilliard Graduate School. However, positive proof has not been forthcoming, and it is equally possible, perhaps even more likely, that they served other purposes. For instance, Brant may well have prepared his arrangement of the *Grosse Fuge* (he later gave it the date "ca. 1933") for his own use as a pianist, for at the time he made several appearances in a piano duo with fellow students Edna Bockstein, Estelle Best, and Betty Lasley. Perhaps it was conceived as an alternative to Beethoven's own arrangement of the piece for piano duet (op. 134), which is rather inconvenient to play, as the players' hands sometimes get in each other's

1 See Wolfgang Rathert, "The ever flowing, changing ways of mind & imagination': Charles Ives, Henry Brant und *A Concord Symphony*," *Mitteilungen der Paul Sacher Stiftung* 31 (2018): 17–24.

2 Frank J. Oteri, "Spaced out with Henry Brant" (Interview with Henry Brant) in *NewMusicBox*, 1 January 2003, https://nmbx.newmusicusa.org/spaced-out-with-henry-brant/3/ (accessed 11 June 2020).

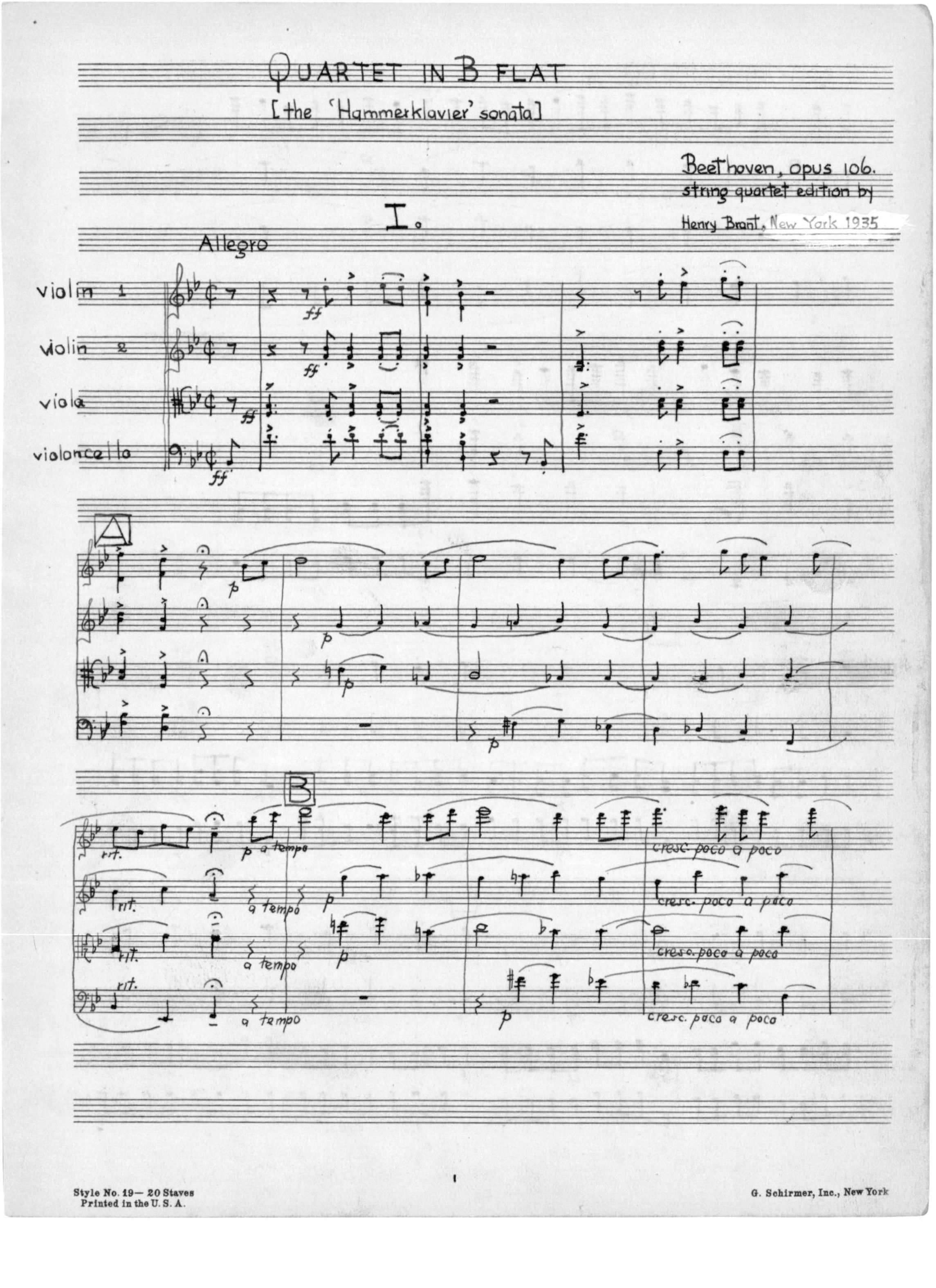

PLATE 1

Henry Brant, String quartet arrangement of Ludwig van Beethoven's Piano Sonata in B-flat major, op. 106 ("Hammerklavier") (c. 1935). Full score fair copy, p. 1

(HENRY BRANT COLLECTION, PSS)

PLATE 2
Henry Brant, Two-piano arrangement of Ludwig van Beethoven's *Grosse Fuge* in B-flat major for string quartet, op. 133 (c. 1933). Cover
(HENRY BRANT COLLECTION, PSS)

PLATE 3
Ludwig van Beethoven, Piano Sonata in B-flat major, op. 106, in *32 Sonatas for the Pianoforte, "Memorial Edition,"* ed. Artur Schnabel (New York: Simon and Schuster, 1935), 691
(HENRY BRANT COLLECTION, PSS)

way. The "Hammerklavier" transcription, dated "1935,"[3] proceeded so to speak in the opposite direction, namely, from the piano to the string quartet, and may have been conceived with a particular ensemble in mind. One possibility is the Toronto-based Hart House String Quartet, with which Brant's father in particular was on friendly terms.

Although the circumstances of their origin are unclear, both Beethoven arrangements can be considered prime examples of "learning from Beethoven." In all of his transcriptions, even those associated with particular occasions, Brant's goal was to deepen his understanding of the works in question. Not least of all, he apparently felt a need in his work as an arranger to perfect his command of instrumentation, of which he was especially proud. (He ultimately passed on his expertise in this area in the form of a weighty, posthumously published textbook.[4]) It comes as no surprise, then, that late Beethoven spurred him to several such efforts at arrangement and self-instruction; after all, the late quartets and piano sonatas, not to mention the *Missa Solemnis*, have always been regarded as unruly, "modern," and hence perennially relevant, even for contemporary music. This was doubtless one of the reasons why Brant always kept several of these works within easy reach, even in advanced age, and why a printed edition of the "Hammerklavier" Sonata lay among the music on his piano at the time of his death.[5]

What makes Brant's quartet arrangement of this work especially interesting is the fact that in several details, even those unrelated to the specific potential and limitations of the chosen ensemble, it departs from every printed edition of the original, including the roughly contemporary "Memorial Edition" published in 1935 by Artur Schnabel, of which Brant likewise owned a copy (**SEE PLATE 3**). This suggests that he was not primarily concerned with a one-to-one transcription with "maximum fidelity to the original," but rather with an interpretation or "resetting" (the term he used on the manuscript's

3 This information in the manuscript is a later emendation; the original date is illegible.
4 Henry Brant, *Textures and Timbres: An Orchestrator's Handbook* (New York: Carl Fischer, 2009).
5 Information kindly supplied by Henry Brant's widow, Kathy Wilkowski, on 14 January 2020. The edition is a partly annotated, partly photo-reproduced copy of the 1923 Schirmer edition by Hans von Bülow and Sigmund Lebert (with translations by Theodore Baker).

dustcover) appropriate to the instruments at hand. What this implies can be seen in the very first bars of the opening movement, where he reduces or "centers" Beethoven's spacious opening gesture, spanning a good four octaves with the outside pitches B♭1 and D5 (E♭5), by transposing the bass part upward and lowering the descant to half of its compass, so that the outside pitches now read B♭2 and D4 (E♭4). Although this procedure facilitates the work's performance, even making feasible Beethoven's extremely fast, if unspecified, tempo indication (half note = 138), it diminishes the explosive impact of the opening gesture. This can be readily heard by comparing it with David Plylar's quartet arrangement of 2015, recorded on CD by the Leipzig String Quartet. Here the spatial proportions of the original are retained, but at the price of transposing the entire work to C major.[6] (In Plylar's version the work begins with C2, the lowest pitch available on the cello.)

In compensation, Brant made all the more sophisticated minor adjustments to the compositional fabric and articulation, adjustments that are no less numerous than the above-mentioned octave transpositions. To take an example, in mm. 5ff., immediately after the *fortissimo* motto, Beethoven's three-voice texture with the cantabile theme in the upper voice is thickened into a four-voice texture by doubling the parts and filling in the implicit harmonies. At the same time, the upper-voice melody is given a more pronounced formal articulation than in the original. In this way, the arrangement also has an element of "analytic instrumentation" of the sort practiced a few years earlier by Arnold Schoenberg and especially Anton Webern.[7] It is precisely this combination of pragmatism (demonstrated here by the changes of register) and analytic inquiry that characterizes Brant's "Hammerklavier" arrangement (and some of his other arrangements), and that comes to the fore again and again in the life's work of a musician open not only to film and radio but equally to experimentation.

Felix Meyer

6 Ludwig van Beethoven, *Arrangements for String Quartet* (Piano Sonata, op. 106, *Leonore* Overture no. 3, op. 72b, and *Fidelio* Overture, op. 72), Leipzig String Quartet (Detmold: Dabringhaus & Grimm, 2018). MDG 307 2072-2.

7 See Carl Dahlhaus, "Analytical instrumentation: Bach's six-part ricercar as orchestrated by Anton Webern" [1969] in idem, *Schoenberg and the New Music: Essays*, trans. Derrick Puffett and Alfred Clayton (Cambridge: Cambridge University Press, 1988), 181–91.

Edgard Varèse
Lecture in Santa Fe
(1937)

Varèse, with Wallingford Riegger, once introduced a combination of left-bank café life and *stammtisch* to New York. [...] They reserved space in a mid-town restaurant and every week more and more musicians came from all sections of New York and the countryside. Everything went along beautifully until [Carl] Ruggles got into an argument with a waiter who said he thought Mozart was greater than Beethoven. Varèse said we cannot have men with such closed minds waiting on us. So we moved the whole group to a restaurant in Greenwich Village for a while.[1]

Although Edgard Varèse (1883–1965) had studied in Paris at the Schola Cantorum (1904–05) and the Conservatoire (1906–07), to the end of his days he saw himself as only marginally representative of French music. For one thing, his relationship to his teachers at those institutions, and still more to their teachings, was by no means unclouded. For another, he felt a close rapport with German musical culture, particularly following his multi-year stay in Berlin, which he decided to undertake immediately after finishing his studies. In the final analysis, national traditions meant far less to him than individual artistic achievements; and since he viewed himself to a great extent as an initiator and innovator, he was mainly interested in those predecessors who had brought about major evolutionary leaps, from Monteverdi and Rameau to Wagner and Musorgsky. It was only natural that Beethoven, too, assumed an important place in this "ancestral gallery."

In the decades between Varèse's student years, when he tried his hand at the *Egmont* Overture in a conducting class headed by Vincent d'Indy,[2] and the end of his career, when he enjoyed great esteem but faced creative aridity, his relation to Beethoven underwent certain shifts of emphasis. In an interview conducted in New York in the 1920s, the period of his greatest successes, he referred to Beethoven as both a great artist and "a bore" of no current relevance.[3] Overstatements of this sort were thoroughly characteristic of Varèse, who, after emigrating to the United States in December 1915, took up the cudgels for modern music as an ad hoc conductor, eloquent proselytizer, and especially as a tireless and militant concert organizer. As such, his gaze naturally tended to point toward the future rather than the past.[4]

In the 1930s, in the throes of the Great Depression, the contemporary music scene suffered an almost complete loss of its material basis, and Varèse, like many of his colleagues, had to seek new bearings. In his case the problems were exacerbated by various ailments and a work block, and the realignment caused him to take on more conducting duties (especially with choruses) and lecture engagements. In keeping with the spirit of the times, this brought him into contact with a "general" non-specialist public, and he increasingly concentrated on combining the music of the present with early music and viewing it as a logical and organic continuation of tradition. Good examples of this are the six lectures that he delivered in August and September 1937 at

1 Otto Luening, Funeral oration for Varèse, delivered in McMillin Theater, Columbia University, on 15 November 1965; published in *Columbia University Forum* 9, no. 2 (spring 1966): 18–20, at 19.

2 See Paul Le Flem's memoir "Vincent d'Indy tel que je l'ai connu," *Musica Disques* 93 (December 1961): 11–15, esp. 15.

3 H.S.G., "Edgar Varèse Interviewed: Shocks for Mus. Docs.," *Musical News and Herald* (London), no. 1682 (21 June 1924): 584–85, at 584.

4 See Felix Meyer, "'The exhilarating atmosphere of struggle': Varèse as a Communicator of Modern Music in the 1920s," in *Edgard Varèse: Composer, Sound Sculptor, Visionary*, ed. Felix Meyer and Heidy Zimmermann (Woodbridge: Boydell, 2006), 82–91.

the Arsuna Galleries in Santa Fe, New Mexico, under the title "Music as Living Matter." Proceeding from the conviction that music must be understood primarily as an acoustical rather than a written phenomenon, he offered his audience a glimpse into the properties of the instruments (or instrument families) of the orchestra. According to the printed announcement, he divided them into "Woodwinds" (10 August), "Brass" (24 August), "Strings" (31 August), and "Harp and Percussion" (7 September), and illustrated their specific use with "Examples from Beethoven's 5th and 7th Symphonies" (14 September) and "Examples from Brahms's 1st Symphony and Ravel's Bolero" (21 September).[5]

Of the partly extant notes to these lectures, we have chosen to exhibit those for the penultimate lecture referring to Beethoven's Seventh Symphony. Here Varèse roughly outlined the work's formal design with special emphasis on its orchestration (SEE PLATE 1). The notes reveal that his lectures were intended for a lay audience, and that he accordingly sought a clear and readily intelligible language. But they also reveal that his attitude toward tradition had changed and deepened since the 1920s: instead of parting company with the music of the past, he now viewed it as an essential breeding ground for the innovations of contemporary music, including his own, which he touched on in the fourth lecture using his percussion piece *Ionisation*. This attitude helps to explain why he also spoke in Santa Fe of Brahms, a composer who until then had barely figured in his musical universe.[6] In contrast, it was fully natural that he should include Beethoven, for unlike Bach, whom he viewed as "the culmination of an epoch and, therefore, the forerunner of decadence," he saw in Beethoven primarily the "originator of a new period in music."[7] His interest in Beethoven may also have been sharpened by an experience he had made in conjunction with a concert performance of the Seventh Symphony: namely, that sounds, like light, can be bundled into rays and can move in space. However contingent this experience may have been to Beethoven's music, he frequently claimed that he derived one of his most important aesthetic concepts from it: the idea of music as a sonic projection in space.[8]

Finally, yet another facet of Varèse's relation to Beethoven came to the fore in his late period, overshadowed by the nagging feeling that he was insufficiently appreciated, not only by the powers-that-be in musical life, but by a good many fellow composers. This feeling was scarcely rooted in reality, for although he no longer stood in the limelight as he had during his breakaway years after the First World War, he was nevertheless revered by many younger musicians, not only from the world of art music. It is probably best understood as an upshot of his declining creativity and a deep dissatisfaction at the fact that he found it increasingly difficult to commit his musical ideas coherently to paper. (In the eleven years following the première of *Déserts* in December 1954, he managed only to complete the *Poème électronique* and part of *Nocturnal*.) In this situation, Beethoven could serve him as a guiding light in two respects: as a fighter who resolutely faced all of life's adversities, and as an artist who, in most cases, could realize his musical ideas only in an arduous process of sketching.

This, in any case, may explain why Varèse, in his later years, kept a small portrait of Beethoven propped up on his studio desk. The furnishings and atmosphere of this studio are captured in various photographs, of which perhaps none is more suggestive than the one shown here (SEE PLATE 2, P. 34). It was taken by the Swiss-born photographer Robert Frank (1924–2019), who emigrated to the United States in 1947 and created a stir, especially with

5 This sequence can be reconstructed from the reviews in the *Santa Fe New Mexican*. In contrast, the printed flyer from which the above titles are taken has the lectures scheduled without exception at weekly intervals, and thus ending on 14 September 1937. Moreover, it reverses the order of the third lecture (on the harp and percussion) and the fourth (on the strings). See the flyer and reviews in the Edgard Varèse Collection, PSS.

6 Shortly before, in 1933, Arnold Schoenberg had stressed Brahms's role as a forerunner of contemporary music in a famous radio broadcast later entitled "Brahms the Progressive," which was not published until 1950 and was thus most likely unknown to Varèse. See Arnold Schoenberg, "Brahms the Progressive," in idem, *Style and Idea* (New York: Philosophical Library, 1950); reprinted in *Style and Idea: Selected Writings of Arnold Schoenberg*, ed. Leonard Stein (London: Faber & Faber, 1975), 398–441.

7 Michael Sperling, "Varèse and Contemporary Music," *Trend* 2, no. 3 (May-June 1934): 124–28, at 124.

8 See e.g. Varèse's statements in "Varèse Envisions 'Space' Symphonies," *The New York Times* (6 December 1936): N7.

PLATE 1
Edgard Varèse, Lecture delivered on 14 September 1937 in the lecture series "Music as Living Matter," Arsuna Galleries, Santa Fe. Handwritten notes, p. 3
(EDGARD VARÈSE COLLECTION, PSS)

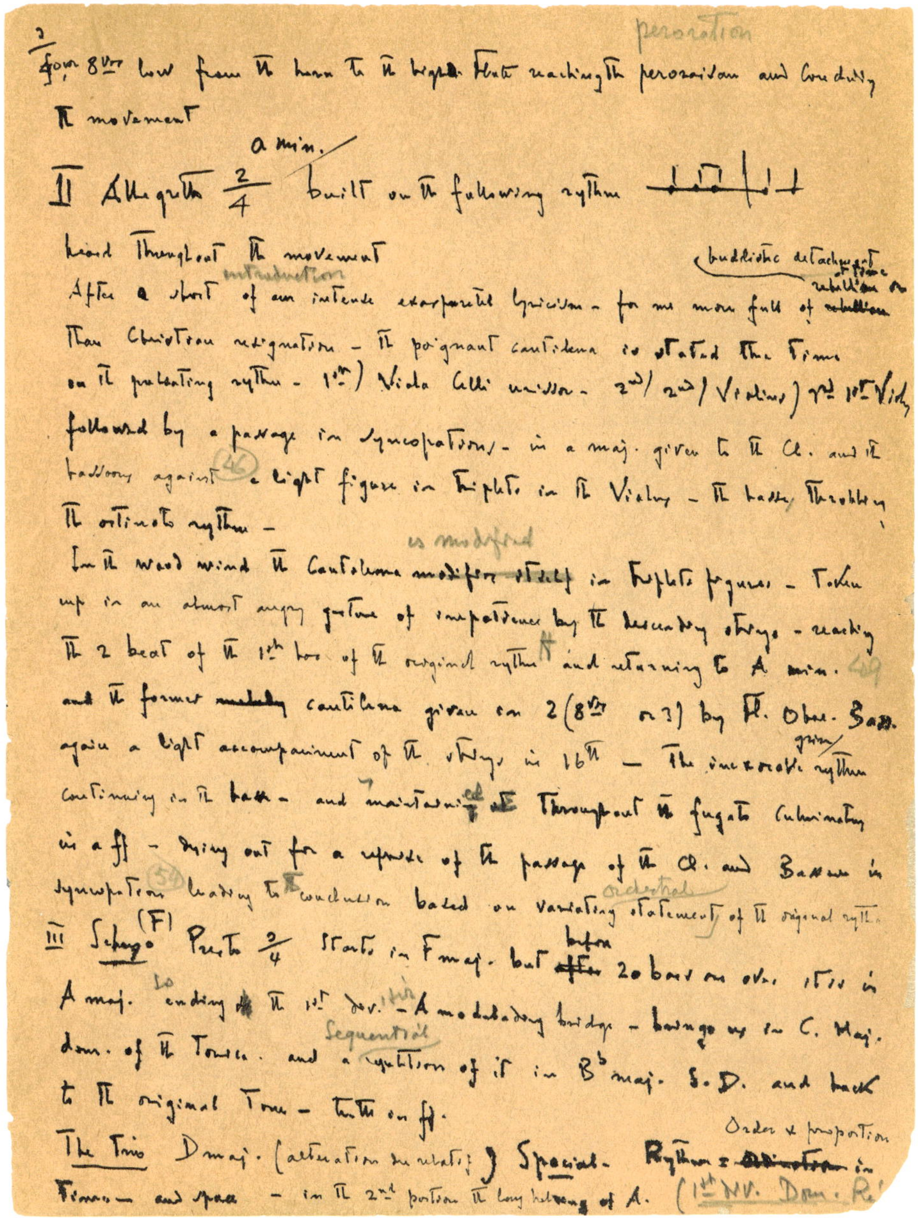

TRANSCRIPTION (FROM LINE 3)

II Allegretto 2/4[,] a min.[,] built on the following r[h]ythm ♩♫|♩♩ heard throughout the movement[.]

After a short introduction of an intense exasperated lyricism – for me more full of rebellion or buddhistic detachment of time than Christian resignation – the poignant cantilena is stated three times in the pulsating r[h]ythm – 1st) Viola Celli unisson [*sic*] – 2nd) 2nd (Violins) 3rd[)] 1st Violins [–] followed by a passage in syncopations – in a maj. given to the Cl. and the bassoons against [46] a light figure in triplets in the Violins – the basses throbbing the ostinato r[h]ythm –

In the wood wind the Cantilena is modified [*corrected from:* modifies itself] in triplets [*sic*] figures – taken up in an almost angry gesture of impatience by the descending strings – reaching the 2[nd] beat of the 1st bar of the original r[h]ythm ff and returning to A min. [49] and the former cantilena given in 2 (8^{vas} or 3) by Fl. Oboe. Bass. again a light accompaniment of the strings in 16th – the inexorable grim r[h]ythm continuing in the basse [*sic*] – and is maintained throughout the fugato culminating in an ff – dying out for a reprise of the passage of the Cl. and Bassoon in syncopation [54] leading to the conclusion based on variating [*sic*] orchestral statements of the original r[h]ythm[.]

III Scherzo (F) Presto 3/4[.] Starts in F maj. but before 20 bars are over it is in A maj. so ending the 1st division – A modulating bridge – brings us in C Maj. dom. of the Tonica and a sequential repetition of it in B♭ maj. S.D. and back to the original Tone – tutti in ff.

The Trio D maj. (alteration du relatif) Special – r[h]ythm = Order + proportion in time – and space – in the 2nd portion the long holding of A. (1st div. Dom. Rel[.)]

PLATE 2
Robert Frank, photograph of Edgard Varèse's desk in New York City (1962)
(EDGARD VARÈSE COLLECTION, PSS)

his documentary picture-book *The Americans.*[9] In the 1960s he was closely connected with New York's downtown scene, where he also met Varèse. Though it shows only the composer's hands, this photograph, published in *Harper's Bazaar* in 1962, vividly conveys the predicament of the ageing artist, with time literally slipping through his grasp.[10] Only orientation on the great achievements of the past, symbolized here by the Beethoven portrait, can give him the hope of likewise leaving behind something lasting and valid.

Felix Meyer

9 Robert Frank, *The Americans,* Introduction by Jack Kerouac (New York: Grove Press, 1959). The volume was first published in French one year previously as Robert Frank, *Les Américains* (Paris: Delpire, 1958).

10 Robert Frank, "Edgar Varèse [–] Willem de Kooning," photo series in *Harper's Bazaar,* no. 3012 (November 1962): 166–69, photo on 168.

Bruno Maderna
Orchestration of the Piano Sonata, op. 7, movt. 1
(c. 1937–38)

It is not uncommon to find in composers' archives exercises dating back to their years of study, often required by the official syllabus. Tasks such as fugues, counterpoint exercises, harmonizations, or orchestrations, often sketched with a still hesitant hand, are made to look even more insecure because of the corrective interventions by the teacher. Such exercises, carried out within an established training process, rarely reflect any special interest of the student concerned; it is only with due caution therefore that they can be considered as genuine reception documents. Nevertheless, they are of extreme interest if one wishes to understand the historical and pedagogical coordinates of an era and to reflect on both the system and the context that have enabled, even indirectly, the emergence or perpetuation of certain models within a process of musical training.

Classifiable in this category are two different orchestrations of the beginning of the first movement of Beethoven's Piano Sonata, op. 7, conserved in Bruno Maderna's papers (SEE PLATES 1 AND 2, PP. 36 AND 39). Both manuscripts are undated and consist of a bifolium, used on all four sides, bearing the logo of the Mario Gasparini company of Venice and the personalized stamp "Bruno Maderna – Verona."[1] This is the typical music paper used by Maderna (1920–1973) from the second half of the 1930s and can be found in almost all the sketch materials of the works of the '40s. This evidence, along with information found in the composer's correspondence and other archival materials, allows us to place the drafting of these two transcriptions with a fair degree of approximation in late 1937 or early 1938. More precisely, these exercises were prepared in the context of rigorous studies taken with Alessandro Bustini at the Santa Cecilia Conservatory in Rome, where Maderna duly completed the advanced composition courses, after years that had been rather disorganized in terms of musical training because of his conducting career as an *enfant prodige*.[2]

It is to Bustini that we can trace the copious handwritten corrections, erasures, and additions that are visible in the first bifolium (PLATE 1), which contains an orchestration consisting of mm. 1–24 of the first movement of the sonata. For example, the strict teacher is responsible for the "div." (*divisi*) added to the cellos in m. 2 or, a little further along on the staff of the same instrumental voice, the indication to entrust to the violas the three lowest notes of the chords that underpin mm. 5–6, emulating the same timbral profile in unison with the bassoons. By comparison, the second orchestration (PLATE 2) is limited to mm. 1–21 of the original and is much less complete. Only the first six measures can be considered fully orchestrated, whereas the following mm. 7–21 are reduced to the main voices.[3]

Despite the incompleteness of the second exercise, certain details can be noted in the choices made by Maderna towards this piano sonata, which, because of its compositional peculiarities, already seems to suggest orchestral sonorities. Both orchestrations are for the so-called "classical orchestra" (with double woodwinds) typical of many Beethoven symphonies. Compared to this orchestral model, perfectly complied with in the second transcription,

1 The bifolium of the second orchestration (Plate 2) was used upside-down. Previously it had already been used for the drafting of an unidentified "5° divertimento" (as is legible, again upside-down, at the bottom of page 4), the traces of which are visible beneath the numerous erasures.

2 Maderna graduated in composition from the Conservatory in Rome on 14 June 1940, after three years of attendance. His initial musical training in the field of composition had been provided by private teachers, including Arrigo Pedrollo.

3 The fundamental orchestration choices are inferable from the notation, but it cannot be assumed with certainty which measures or, to be more precise, staves left blank are to be meant simply as rests.

PLATE 1
Bruno Maderna, Orchestration of Ludwig van Beethoven's Piano Sonata in E-flat major, op. 7, movt. 1 (c. 1937–38). 1st full score with annotations by Alessandro Bustini, p. 1
(BRUNO MADERNA COLLECTION, PSS)

the absence of trumpets in the first orchestration is striking. It is precisely this difference that distinguishes the opening gesture, marked by the repeated tonic for 2+2 measures, in the two instrumentations. In the first version, the repeated notes of the left hand are entrusted to the timpani and the double bass, with the latter precisely observing the dynamic articulation and the octave leap of the original. In the second orchestration, the presence of the trumpets makes the sound profile much more martial and allows additional experimentation with the dynamic levels (and the contrast between the initial *piano* and the *sforzato* of m. 3) by means of timbre. The double basses no longer slavishly follow the original: the initial "reinforcement," provided by the octave leap in the sonata, is realized in m. 1 in the form of an accent placed on the first eighth note in the double basses and timpani, while the *sforzato* in m. 3 is further emphasized by the entrance of the trumpets (in octaves) and by the move of the repeated E♭ to the lower octave in the double bass. In general, the first orchestration appears more conventional in terms of the subdivision of the main voices and the filling out of string and wind parts, while the second exercise, despite its incompleteness, seems to reveal writing that is more skillful and independently thought out.

In both orchestrations we recognize the traces of a concept of instrumentation suited to a specific period of apprenticeship, as well as signs of the highly conflicted relationship that Maderna had at the time with Bustini because of his teaching methods,[4] which were utterly traditional and faithful to the requirements of a recently introduced curriculum. It must be remembered that the new "Norme per l'ordinamento dell'istruzione musicale e approvazione dei nuovi programmi di esame" (Rules for the organization of music education and approval of new examination programs) had been approved in Italy only on 11 December 1930, with Royal Decree No. 1945.[5] After years of complaints and uncertainties concerning the previous official rules,[6] the teaching of composition was adjusted to ten years (with three different levels, "lower," "middle" and "upper," of 4+3+3 years) and divided into the subjects harmony, counterpoint, fugue, composition, and instrumentation. From the end of 1930, therefore, instrumentation became mandatory in the examination program of the upper level, thus becoming an integral part of the teaching in Italian conservatories.

The composers and models that were to be the subjects of instrumentation, however, were the prerogative of the teacher on duty, who chose according to his own ideas, without taking into account those of the student. Or, at least, so it was in the case of Bustini, who was quick to mock in class the orchestral models that Maderna loved at the time (Debussy, Hindemith, and, above all, Stravinsky), imposing instead the traditional greats, especially the German ones.

Thus, it could almost be hypothesized that Maderna began the second draft precisely to give free rein to his own independent orchestral transcription of the Beethoven sonata, free from his teacher's basic corrections. A teacher who had always tried to control and subdue the overflowing talent of his young pupil, and who seemed unable to forgive the fact that the seventeen-year-old boy, who was trying to stand up to him in class, was the same Brunetto Grossato who at the age of thirteen had already conducted the Adagio of Beethoven's Fourth Symphony or the entire Fifth.[7] A teacher who "went wild" when the student gave rein to his imagination in preparing his musical exercises and who agreed to accept certain liberties of content only on condition that "the form would be Beethovenian."[8] A teacher to whom perhaps much is owed if indeed, as a result, Maderna would always experience Beethoven as a barrier, so much as to openly state that he had "great difficulties" with his music.[9]

4 See, on this matter, the anthology "Per un ritratto di Bruno Maderna: estratti dalla corrispondenza," in Bruno Maderna, *Amore e curiosità: Scritti, frammenti e interviste sulla musica*, ed. Angela Ida De Benedictis, Michele Chiappini, and Benedetta Zucconi (Milan: il Saggiatore, 2020), 541–638, esp. 551–66.

5 In this regard, see Orazio Maione, *I Conservatori di musica durante il fascismo: La riforma del 1930: storia e documenti* (Turin: De Sono, 2005), 87–94.

6 The old curriculum, issued in 1899, was modeled almost *tel quel* on the rules of the Paris Conservatory. Maderna himself remarked in several interviews that his apprenticeship at the Santa Cecilia Conservatory had been conducted following "the same programs as the Paris Conservatory." See "Intervista con Georges Caraël" [1968], in Maderna, *Amore e curiosità* (see note 4), 345–57, at 345.

7 In this regard, see Angela Ida De Benedictis, "More than conducting, more than composing: Hermann Scherchen, Bruno Maderna, Luciano Berio," in *Komponieren & Dirigieren: Doppelbegabungen als Thema der Interpretationsgeschichte*, ed. Alexander Drčar and Wolfgang Gratzer (Freiburg im Breisgau: Rombach, 2017), 371–400, esp. 380–82.

8 Bruno Maderna, Letters of 10 and 11 January 1939 to Irma Manfredi, Maderna's adoptive mother (Bruno Maderna Collection, PSS); the second is published in Maderna, *Amore e curiosità* (see note 4), 556–57.

9 Stated in 1966 in an interview with Bibeb (pseudonym of Elisabeth Maria Lampe-Soutberg), now in ibid., 132–45, at 138.

A teacher, however, to whom a great merit must be attributed: that of having indelibly amplified and strengthened, by his very impositions, a character pervaded by an indomitable sense of independence. Because even the ability to irritate and provoke dissent, after all, can be seen as a gift – a life lesson, which, in the case of Maderna, ultimately strengthened the student's quasi-Beethovenian willpower:

"I'm a little depressed because of my Sonata. Bustini has really turned out to be a jerk. As soon as he saw that it was actually my music, he went wild, without even thoroughly examining the work. This does not make me love composition; it only strikes at my susceptibility more and more. [...] It means that I will go on with the legs of Bach, Beethoven, and the nineteenth-century romantics. That's school for you. But should the Eternal Father come down in person, I will not renounce my personality!"[10]

Angela Ida De Benedictis

10 "Sono un po' depresso per via di quella mia Sonata. Bustini si è proprio rivelato un cafone. Appena ha visto che si trattava di musica veramente mia è montato in bestia, senza neanche esaminare a fondo il lavoro. Così non mi fa prendere amore per la composizione [...]. Vuol dire che andrò avanti con le gambe di Bach di Beethoven e dei romantici ottocenteschi. È la scuola. Ma dovesse venir giù il Padre Eterno in persona, io alla mia personalità non rinuncio!" Maderna, letter to Manfredi of 11 January 1939 (see note 8). The "Sonata" referred to in the letter is a study work for violin and piano (lost).

PLATE 2
Bruno Maderna, Orchestration of Ludwig van Beethoven's Piano Sonata in E-flat major, op. 7, movt. 1 (c. 1937–38). 2nd full score, p. 1
(BRUNO MADERNA COLLECTION, PSS)

Earle Brown
Analysis of the Piano Sonata, op. 81a
(c. 1949)

With his graphic notation, mobile work conceptions, and other innovations, Earle Brown (1926–2002) contributed significantly to the evolution of music in the latter half of the twentieth century. That he became an avant-garde composer at all seems more than astonishing in view of his origins and training. Born and raised in Lunenburg, Massachusetts, a small town forty-six miles west of Boston with a mere 1,600 inhabitants in the 1920s, Brown grew up with the everyday music of his social surroundings: local bands, church music, and radio.[1] Rarely did it include classical pieces, much less contemporary art music. As he later recalled, "there were no string quartets or orchestras close by that I could listen to except on the radio." Instead, his early musical influences and activities consisted in jazz and popular music. "I started playing the trumpet at about ten years of age [...]. When I was [in] high school I formed a dance band, and later I played with large jazz orchestras."[2] He continued these musical activities during the year he spent studying mechanical engineering and mathematics at Northeastern University, Boston (1944–45), and during his military service (until 1946), where, after basic training, he played in military bands, dance ensembles, and concert orchestras. It was then that he resolved to become a professional musician.

To receive his training, Brown chose the Schillinger House School of Music in Boston (now Berklee College), established only one year earlier by the Schillinger pupil Lawrence Berk. It differed from conventional conservatories in two essential ways. First, the four-year course of study began with a heavy bias toward theory, building on *The Schillinger System of Musical Composition*.[3] Whether the students later focused on performance, composition and arranging, or teaching the Schillinger System,[4] they first had to pass two years of progressively structured theory courses divided into specific areas (rhythm, scales, melody, and harmony, each with its own geometrical transformation procedures) and related advanced courses (called "Schillinger Problems"). Second, the repertoire they studied was not limited to classical music, but aimed at past forms of music no less than at contemporary counterparts (in a comprehensive sense). This appealed mainly to students who were either active as, or sought to become, jazz and film musicians. As a result, in its early years, Schillinger House was "primarily a school for jazz musicians."[5] Given Brown's musical background, it was only logical that he should receive his training at Schillinger House, particularly since, as he recalled decades later, after leaving military service he considered the option of becoming a film composer: "So I thought of the Schillinger thing. A lot of film composers had studied with Schillinger."[6] But at the same time he developed a very strong interest in contemporary art music, which led him to take private lessons from the twelve-tone composer Roslyn Brogue Henning, a pupil of Walter Piston, from 1947 to 1950.

Yet the course material at Schillinger House by no means excluded classical music, and Brown's surviving notes and assignments from his student years contain also exercises in the classical repertoire. One example is a seven-page analysis of Ludwig van Beethoven's "Les Adieux" Piano Sonata, op. 81a (SEE PLATE 1). It probably originated during a course on "Directed Listening"

1 There are clear parallels between Charles Ives and Earle Brown in their respective origins, musical backgrounds, and to some extent their resultant creative work, as Brown himself suggested; see Earle Brown, "Earle Brown, Composer," in *Beyond Notation: The Music of Earle Brown*, ed. Rebecca Y. Kim (Ann Arbor: University of Michigan Press, 2017), 291–301, esp. 291; text initially published in Deena and Bernard Rosenberg, *The Music Makers* (New York: Columbia University Press, 1979), 80–91.

2 David Ryan, interview with Earle Brown (1999), quoted from Louis Pine, "Earle Brown's Study and Use of the Schillinger System of Musical Composition," in *Beyond Notation* (see note 1), 27–79, at 27.

3 Joseph Schillinger, *The Schillinger System of Musical Composition*, 2 vols., ed. Arnold Shaw and Lyle Dowling (New York: Carl Fischer, 1946).

4 Brown majored in composition and arranging, but also received certification to become a Schillinger teacher. From 1950 to 1952 he ran an accredited studio in Denver, where he taught the Schillinger technique.

5 Carolyn Brown, "The Early Years," in *Beyond Notation* (see note 1), 21–26, at 25. See also Pine, "Earle Brown's Study" (see note 2), 28–38.

6 John Yaffé, "An Interview with Composer Earle Brown" [1995], *Contemporary Music Review* 26, nos. 3–4 (2007): 289–310, at 291.

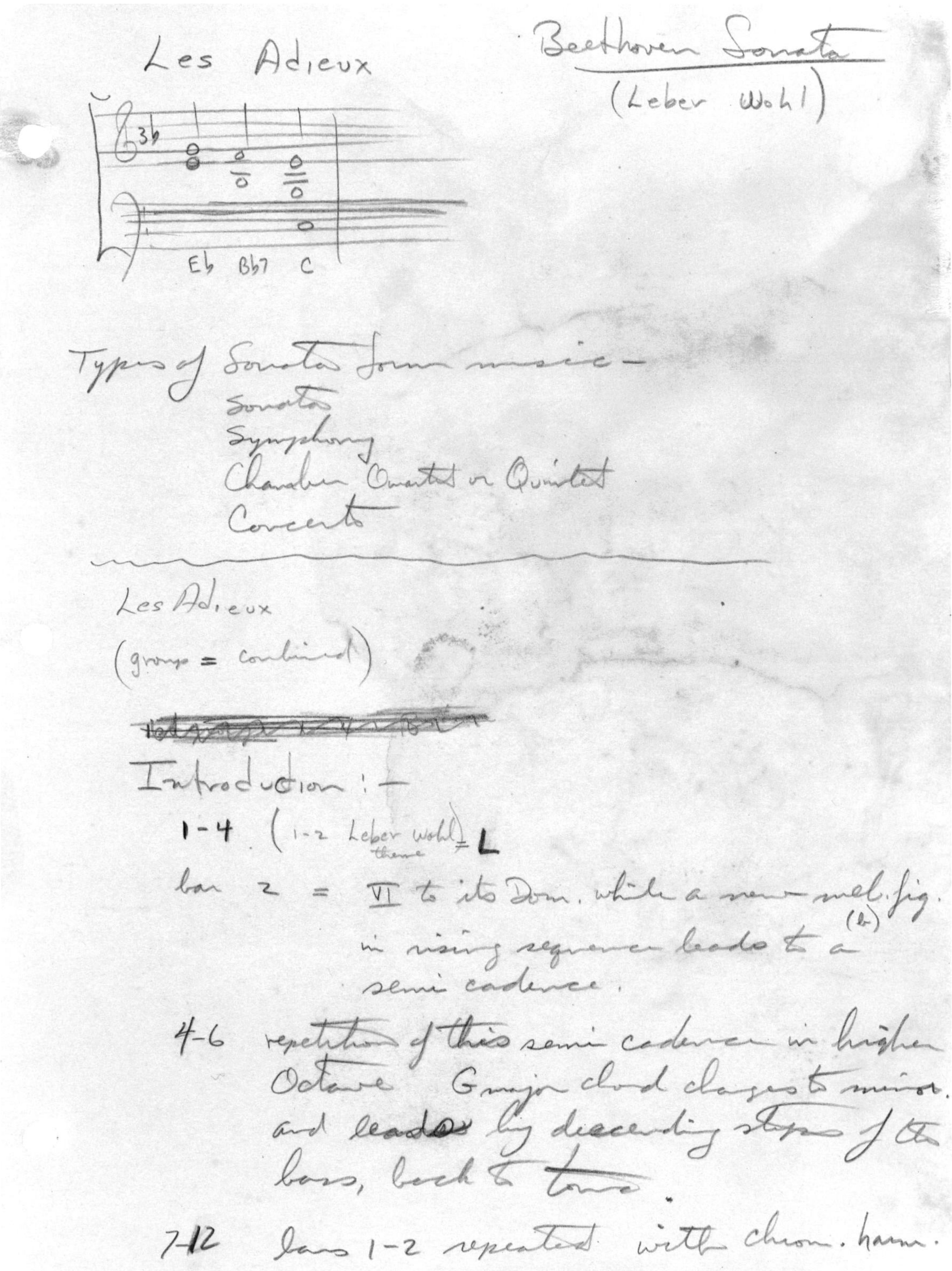

Les Adieux

Beethoven Sonata
(Leber Wohl)

Eb Bb7 C

Types of Sonata form music —
Sonata
Symphony
Chamber Quartet or Quintet
Concerto

Les Adieux
(groups = combined)

Introduction: —
1-4 (1-2 Leber Wohl theme) = L
bar 2 = VI to its Dom. while a new mel. fig. in rising sequence leads to a (b) semi cadence.
4-6 repetition of this semi cadence in higher Octave G major chord changes to minor. and leads by descending steps of the bass, back to tonic.
7-12 bars 1-2 repeated with chrom. harm.

PLATE 1
Earle Brown, Analysis of Ludwig van Beethoven's Piano Sonata in E-flat major, op. 81a ("Les Adieux") (c. 1949). Manuscript, p. 1
(EARLE BROWN COLLECTION, PSS)

that Brown, according to the school's curriculum, attended in his seventh semester, thus in 1949. Admittedly, the contents of the course are described in the "Schillinger House Catalogue" rather vaguely as a "Laboratory course in assigned record and score analysis,"[7] but we learn more from the notes Brown wrote down in one of his student notebooks: beneath the title of the course we find not only the Beethoven analysis, but descriptions of listening impressions (both structural and semantic) of Ravel's *Ma mère l'Oye,* Debussy's "Fêtes" from *Trois Nocturnes,* and Elie Siegmeister's *Ozart Set,* plus formal analyses of two Bach fugues (in E minor from *WTC* I and D major from *WTC* II).

That said, Brown's Beethoven analysis consists essentially of excerpts from the published analysis by Donald Francis Tovey.[8] He adopts Tovey's labels for motifs ("L", for example, stands for the "Lebewohl" motif),[9] Tovey's formal divisions, including bar numbers (Tovey starts again at m.1 for the Allegro section following the slow introduction to the first movement), and the names Tovey assigned to formal sections and characters (he refers to the second movement as "Intermezzo"). Only rarely do we detect the Schillinger student, as when Brown writes the chord symbols "E♭ B♭7 C" beneath the three sonorities of the "Lebewohl" motif – incorrect labels from the standpoint of classical harmonic theory, but perfectly acceptable in jazz. (Of course Brown knew that the open fifth B♭–F was not a B-flat 7th chord; rather, he used the "7" to indicate a dominant function.) Moreover, the concluding group of the first-movement exposition (mm. 62–65), which both Brown and Tovey describe as an "Imitative figure in double diminution," receives the notation "t = ♩ | t = 𝅘𝅥𝅯" in Brown's analysis. According to the Schillinger System, "t" indicates a "duration-unit,"[10] usually referring to the denominator of a time signature. But it can also specifically indicate the basic rhythmic unit of a motif, as in this case. The diminution value that Brown notates here is 4:1, i.e. the ratio between the "Lebewohl" motif in bars 50 to 52 (in whole notes) and the "imitative figure" derived from this motif in bars 62 to 65 (with quarter notes as the basic unit).

This is not to say that Brown, by excerpting Tovey, wanted to avoid making his own analysis. It was probably standard practice at Schillinger House to have students take their bearings from existing analyses of historical repertoires in order to master the classical forms. (Another notebook from Brown's years of study, for example, contains excerpts from Roger Fiske's book on the late Beethoven quartets and Ernst Toch's textbook on form, both with bibliographical references.[11]) Tovey's analyses must have been attractive to Schillinger students and teachers because they inductively develop the form of a piece from small units, such as motifs, phrases, or groups of measures. Tovey's ultimately empirical approach was thus compatible with the Schillinger technique, despite their obvious theoretical differences, for it proceeds from musical phenomena rather than prefabricated formal laws. The Schillinger technique, too, starts with small musical units and reaches larger forms via specific processes of transformation.

Simon Obert

7 Two copies of the "Schillinger House Catalogue" are preserved in Brown's posthumous papers. The catalogue consists of eight hectographed pages containing the eight-semester curriculum, course descriptions, tuition fees, and semester dates. One copy stems from the 1947–48 academic year; the other lacks a title page but probably dates from the final year of Brown's studies (1949–50), since he checks off several of the courses listed there. A copy of the "Schillinger House Catalogue, 1949–1950" from the Berklee College archives can be consulted online at https://archives.berklee.edu/1949-1950-schillinger-house-catalog/20175#page/1/mode/2up (accessed 2 June 2020).

8 Donald Francis Tovey, *A Companion to Beethoven's Pianoforte Sonatas (Bar-to-bar Analysis)* (London: The Association Board of the Royal School of Music, 1948), 197–207.

9 Brown, who knew no German at the time, referred to the sonata's nickname as "Leber Wohl," an involuntary blooper occasionally encountered elsewhere.

10 Schillinger, *Schillinger System* (see note 3), vol. 2, 1363.

11 Roger Fiske, *Beethoven's Last Quartets* (London: Oxford University Press, 1940); Ernst Toch, *The Shaping Forces in Music: An Inquiry into Harmony, Melody, Counterpoint, Form* (New York: Criterion Music, 1948).

György Ligeti
The System of Classical Harmony (1956)

György Ligeti ended one of his final public lectures with a "message to young composers": "Try to obtain the best possible training in traditional subjects, such as harmony and counterpoint, for they are the foundation of the composer's craft."[1] Ligeti himself had received solid training in the craft of composition, first in Cluj, then in Budapest with Ferenc Farkas, Pál Kadosa, and Sándor Veress, while at the same time studying mathematics and physics. In autumn 1950 he accepted a teaching position for harmony, counterpoint, and formal analysis at the Franz Liszt Academy in Budapest, a position he retained until he left Hungary in late 1956. His classes were attended mainly by instrumental students rather than budding composers. Given the political conditions that reigned under the Rakosi regime from 1949, he was not unhappy to focus on handing down the classical-romantic tradition: teaching, along with researching and arranging folk music, offered him the best way to conduct serious work without compromises under Communist rule. His own composing, however, became an increasingly private affair, and his more daring works, such as *Musica ricercata* or the First String Quartet, had to wait years before they were finally premièred in the West.

Initially Ligeti published an introduction to the fundamentals of harmony in 1954.[2] Two years later he drew the sum total of his musico-theoretical investigations in a two-volume textbook on the classical theory of harmony.[3] There he limited himself explicitly to the period from the Baroque to Viennese Classicism and excluded Romanticism and the twentieth century, for which he referred to the relevant textbooks by Antal Molnár and Leó Weiner.[4]

In *A klasszikus harmóniarend,* Ligeti operates exclusively with music examples in order, as he puts it in the preface, to combine theory with practice and to illustrate the "living" application of the basic rules of harmony.[5] Starting with the simplest of materials (the I–V–I cadence), the harmonic vocabulary is successively expanded up to and including ninth and altered chords. The examples range chronologically from Buxtehude and Purcell to Beethoven, with the emphases clearly falling on Bach, Mozart, and Beethoven. Some ninety per cent of the examples are based on his own knowledge of the literature and his broad study of scores. The remainder, all meticulously referenced, come from the textbooks of Ebenezer Prout and Antal Molnár[6] as well as from several colleagues with whom he shared his analytical interests in the early 1950s. In particular, he expressly thanks Lajos Bárdos, János Breuer, Zoltán Gárdonyi, Erzsébet Hegyi, and Molnár.

In the history of music theory, Ligeti's approach – to design a harmony textbook as an extensive collection of examples with slender accompanying commentary – is interesting in that it had almost never before been pursued with such rigor, at least not in the German-language tradition. Equally unusual are the assignments and exercises it offers, based on individual examples. That said, his textbook is barely known outside of Hungary, where it was long used as teaching material, and has yet to appear in translation.

Ligeti's collection of examples devotes a total of sixty-nine excerpts to Beethoven; the only composers to appear more frequently are Bach and

1 György Ligeti, "Zwischen Wissenschaft, Musik und Politik" [2001], in idem, *Gesammelte Schriften,* ed. Monika Lichtenfeld (Mainz: Schott, 2007), vol. 2, 33–50, at 50.
2 György Ligeti, *Klasszikus összhangzattan: Segédkönyv* (Classical harmony: a guide) (Budapest: Zeneműkiadó Vállalat, 1954).
3 György Ligeti, *A klasszikus harmóniarend: Összhangzattani példák a barokk és a bécsi klasszikus zeneirodalomból* [The System of Classical Harmony: Examples of Harmony in Music from the Baroque Era to Viennese Classicism], 2 vols. (Budapest: Zeneműkiadó Vállalat, 1956); photographic reproduction in a single volume with new pagination (Budapest: Editio Musica, 2014). The quotations below are taken from the latter edition.
4 Ligeti, *A klasszikus harmóniarend* (see note 3), 10.
5 Ibid., 9.
6 Ebenezer Prout, *Harmony: Its Theory and Practice,* 27th edn. (London: Augener, 1903); Antal Molnár, *Összhangzattan összes példány,* 2nd edn. (Budapest: Dante Könyvkiadó, 1943). See Péter Halász, "Tradíció és kreativitás: Ligeti György Klasszikus összhangzattanáról," *Muzsika* (May 1998): 15–17.

PLATE 1
György Ligeti, *A klasszikus harmóniarend* [The System of Classical Harmony] (1956). Handwritten music example 162 (belonging to example 203 in the book) showing the opening of Ludwig van Beethoven's Piano Concerto No. 4 in G major, op. 58
(GYÖRGY LIGETI COLLECTION, PSS)

EXAMPLE 1
Ludwig van Beethoven, Piano Sonata in E-flat major, op. 81a ("Les Adieux") (1809), mm. 1–2

EXAMPLE 2
György Ligeti, Trio for violin, horn, and piano (1982), mm. 1–2

Mozart, with 73 and 110 examples each. The excerpts are taken primarily from his piano music, the string quartets, and a few movements of the symphonies and largely occupy the more complex second volume of the textbook ("Alteration and Figuration"). Our plate shows Ligeti's handwritten copy of the opening bars of Beethoven's Fourth Piano Concerto, op. 58 (SEE PLATE 1), to illustrate the use of secondary dominants in root position and first inversion. This document comes from one of the two production masters for his harmony treatise, the first being a fifty-two-page typescript which contains his entire commentary and lists all 343 examples, the other consisting of ninety-six pages of handwritten music examples that bear impressive testimony to his collecting and categorizing activities. The excerpts, written on widely varying manuscript paper, were gradually placed in systematic order, mounted on larger sheets of paper, and numbered from 1 to 283. The scrap paper used for mounting the excerpts includes several hectographed course schedules for the Budapest Academy of Music, where Ligeti was a teacher and examiner for music theory and solfège.[7]

Music Example 162, belonging to Example 203 in the book, presents the Fourth Piano Concerto's striking opening for solo piano (*zongora*) and the first eight bars of the orchestra (*zenekar*), beginning in the mediant key of B major. In the first phrase, only the tonic key is marked; from bar 6, Ligeti assigns the symbols of functional harmony to the chords and adds the analogous solmization syllables in the lower line. In bar 10 he goes on to propose an exercise: "How might this sequence be continued?"[8] The solmization relates to Lajos Bárdos's textbook, from which the example has been taken, as the caption conscientiously points out. Bárdos was a theorist who taught at the Budapest Academy of Music from 1928 to 1968. Ligeti held him in such high esteem that he sat in on his analysis courses until well into the 1950s, even though "this raised eyebrows among teachers and students, it not being customary to attend the classroom instruction of a colleague."[9] What fascinated him was the systematic approach with which Bárdos kept his eye equally on rhythm, harmony, and formal design.[10] Earlier, in 1947, Ligeti had displayed the same interest in holistic analysis during Bence Szabolcsi's course on the Beethoven string

7 Ligeti held some courses together with his colleague Erzsébet Hegyi (1927–2017), who also provided him with eight examples from Bach's music for his harmony textbook.

8 Ligeti, *A klasszikus harmóniarend* (see note 3), 82, Example 1.

9 Ove Nordwall, *György Ligeti: Eine Monographie* (Mainz: Schott, 1971), 220. See also Ligeti's assessment of Bárdos in *Träumen Sie in Farbe? György Ligeti im Gespräch mit Eckhard Roelcke* (Vienna: Zsolnay, 2003), 65.

10 See e.g. the analytical comments on Beethoven's piano sonatas in Lajos Bárdos, *Selected Writings on Music* (Budapest: Editio Musica, 1984), 11–20.

quartets, choosing the first movement of op. 18, no. 1, "because the entire fabric emerges from an almost inconsequential germ motif."[11] Beethoven was one of Ligeti's formative musical experiences, and his music remained a central point of reference even in Ligeti's later career. The string quartets and piano sonatas also played a key role in Ligeti's analysis courses during his Hamburg professorship.[12] And, in 2000, when the *Frankfurter Allgemeine Zeitung* asked him about nationality, he declared himself to be "an enemy of nationalism of any stripe," only to concede that he felt "bound to the German tradition" in that "Beethoven and especially Bach" were of "paramount importance" to him.[13]

From today's perspective, the importance of Ligeti's harmonic theory is by no means limited to the function of an elementary textbook. Rather, it illuminates his entire musical cosmos and his analytical approach to classical masterpieces. It also sheds light on later stages of his compositional career, as is impressively shown by the Beethoven example with which his treatise comes to an end. It is perhaps the best-known motif of farewell in music history: the "Lebewohl" motif from the first movement of the Piano Sonata in E-flat major, op. 81a ("Les Adieux"), where Beethoven adopts the *topos* of horn fifths. Using the movement's coda, Ligeti demonstrates the superposition of tonic and dominant as an example of compound harmonic functions.[14] His commentary stresses the harmonic peculiarity of this passage with its echo effect.[15] It also anticipates his own Horn Trio (1982), where he employs a dissonant, out-of-tune "Lebewohl" motif both as a false Beethoven quotation and as the germinal idea of the first movement (SEE EXAMPLES 1 AND 2, P. 45).

Heidy Zimmermann

11 Thus as recalled by György Kurtág in "Laudatio auf György Ligeti," in idem, *Drei Gespräche mit Bálint András Varga und Ligeti Hommagen*, ed. Bálint András Varga (Hofheim: Wolke, 2010), 151–63, at 158. See also Ligeti's epistolary comments on Beethoven references in his Second String Quartet, in Harald Kaufmann, *Von innen und außen: Schriften über Musik, Musikleben und Ästhetik*, ed. Werner Grünzweig and Gottfried Krieger (Hofheim: Wolke, 1993), 249–50.

12 Even in his Budapest period, pocket scores of practically all of Beethoven's string quartets formed part of his personal library. See also the live tape recordings of several Hamburg courses in the György Ligeti Collection (PSS).

13 György Ligeti, "Bagatellen," in idem, *Gesammelte Schriften* (see note 1), vol. 2, 68–71, at 71.

14 Ligeti, *A klasszikus harmóniarend* (see note 3), 144.

15 This observation was further developed, with thoughts on the dissociation of musical time, in the essay "Wandlungen der musikalischen Form," where Ligeti traces such tendencies back to Beethoven, including the "strange coda to the first movement of the 'Les Adieux' Sonata, where imitations of horn calls intermingle with their own echo." György Ligeti, "Wandlungen der musikalischen Form" [1960], in idem, *Gesammelte Schriften* (see note 1), vol. 1, 85–104, at 101.

György Kurtág
Analysis of the String Quartet, op. 132, movt. 1
(early 1960s)

György Kurtág (b. 1926), who began his oeuvre systematically with a String Quartet op. 1, is unquestionably a modernist composer, but just as unquestionably "anchored in the European tradition," as György Ligeti once put it. Although Béla Bartók and Anton Webern could be named as his "points of orientation," the foundation of his modernism is the music of Beethoven. All the same, Ligeti maintains, there are no discernible direct ties to Beethoven's style; instead, an "underground connecting line extends directly from Beethoven to Kurtág."[1] Reason enough to cast a glance at his eighteen-page bar-by-bar analytical transcription of the opening movement of Beethoven's A-minor String Quartet, op. 132 (SEE PLATE 1, P. 48).

Kurtág's analysis, prepared in the early 1960s, lays bare the deep structures of a tonal composition as seen through eyes schooled in atonality. He approached this string music from the piano, notating the four-voice original on two staves and adding new staves for comments as necessary (four and five on page 1). The very first page of the transcription reveals his analytical acumen: the contrasts of tempo, texture, and character, rather than defining a conventional sonata form, gain flexibility through the ever-present possibility of sudden change from an invariant nucleus. For this reason "late" Beethoven, including this piece from his final five string quartets, opp. 127 to 135 (chronologically the second, despite its opus number), also stands, with its jolting discontinuities, as a symbol of aesthetic freedom, even a premonition of universal freedom for humanity.[2] Kurtág identifies the aforementioned four-note nucleus, first heard in the cello at the bottom of page 1 (mm. 1–2: G♯-A-F-E), with the abbreviation "a = Leitmotiv (Lm)" and defines it on a separate sheet with the words "az alaptípus 2 szer 2 hangbólálló egység" ("the basic type is 2 times 2 sound units").[3] The first page, reproduced here, contains four sigla:

"a = Leitmotiv (Lm)"	main motif
"aJ = a Inversióban"	inversion of main motif
"aP = a permutációban"	permutation of main motif
"aV = a hangkozvariáns"	intervallic variant of main motif (referring to the middle interval)

The focus of Kurtág's analytic interest is centered on Beethoven's dialectical art of composition, in which everything derives from a single nucleus. This applies, for example, to the strict contrapuntal texture of the first eight measures ("Assai sostenuto"), where Kurtág divides the music into an ascending and a descending half step above the harmonic foundation "D-T-S^{VI}-D^{V}" (V-I-IV-V) and embeds it in a larger harmonic framework of two-bar units. But it is equally evident in the free texture beginning at bar 9 ("Allegro"): the virtuosic figuration in the first violin, concentrated in a single rhombus F5, leads to the thematic phrase in the high cello (mm. 11–12). In the "Assai sostenuto" (an introductory exposition), Kurtág's transcription shows no fewer than twelve leitmotifs, indicated with brackets and sigla, and another seven in the contrasting "Allegro" (mm. 9–13).

The arrows with which Kurtág identifies the ascending and descending half-steps are omnipresent,[4] regardless of their rhythmic duration or their metrical or diastematic position within the fabric. These arrows, iconic symbols

1 "Drei Komponisten der europäischen Tradition dienen als Orientierungspunkte für seine Musik, [...] Beethoven, Bartók, Webern. [...] Die unterirdische Verknüpfungslinie spannt sich direkt von Beethoven zu Kurtág." György Ligeti, "Laudatio auf György Kurtág" [2000], in idem, *Gesammelte Schriften*, ed. Monika Lichtenfeld (Mainz: Schott, 2007), vol. 1, 485–89, at 488–89.

2 Thus Hans-Joachim Hinrichsen, *Ludwig van Beethoven: Musik für eine neue Zeit* (Kassel: Bärenreiter; Berlin: Metzler, 2019), 203–06 and 294–314. Occasionally Kurtág's analysis refers to related structures in other Beethoven works, e.g. the first movement of String Quartet, op. 135 (p. 3), the *Pastoral* Symphony, op. 68 (p. 5), or the second movement of the "Les Adieux" Piano Sonata, op. 81a (p. 10).

3 György Kurtág, Analysis of Beethoven's String Quartet, op. 132, draft, headed "Vezérhangelv az op. 132ben." ("leading note principle in op. 132"), György Kurtág Collection, PSS. I am grateful to Simone Hohmaier (Berlin) for kindly helping me to understand the Hungarian.

4 Admittedly Kurtág also placed arrows in mm. 8–9 and 10–11 of the cello part to define the meter of upbeats and downbeats (marked with ∪ and ∩): m. 9 B, m. 11 C, where the latter pitch, being only imaginary, is enclosed in square brackets.

PLATE 1
György Kurtág, Analysis of Ludwig van Beethoven's String Quartet in A minor, op. 132, movt. 1 (early 1960s). Manuscript fair copy, p. 1
(GYÖRGY KURTÁG COLLECTION, PSS)

PLATE 2
György Kurtág, Analysis of Ludwig van Beethoven's String Quartet in A minor, op. 132, movt. 1 (early 1960s). Manuscript fair copy, p. 17
(GYÖRGY KURTÁG COLLECTION, PSS)

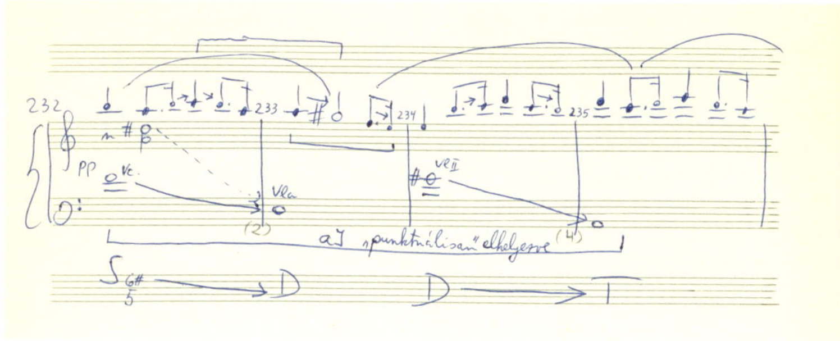

for the kinetic forces of the tonal structure, indicate not so much pitch progressions as indwelling energies of the sort that also prevail in Kurtág's own music.[5] In Beethoven's fabric, almost all the notes in bars 1 to 8 are written as half notes; in contrast, Kurtág's transcription of the contrapuntal texture distinguishes between half notes (for "a̲" and "a̲J") and stemless dots (for "a̲P" and "a̲V"). The latter sigla, despite their systematic nature, are more remote than the former from motivic intelligibility, a quality well captured in Kurtág's choice of the term "leitmotif." A quarter of a century later Carl Dahlhaus, using Beethoven's op. 132, coined the neologism "subthematic" for "leitmotivic" flexibility of the sort recognized by Kurtág. The "subthematic" substrate, he explained, is not "a specific series of intervals that could be identified by the letters of the alphabet by which notes are known, but only a formula as nebulous as 'the configuration of two rising or falling semitone steps with a variable interval between them' serves as the substratum of the 'subthematic' – the stratum into which thematicism's function of establishing musical coherence has to some extent withdrawn."[6]

Western and Hungarian traditions interweave in this Beethoven analysis. On the one hand, for bars 232 to 235 Kurtág writes "a̲J 'punktuálisan' elhelyezve" (a̲J placed pointillistically) (**SEE PLATE 2**), thereby drawing more on Stockhausen's concept of "pointillist music" than on the traditional doctrine of counterpoint ("punctus contra punctum"). The semitone context of two pitches separated by one or almost two octaves (marked with arrows) demonstrates that the Hungarian analyst has incorporated theories from the European avant-garde into his study. He views Beethoven as an early creator of modernist music.

On the other hand, the Hungarian tradition as represented in the theoretical writings of Lajos Bárdos (1899–1986)[7] also has relevance for Kurtág. His analysis of the opening movement of op. 132 arose in conjunction with a course headed by Bárdos at the Budapest Academy of Music. Like Ligeti,[8] Kurtág had a high opinion of Bárdos as a teacher.[9] The predominance of semitone arrows in the four forms of "leitmotif" in his Beethoven analysis appears to be typically Hungarian if we consider Bárdos's semitone-laden reading of Kodály.[10] Nonetheless, Kurtág did not espouse a Hungarian nationalism of the sort that Bárdos lauded in Kodály; his concern was, and remains, not "Hungarian" music, still less "German" music, but the idea of a "classical" music that becomes "his" in dialogue with others. As Kurtág's works generally arise within an intertextual horizon,[11] his transcription of Beethoven's quartet movement closely parallels his own creative poetics. To the end of his days Beethoven himself copied out works by revered "forebears," initially to find his own voice, later to solve his own compositional problems. The distinguishing features of György Kurtág, the Hungarian admirer of Beethoven, come to the fore in the hybrid overlapping and idiosyncratic commingling of perspectives displayed in this document.

Hermann Danuser

5 It need hardly be mentioned that the Hungarian form of solmization (with ascending syllables do di re ri mi fa fi sol si la li ti do, and descending syllables do ti ta la le sol fi fa mi ma re ra do) also plays a role.

6 Carl Dahlhaus, "Subthematicism," in idem, *Ludwig van Beethoven: Approaches to His Music*, trans. Mary Whittall (Oxford: Clarendon Press, 1997), 202–18, at 205.

7 See Lajos Bárdos, *Selected Writings on Music*, trans. Alexander Farkas and Kata Ittzés (Budapest: Editio Musica, 1984).

8 See Heidy Zimmermann's article on Ligeti's treatise on harmony in the present volume, 43–46.

9 Kurtág made Lajos Bárdos the dedicatee of his op. 12, *Eszká emlékzaj / S. K. – Remembrance Noise:* Seven songs on poems by Dezső Tandori for voice and violin.

10 Bárdos's essay on the Locrian mode in Kodály's music emphasizes the half step in much the same way as the "subthematic leitmotif" that forms the focus of Kurtág's analysis of the first movement of Beethoven's op. 132. See Lajos Bárdos, "The Modus Locricus in the Works of Zoltán Kodály: A 'Sorrowful' Tonality," in idem, *Selected Writings* (see note 7), 230–87, esp. 231 and 273.

11 See Simone Hohmaier, *"Meine Muttersprache ist Bartók ...": Einfluß und Material in György Kurtágs "Quartetto per archi" op. 1 (1959)* (Saarbrücken: Pfau, 1997); idem, *"Ein zweiter Pfad der Tradition": Kompositorische Bartók-Rezeption* (Saarbrücken: Pfau, 2003); Rachel Beckles Willson, *Ligeti, Kurtág, and Hungarian Music during the Cold War* (Cambridge: Cambridge University Press, 2007); and Tobias Bleek, *Musikalische Intertextualität als Schaffensprinzip: Eine Studie zu György Kurtágs Streichquartett* Officium breve *op. 28* (Saarbrücken: Pfau, 2010).

2

IDEALIZATIONS

Michelle Ziegler

Lofty Values, Empty Words
Ideological Levels in the Reception of Beethoven

Reception mechanisms more than a century old cannot be switched off overnight. If Beethoven's music already bore a heavy ideological burden in the nineteenth century, myriad twentieth-century attempts to free his sounds from these fetters miscarried. Claude Debussy's early critique of 1901 was, for example, itself not free of ideological taints. Writing in a concert review of the Ninth, the sharp-tongued French composer stated that it "has long been surrounded by a haze of adjectives."[1] It goes so far, he continued, that one marvels that the work had not been buried long ago beneath the avalanche of prose. Explaining that Beethoven's thought was entirely musical, he attempted to divest it of the "stupid comments" that the work has excited. Yet his line of argument ended in the conclusion that an "excess of humanity" has burst the conventional bounds of the symphony, which sprang from a soul "drunk with the idea of freedom."[2] His attempt to break away from the reception tradition thus perpetuates one of its powerful *topoi:* the Ninth as a monument to liberty. In short, the attribution of ideas to Beethoven's works continues stubbornly apace. Nor are the attributions limited to verbal discussion: they equally mark the music's performance and find reflection in the visual depiction of Beethoven and his music. Even composers fall under their spell, either strengthening or interrogating them by their references to Beethoven.

If the tradition of ideological attributions can't be easily dispensed with, the things attributed are at once constant and variable: some clichés, such as romanticized heroism or the narrative of overcoming adversity, have been stubbornly perpetuated since the dawn of Beethoven reception; other attributions emerge from specific historical contexts, receive contradictory interpretations, and are often

I wish to thank Heidy Zimmermann for her conversations and her reading of this essay, Simone Hohmaier and Anne C. Shreffler for their helpful suggestions, and Tina Kilvio Tüscher (Paul Sacher Stiftung) as well as Stefanie Kuban and Dorothea Geffert (Beethoven-Haus, Bonn) for assisting me in various ways during my research.

1 Claude Debussy, "The Ninth Symphony," in *Debussy on Music: The Critical Writings of the Great French Composer,* ed. François Lesure, trans. Richard Langham Smith (New York: Knopf, 1977), 29–32, at 29; first published in *La Revue blanche* (1 May 1901).

2 Ibid., 30.

short-lived for that very reason. The constants seem to appeal to general needs for understanding, whereas the variables offer a broad range of possibilities for political, cultural, or philosophical appropriation. Perpetuations and reinterpretations form part of a complex system of meaning.[3] By being endlessly repeated, they impart recognizability while broadening the spectrum of musings on "the Beethoven myth."[4] The constants will be briefly presented below with a backward glance at the nineteenth century. Then, proceeding from four documents on reception, the interplay of variable interpretations will be discussed insofar as they clarify specific twentieth-century Beethoven labels: the humanist, the revolutionary, the patriot, and the virile male. These interpretive approaches will be examined with regard to their ambiguity, self-contradictions, and mutability, then slotted into their historical context to unveil their political, cultural, or philosophical appropriations.

Conceptual Fixity as a Prerequisite

Already during his lifetime Beethoven's music was said to have "spiritual content." Beethoven himself invited ideational interpretations by giving his works such eloquent titles as *Grande Sonate pathétique* or *Sinfonie pastorale,* taking part in salon conversations, and sanctioning, if not defining, the then current practice of adding words to his instrumental music. In this way his symphonies became a "listening chamber and arena for world-views."[5] Their creator was recognized as an authority who "enthusiastically encouraged momentous approaches to interpreting his oeuvre as an 'art-work of ideas.'"[6] Building upon this, the belletristic music criticism of E. T. A. Hoffmann and Adolph Bernhard Marx in particular was responsible for the apologetics of the nineteenth century.[7] They left their mark on the cult of genius with two seemingly antithetical alignments. On the one hand, they divested Beethoven's music, being a "music of ideals," of its immediate ties to the world and granted it extra-temporal ethical values, thereby elevating the composer to a "specialist for every manner of coping with reality."[8] On the other hand, the quest for a message in the music caused his works to be interpreted from the life story of their creator, thereby leading to the model of a problematical "identification" of Beethoven the artist and Beethoven the man.[9] Ultimately, the ideological appropriators in this line of reception found an influential advocate in Richard Wagner, who, in his memorial essay *Beethoven* (1870), emphasized the sublimity and eternal validity of Beethoven as well as the power of the German spirit, thereby opening up channels for a multitude of currents. Thus, the engagement with Beethoven's music and personality in the nineteenth century produced an inventory of formulae that allowed Beethoven to appear as a man of suffering, despair, and yet determination, as a brilliant child of nature, a revolutionary, a sorcerer, and a titan. Not only did this mode of reception take hold – i.e. the view of Beethoven's music as an "art-work of ideas" and the merging of musical description and biography – so did its ideational core: the *topoi* of struggle and triumph.

It was on such well-entrenched constants that Hans Heinrich Eggebrecht focused in a study of unparalleled scope, originally delivered as a lecture for the Beethoven Bicentennial in 1970 and later published with the title *Zur Geschichte der Beethoven-Rezeption* (On the History of Beethoven Reception). Drawing

3 Roland Barthes attributed ambiguous features, at once musical and psychological, to what he called the "système de sens qu'est le Beethoven romantique." See Barthes, "Musica Practica," *L'Arc* 40 (1970): 15–18, at 16.

4 See Alessandra Comini, *The Changing Image of Beethoven: A Study in Mythmaking* (New York: Rizzoli, 1987); *Mythos Beethoven: Ausstellungskatalog,* ed. Rainer Cadenbach (Laaber: Laaber, 1986); and *Ludwig van: Le Mythe de Beethoven* [exhibition catalogue], ed. Colin Lemoine and Marie-Pauline Martin (Paris: Gallimard, 2016).

5 Hermann Danuser, *Weltanschauungsmusik* (Schliengen: Argus, 2009), 35.

6 Hans-Joachim Hinrichsen, "'Seid umschlungen, Millionen': Die Beethoven-Rezeption," in *Beethoven Handbuch,* ed. Sven Hiemke (Kassel: Bärenreiter; Stuttgart: Metzler, 2009), 568–609, at 573.

7 See Elisabeth Eleonore Bauer, *Wie Beethoven auf den Sockel kam: Die Entstehung eines musikalischen Mythos* (Stuttgart: Metzler, 1992).

8 Andreas Kuhlmann, "Hohes Wort, große Tat: Zur Beethoven-Rezeption," *Merkur* 43, nos. 487–88 (1989): 940–46, at 946.

9 Carl Dahlhaus, *Ludwig van Beethoven: Approaches to his Music,* trans. Mary Whittall (Oxford: Clarendon Press, 1991), 35.

on recent research in the reception of literature, he investigated the verbal reception of Beethoven "on a material level of maximum breadth."[10] His classification and evaluation of the material aimed at durable attributions: he sought to argue that the discussion of Beethoven could, from the very beginning, be boiled down to a few constants, to a "particular way of speaking about Beethoven that has, basically, continued to the present day."[11] Even if his procedure of assigning textual passages to "conceptual fields" is not always intelligible down to the slightest detail,[12] and his conclusion that the constants "capture and reveal Beethoven for what he is" had already encountered criticism in the 1970s,[13] Eggebrecht's thorough analysis of the patterns of reception has retained its currency. In weighing the verbal attributions and explaining their mutual interaction, he was able to unearth a "homogeneous base layer"[14] in the reception of Beethoven. Its essence is made up of the threefold concepts of suffering, struggle, and triumph, connected with the reception cliché of romanticized heroism and the ethos of a "transferal of an ethical impulse proceeding from suffering."[15] These three basic elements (surmounting adversity, cult of the hero, and ethics) form the key to the reception of Beethoven, which was invariably grounded in morality. At the same time, Eggebrecht himself pointed to the abstract and overly generalized nature of these constants.[16] They harbor an ambiguity and open-endedness that make them amenable to any and all sorts of appropriation. In this way, they determined the tortuous course of their ideological misappropriation in the twentieth century.

1903: The Man Beethoven as Generational Role Model (Romain Rolland)

"He was short and thick-set, broad-shouldered and of athletic build." Thus reads the bland opening sentence of Romain Rolland's *Vie de Beethoven,* published in *Cahiers de la Quinzaine* in 1903.[17] Rolland, at that time still an unknown French writer and music critic, allowed Beethoven to appear as a human being. He focused on the composer's personality and life, speaking of "a sad, even brutal fight for existence,"[18] which he now and then tapped for his works. At the same time, by stressing his powers of surmounting obstacles, Rolland turned Beethoven into a role model for humanity, into one of those noble heroes referred to in his preface as "made great by goodness of heart."[19] With this essay Rolland, a music history teacher who had written a doctoral dissertation on opera before Lully and Scarlatti, was less intent on historical depiction than on moral fortification. He derived the need for edification from the crisis of his day: "The air is heavy around us. Old Europe is stifled by a thick and vitiated atmosphere – an undignified materialism which weighs on the mind, hindering the work of governments and individuals alike." But the individual is not alone in his struggle, for Beethoven can show him the way, "animated by the example of this man's faith in life and his quiet confidence in himself."[20] Rolland's essay, in its psychologizing drift, drew on nineteenth-century tradition while creating a role model for his contemporaries within the fashionable genre of historical biography.[21] This strategy coincided with the intentions of his publisher Charles Péguy, a left-wing *littérateur* whose *Cahiers de la Quinzaine* addressed a young readership in the atmosphere of disappointment

10 Hans Heinrich Eggebrecht, *Zur Geschichte der Beethoven-Rezeption,* 2nd edn. (Laaber: Laaber, 1994), 7. This is an expanded version of a lecture entitled "Beethoven 1970" that Eggebrecht delivered at the plenary session of the Academy of Sciences and Literature, Mainz, on 10 April 1970.

11 Ibid., 43.

12 The "conceptual fields" (*Begriffsfelder*) are very broadly conceived and seem to belong to conflicting categories. Some indicate the actual contents of the reception (e.g. *Überwinden*), while others indicate underlying modes of reception (*Erlebensmusik*). Specific labels (e.g. chauvinistic readings) are skipped altogether in the absence of relevant "conceptual fields." (Eggebrecht catalogued nationalistic statements merely as forms of *Inbegriff* and as evidence of the "utility" of Beethoven's music.)

13 Eggebrecht, *Zur Geschichte der Beethoven-Rezeption* (see note 10), 8. A critique of this study and the subsequent "Theory of Aesthetic Identification" can be found in the round table discussion "Beethoven's Wirkungsgeschichte," published in *Bericht über den Internationalen Beethoven-Kongreß, 20. bis 23. März 1977 in Berlin,* ed. Harry Goldschmidt, Karl-Heinz Köhler, and Konrad Niemann (Leipzig: VEB Deutscher Verlag für Musik, 1978), 467–91.

14 Eggebrecht, *Zur Geschichte der Beethoven-Rezeption* (see note 10), 74.

15 Ibid., 73.

16 See ibid., 102.

17 "Il était petit et trapu, de forte encolure, de charpente athlétique." Romain Rolland, *Vie de Beethoven,* 4th edn. (Paris: Hachette, 1910), 9.

18 Ibid., 11.

19 Ibid., 5.

20 "L'air est lourd autour de nous. La vieille Europe s'engourdit dans une atmosphère pesante et viciée. Un matérialisme sans grandeur pèse sur la pensée, et entrave l'action des gouvernements et des individus. [...] Ranimons à son exemple la foi de l'homme dans la vie et dans l'homme." Ibid., 3–4 and 7.

21 See Marie Gaboriaud, *Une vie de gloire et de souffrance: Le mythe de Beethoven sous la Troisième République* (Paris: Classiques Garnier, 2017), 143–49.

following the Dreyfus Affair. The moral appeal leaning on Beethoven brought about the breakthrough of publisher and author alike: the slender volume quickly vanished from the shelves and drove the Beethoven cult in France to new heights.

In the wake of this veneration, Beethoven even became a surrogate for religion.[22] The critic Raymond Bouyer, for example, referred in a series of ten articles to a "God of 1905,"[23] and sculptors such as Antoine Bourdelle turned out idealized busts. In the aftermath, this form of adoration faced two opposing currents, both essentially sustained by composers, but fundamentally different in their view of him. Established composers in the Schola Cantorum rejected this fanatical appropriation but remained true to the line of musical tradition. Vincent d'Indy, for example, in his 1911 biography, defended Beethoven the Catholic, whose works had driven him to surmount his sorrow and suffering "in accordance with Biblical law."[24] On the opposite side, a young group of composers associated with the Société Musicale Indépendante (founded in 1910), including Maurice Ravel, turned against both the aesthetic of meaning and the musical discipleship, which they regarded as conservative. As a result of such new aesthetic precepts, coupled with a rise in nationalism, the 1920s witnessed what might well be called a Beethoven crisis. Notwithstanding this change of currents and the criticism of his essay's inaccuracies, Rolland declined to revise his book and, in 1927, offered a justification for reissuing the original version: he wrote it, he said, for the readers of its day, who had since fallen in the war. In this way, he turned his book *ex post facto* into a tribute to the "living of yesterday."[25]

1926: Beethoven as Model Revolutionary (Anatoly Lunacharsky)

In 1926 plans were already underway for the events to be mounted in 1927 for the first centennial of Beethoven's death. Memorial concerts were foreseen not only in cities throughout Europe, but as "world cultural events" in Asia and the Americas.[26] In the young Soviet Union, the Commissar for Education, Anatoly Lunacharsky, diplomatically addressed the portrayal of Beethoven the Revolutionary: in an article entitled "Great Sisters," published in the first issue of the periodical *Music and Revolution* (1926), he argued that music and revolution were related. Following the poetic outburst "Every revolution is a grandiose symphony," he argued that Beethoven was a phenomenon in the history of music because, inspired by the French Revolution, he was able to "plunge into the deepest musical poetry." According to Lunacharsky, both Beethoven's music and his personality were imbued by the revolutionary posture: "Expressed in the language of human consciousness, this poetry raises mountainous problems, struggles, and victories; expressed in the pure language of music, it occasions the severest violations of musical balance, and artful guidance to a harmonious resolution."[27] Lunacharsky positioned the revolutionary Beethoven as a model for transferring dialectical materialism into musical forms: tensions between opposing musical forces leading to a peaceful resolution. Departing from the widespread view that reduced the revolutionary element in Beethoven's music to innovations and radical modernizations in music's resources, he presented a dramaturgical model that permitted a wide array

22 See Gabriele Johanna Eder, "Beethoven, die Musikwissenschaft, die Dichtung und die Politik: Romain Rolland, ein Grenzgänger zwischen den Welten," in *Musik-Wissenschaft an ihren Grenzen: Manfred Angerer zum 50. Geburtstag*, ed. Dominik Schweiger, Michael Staudinger, and Nikolaus Urbanek (Frankfurt am Main: Peter Lang, 2004), 447–58, esp. 449.

23 Raymond Bouyer, *Le Secret de Beethoven* (Paris: Fischbacher, 1905), 9; first published in *Le Ménestrel* (26 March and 25 June 1905).

24 Vincent d'Indy, *Beethoven* (Paris: Henri Laurens, 1911), 148.

25 Romain Rolland, "Préface" [1927], in idem, *Vie de Beethoven*, ed. Jean Lacoste (Paris: Bartillat, 2014), 81–83, at 83.

26 Kuno Klebelsberg, "Kulturelle Weltereignisse" [unidentified newspaper clipping, 6 February 1927] (Beethoven-Haus, Bonn, Z 250 n / 12).

27 Anatoly Lunacharsky, "Musik und Revolution" [originally "Velikie sestry" (Great sisters), 1926], in idem, *Musik und Revolution: Schriften zur Musik*, ed. and trans. Guido Bimberg (Leipzig: Reclam, 1985), 141–50, at 145.

of aesthetic implementations. By adopting this stance, the Commissar secured a neutral position in the culture – political power plays of the 1920s – a position in which he sought to mediate between "left-wing" progressive artists, "realistic" proletarian associations, and traditionalists.

The plan to position Beethoven as a model for all factions of Soviet music-making also pervades Lunacharsky's speeches for the 1927 Beethoven Centennial.[28] In an address before a Moscow concert of the conductorless orchestra Persimfans, he took aim at two revolutionary standpoints for having turned away from Beethoven. Unlike actual revolutionaries, the modernists, being "revolutionaries of form," merely seek "crass formal innovations" in a single area rather than demanding a transformation of social life in its entirety. In their organic notion of history, they take their bearings from the most recent past and regard Beethoven as a "museum." The "genuine revolutionaries," in contrast, oppose Beethoven, for they see themselves as classics and do not wish to cloak themselves in "old cultural rags."[29] Lunacharsky sought to refute both standpoints by pointing out Beethoven's close proximity to current cultural productivity, claiming that his music reflects the spirit of the French Revolution, man's capability for self-assertion, and thus the beginning of a new consciousness. For this reason, creative Soviet musicians had to uphold him as a "harbinger" of the music that would usher in the revolution of the proletariat.[30]

Lunacharsky's recruitment of Beethoven for Soviet cultural policy dominated the official line of the 1927 celebrations. Memorial concerts, readings, and plays expressed the special position that Beethoven had occupied for the Bolsheviks since the October Revolution of 1917. In keeping with Vladimir Ilyich Lenin's admiration for the "Appassionata" as an "astonishing and superhuman work of music,"[31] he was celebrated in the young Soviet Union as the most significant composer in music history, and his music was performed from one end of the country to the other.[32] In contrast, the propagation of Beethoven as a model for national symphonic music struck out on new paths. In an age of conflicting views as to what the revolution should mean for creative musicians, this appropriation of Beethoven laid the cornerstone of a new policy for music. Admittedly the composers did not immediately respond: none of the memorial compositions written by Joseph Schillinger, Nikolai Roslavets, or Aleksandr Mosolov for the tenth anniversary celebrations of the October Revolution – celebrations that followed directly upon the Beethoven Centennial festivities in autumn 1927 – went so far as to quote Beethoven.[33] Only Dmitry Shostakovich's Second Symphony ("To October"), op. 14 (1927), adhered to Lunacharsky's dramaturgical arc from lawlessness to order and fell back on Beethoven's Ninth in its final chorus. In the aftermath, an orientation on the classics became a central precept of Socialist Realism in music.

A broad array of interpretations of Beethoven the revolutionary was revealed by the anniversary celebrations in the former state of East Germany in 1952 and 1970. The 1952 campaign to commemorate the 125th anniversary of Beethoven's death was staged as a national mission.[34] Among other things, it included a traveling exhibition in which Harry Goldschmidt sought to demonstrate "Beethoven's genuine revolutionary awareness."[35] The central committee in charge made it known that the memorial day was taking place in a period during which

28 Lunacharsky's countless speeches and articles on Beethoven during the 1927 Centennial derive from three main texts: "Chto zhivo dlia nas v Betkhovene" [What is alive for us in Beethoven?], "Pochemu nam dorog Betkhoven" [Why Beethoven is dear to us], and "Betkhoven i sovremennost" [Beethoven and the present]. See Amy Nelson, *Music for the Revolution: Musicians and Power in Early Soviet Russia* (University Park: Pennsylvania State University Press, 2004), 282–83, n. 10.

29 Anatoly Lunacharsky, "Warum uns Beethoven teuer ist" [1927], in idem, *Das Erbe: Essays – Reden – Notizen*, ed. and trans. Franz Leschnitzer (Dresden: VEB Verlag der Kunst, 1965), 17–29, esp. 17–18.

30 Ibid., 26.

31 In the second part of this statement, usually studiously ignored, Lenin argues that he cannot listen to it often for it induces us to "caress people on the head," whereas the point now is to "strike them on the head, strike them without mercy." The passage was handed down by Maxim Gorky in *W. I. Lenin*, ed. N. Krutikova (Moscow: APN-Verlag, 1973), 53–54.

32 Alexander Friedman, "'Unser Beethoven': Rezeption des Komponisten und seiner Musik in der Sowjetunion vor dem deutschen Überfall 1917–1941," in *Inklusion & Exklusion: "Deutsche" Musik in Europa und Nordamerika 1848–1945*, ed. Sabine Mecking and Yvonne Wasserloos (Göttingen: V&R unipress, 2016), 195–211, esp. 197.

33 Nelson, *Music for the Revolution* (see note 28), 204.

34 Christina M. Stahl, *Was die Mode streng geteilt?! Beethovens Neunte während der deutschen Teilung* (Schott: Mainz, 2009), 117.

35 Harry Goldschmidt, *Ludwig van Beethoven und seine Zeit: Illustrierter Führer durch die deutsche Beethoven-Ausstellung* (Berlin: Staatl. Kommission für Kunstangelegenheiten, 1952), 41.

"the American imperialists threatened to poison German national consciousness" and the cultural heritage of the German nation.[36] Hanns Eisler stood up against such tendentious misappropriations when Egon Rentzsch, a member of the central committee, asked for his comments on the draft statement, which later underwent minimal adaptations. In his reply, Eisler basically argued that it simplified historical eras and figures by tailoring them to suit "day-to-day politics"; instead, he said, they should be viewed in all their complexity and contradictions.[37] By this point, Eisler had disembarrassed himself of the martial tone of his earliest publication on Beethoven, issued in *Die Rote Fahne* in 1927, in which he still sought to enlist Beethoven's "strong" and "life-affirming" music for the working class.[38] The more sophisticated understanding of Beethoven in his later pronouncements derives from the deep study he undertook during his exile in the United States, when he gave various lectures and planned to produce a new edition of Beethoven's sketchbooks.[39] This understanding came to the fore in 1952, for example, when he coined the aphorisms "heroism without bombast" and "feeling without sentimentality" for the weekly periodical *Sonntag* to describe the expressive power of Beethoven's music.[40] In the 1960s he turned against an "inflated 'world-view'" in current music, "this 'through darkness to light' metaphor," which, he felt, no longer meant anything to his contemporaries: "It had meaning in Beethoven's case, but for us it's as cheap as blackberries."[41] Later, other composers tried, with different levels of pretension, to combine their political and artistic aims. Karl Ottomar Treibmann, in his four-movement choral symphony *Der Frieden* (1983), sought to draw on popular culture with reflections and rhythmicizations of the Joy theme as a "modern pilgrim's chorus."[42] In contrast, Paul Dessau created an ingenious montage in his *Orchestermusik Nr. 3 (Lenin)* of 1970, where he honored the centennial of Lenin's birth, and the bicentennial of Beethoven's, with an "Appassionata" paraphrase peppered with quotations from his own music and references to Schoenberg.[43]

1944: Beethoven the Patriot and his Opposite Number (Max Unger)

The formula "Beethoven's patriotic music" was as potent in his nationalistic appropriation in the Third Reich as Max Unger's like-named article on its historical underpinnings was meager. Unger, a German musicologist and former custodian of Hans Conrad Bodmer's collection of Beethoveniana, opened his article with a description of Beethoven as a "modern man" who stood in the midst of life and nurtured his own political inclinations. But given Beethoven's vacillating political sympathies, Unger had a hard time emphasizing the composer's commitment to the fatherland. Nonetheless, he followed the war propaganda by singling out Beethoven's republican convictions and depicting his profession of faith in the French Revolution as "rebellion against monarchical power and its abuse" – a rebellion that could not, however, affect "well-intentioned rulers."[44] When composing the *Eroica*, Unger continued, Beethoven hardly had in mind a particular individual (Napoleon), but rather an "impersonal hero."[45] These reinterpretations must be seen in relation to the time when the article was written and the organ in which it was published. *Musik im Kriege* was a fusion of four party-affiliated music periodicals

36 Zentralkomitee der Sozialistischen Einheitspartei Deutschlands, "Zum 125. Todestag Ludwig van Beethovens am 26. März 1952," *Neues Deutschland*, no. 60 (11 March 1952): 6.

37 Hanns Eisler, "Bemerkungen zum Entwurf eines Beschlusses des ZK der SED zum 125. Todestag Ludwig van Beethovens," in idem, Gesammelte Werke, ser. III, vol. 2: *Musik und Politik: Schriften 1948–1962*, ed. Günter Mayer (Leipzig: VEB Deutscher Verlag für Musik, 1982), 194–211, esp. 194.

38 Hanns Eisler, "Ludwig van Beethoven: Zu seinem 100. Todestage am 26. März" [1927], in idem, Gesamtausgabe, ser. IX, vol. 1.1: *Gesammelte Schriften 1921–1935*, ed. Tobias Fasshauer and Günter Mayer (Wiesbaden: Breitkopf & Härtel, 2007), 42–46, esp. 45.

39 See Lynn Matheson, "'Ein Thema hat ungefähr so viele Möglichkeiten wie ein Mensch': Zur Beethoven-Rezeption Hanns Eislers," in *Hanns Eisler: 's müßt dem Himmel Höllenangst werden*, ed. Maren Köster (Hofheim: Wolke, 1998), 107–19, esp. 109–13.

40 Hanns Eisler, "Zu Beethovens Todestag," *Sonntag: Wochenzeitung für Kultur, Politik und Unterhaltung* (23 March 1952): 4; reprinted in idem, *Musik und Politik* (see note 37), 214–15, esp. 214.

41 Hanns Eisler in conversation with Hans Bunge, 6 November 1961, in Eisler, Gesammelte Werke, ser. III, vol. 7: *Gespräche mit Hans Bunge: Fragen Sie mehr über Brecht*, ed. Hans Bunge (Leipzig: VEB Deutscher Verlag für Musik, 1975), 233.

42 Karl Ottomar Treibmann, "Werkstationen: Notizen eines Komponisten," in Ulrike Liedtke, *Karl Ottomar Treibmann: Klangwanderungen* (Altenburg: Kamprad, 2004), 51–88, esp. 76.

43 See Matthias Tischer, "Dessau, Beethoven, Lenin, (Ulbricht) – und Schönberg? Zu Paul Dessaus *Orchestermusik Nr. 3* (Lenin)," in *"Vom Erkennen des Erkannten": Musikalische Analyse und Editionsphilologie: Festschrift für Christian Martin Schmidt*, ed. Friederike Wissmann, Thomas Ahrend, and Heinz von Loesch (Wiesbaden: Breitkopf & Härtel, 2007), 465–72.

44 Max Unger, "Beethovens vaterländische Musik," in *Musik im Krieg: Organ des Amtes Musik* 1, nos. 9–10 (1943–44): 170–75, at 170.

45 Ibid., 171.

that merged, in April 1943, in the wake of the proclamation of total war. Its mission was to serve the cause of German music so as to "contribute to the realization of the great Reich of the Germans, the Reich of the Führer."[46] Headed by the Nazi ideologue Herbert Gerigk, the ten double issues that eventually appeared, and their references to Beethoven, served the purposes of edification, racist agitation, and bolstering national sentiment. Unger, a Beethoven expert, had been denounced as a "musical Bolshevik" in 1935, only to be rehabilitated by the party and installed in the Amt Rosenberg (Rosenberg Office) in 1942. In this periodical he not only probed Beethoven's music for its patriotic leanings, but provided information in another article on Beethoven's military marches.[47] Hans Joachim Moser spread racist slurs in an article entitled "Meyerbeer contra Beethoven," in which he dismissed Giacomo Meyerbeer's analytical inscriptions in a score of Beethoven's String Quartet, op. 127, as "Jewish presumption."[48]

Although Beethoven did not have the same status in the régime's "symbolic internal order" as such Nazi icons as Richard Wagner and Anton Bruckner,[49] he occupied a firm place in the cultural policy of the Third Reich. The Ninth Symphony resounded in lavishly staged performances for Hitler's birthday in 1937, and again in 1942; his famous works were programmed on radio and in film to strengthen national cohesion, and helped to attain a cultural rapport with local music-lovers in areas of occupation.[50] As appropriated by the Nazis, traditional images of Beethoven were expanded to include racist components, such as an emphasis on his Nordic ancestry (overlooking his Flemish roots), and Jewish musicians were forbidden to play his music.[51] Basically, the appropriation activated chauvinistic lines of tradition in which Beethoven had already been embroiled in the nineteenth century for the purpose of constructing a national cultural identity and personifying the superiority of German music.[52] Beethoven's Germanness was magnified into the titanic, the strong, into superiority over the non-German. The Nazi composer and Reger pupil Hermann Unger, for example, writing in the *Deutsche Militär-Musik-Zeitung* in 1942, exclaimed, alluding to Bismarck and Wagner, "When I hear Beethoven, I become more valiant."[53] By joining up with the nationalist tradition of the Third Reich, the appropriation built upon a consensus and an identification that Germany's rulers shared with its musicians and music-lovers (SEE PLATE 1, P. 62).

This "zone of consensus between idealistically inflated German cultural chauvinism and Nazi ideology"[54] is also where Wilhelm Furtwängler's writings on Beethoven are positioned. This German conductor had issued an appeal to the German people as far back as 1920, in an article for the Beethoven Jubilee entitled "Beethoven the Victor": the "superhuman strength of Beethoven's will to victory" was, he opined, derived from "a sort of unbounded trust" that he referred to, "even at the risk of being misunderstood," as "German destiny."[55] In 1936 he brought his chauvinistic outpourings to a head in the preface to Walter Riezler's Beethoven biography: "By no one is the force and grandeur of German sensibility and essence expressed with greater urgency."[56] Finally, in an article of 1942 on Beethoven's "worldwide validity," he pointed to the universal significance of this German composer.[57] Was this reading merely an expression of Furtwängler's chauvinism or a link with Nazi policy? Furtwängler himself was, to be sure, never a member of the party and

46 Herbert Gerigk, "An unsere Leser," *Musik im Kriege: Organ des Amtes Musik* 1, no. 1 (1943): 1.

47 Max Unger, "Beethovens Militärmärsche," *Musik im Kriege: Organ des Amtes Musik* 1, nos. 7–8, (1943): 121–24.

48 Hans Joachim Moser, "Meyerbeer contra Beethoven," in ibid.: 131–32, at 132.

49 Esteban Buch, "Beethoven und das 'Dritte Reich': Porträt eines konservativen Titanen," in *Das "Dritte Reich" und die Musik*, ed. Stiftung Schloss Neuhardenberg and Cité de la musique (Paris: Cité de la musique; Berlin: Nicolai, 2006), 39–53, esp. 39.

50 See Esteban Buch, *Beethoven's Ninth: A Political History*, trans. Richard Miller (Chicago: University of Chicago Press, 2003), 201–19, and David B. Dennis, *Beethoven in German Politics, 1870–1989* (New Haven: Yale University Press, 1996), 142–74.

51 See Heribert Schröder, "Beethoven im Dritten Reich: Eine Materialsammlung," in *Beethoven und die Nachwelt: Materialien zur Wirkungsgeschichte Beethovens*, ed. Helmut Loos (Bonn: Beethoven-Haus, 1986), 187–221, esp. 205–10.

52 The hypothesis of the "pre-eminence of German music" remained in effect even after the Second World War; see Anselm Gerhard, "Die 'Vorherrschaft der deutschen Musik' nach 1945 – eine Ironie der Geschichte," in *Deutsche Leitkultur Musik? Zur Musikgeschichte nach dem Holocaust*, ed. Albrecht Riethmüller (Stuttgart: Franz Steiner, 2006), 13–27.

53 Hermann Unger, "'Wenn ich Beethoven höre, werde ich tapferer': Eine Untersuchung über das Thema 'Kriegsmusik,'" *Deutsche Militär-Musiker-Zeitung* 64 (1942): 105–07, reproduced in Schröder, "Beethoven im Dritten Reich" (see note 51), 216.

54 Peter Gülke, "Hätte er gehen müssen? Furtwängler oder: Kein Ende beim Thema 'Musik und Politik,'" in *Musik – Politik – Ästhetik: Detlef Altenburg zum 65. Geburtstag*, ed. Axel Schröter and Daniel Ortuño-Stühring (Sinzig: Studio, 2012), 210–16, at 211.

55 Wilhelm Furtwängler, "Beethoven der Sieger," *Frankfurter Zeitung und Handelsblatt* (16 December 1920), 1st morning edition: 3; reprinted in *Braunschweiger neuste Nachrichten – Der Sonntag* (20 March 1927), fol. 2 (Beethoven-Haus, Bonn, Z 32 / 3) and the program booklet of the Potsdam City Concerts 1938–39 (Leipzig: Max Beck, n.d.) (Wilhelm Furtwängler Collection, Zurich Zentralbibliothek).

56 "Durch Niemanden wird Gewalt und Größe deutschen Empfindens und Wesens eindringlicher zum Ausdruck gebracht." Wilhelm Furtwängler in the preface to Walter Riezler, *Beethoven* (Berlin: Atlantis, 1936), 9–10, at 9.

57 Wilhelm Furtwängler, "Die Weltgültigkeit Beethovens" [1942], in *Ton und Wort: Aufsätze und Vorträge 1918 bis 1954* (Wiesbaden: F. A. Brockhaus, 1954), 184–87, esp. 185.

PLATE 1
Wreath laid in the so-called "birth room" of the Bonn Beethoven-Haus during the visit of the medical corps of the 58th SS Standarte, June 1936. Photograph by Max Ehlert
(BEETHOVEN-HAUS BONN, B 789)

distanced himself again and again from the régime. Yet he let himself regularly be listed by the party as a conductor, as in the celebrations staged by Goebbels for Hitler's birthday in 1942. While Furtwängler himself justified his activities by referring to the autonomy of art, the assessments of his contemporaries and posterity alike[58] vacillate between staunch defense and equally staunch accusation. As early as 1934 Samuel Becket described him as "covered with interwoven swastikas."[59]

Meanwhile, on the side of the allies, Beethoven was also dispatched to the front as war propaganda. The British, in an effective promotional strategy, emphasized the values of a common European musical tradition and Beethoven's universal message. The German service of the BBC announced its war reports with a signal consisting of three short and one long note-value, at once Morse code for the letter "V" (for "victory") and the world-famous opening of the Fifth Symphony. America's *Real Life Comics* went so far as to present Beethoven as a veritable war hero who had composed the Fifth as a symbol of democracy.[60] This did not prevent him from returning, at the end of hostilities, to his role as the lodestar of international reconciliation, though Wagner, of all people, served as a point of reference. In late 1945 the journalist Hans Borgelt presented Beethoven as "a friend of humanity" and even referred to Wagner's 1870 preference for "world benefactor," as opposed to "world conqueror," as a "warning."[61] Heinrich Steger, a member of the board of Vienna's Gesellschaft der Musikfreunde, had been no less unscrupulous in 1920 when he opened the week-long Beethoven Festival of the Gesellschaft with a crypto-quotation, turning the "world benefactor" into the "world conqueror" and "world ruler" in the "realm of music and the spirit."[62]

58 For a detailed assessment see Gülke, "Hätte er gehen müssen?" (see note 54), and idem, "Der Erwählte: Zum 30. November 2004," *Musik & Ästhetik* 9, no. 34 (2005): 93–114.

59 Letter of 27 January 1934 from Samuel Beckett to Morris Sinclair, in *The Letters of Samuel Beckett*, vol. 1: *1929–1940*, ed. Martha Dow Fehsenfeld and Lois More Overbeck (Cambridge: Cambridge University Press, 2009), 180–83, at 182. See Michael Kunkel, "'Mine is a faint voice', Beckett selon Beethoven – Beethoven selon Beckett," *Neue Zeitschrift für Musik* 177, no. 6 (2016): 30–35, esp. 34.

60 "Ludwig van Beethoven," *Real Life Comics*, no. 15 (January 1943), reprinted in Michael Broyles, *Beethoven in America* (Bloomington: Indiana University Press, 2011), 341.

61 Hans Borgelt, "Ludwig van Beethoven: zur 175. Wiederkehr seines Geburtstages" [unidentified newspaper clipping of 1945] (Beethoven-Haus, Bonn, Z 3123).

62 Quoted from "Die Beethoven-Festwoche der Gesellschaft der Musikfreunde," *Neue Freie Presse*, no. 20220 (12 December 1920): 8.

PLATE 2
Cover of the magazine *High Fidelity* 23, no. 2 (February 1973), detail

1973: The Virile Beethoven with Wig and Lipstick (*High Fidelity*)

In 1973 Beethoven appeared on the title page of the music periodical *High Fidelity* in a special outfit: a collage showed a bust of the composer sporting a long reddish-brown wig with his lips colored red (SEE PLATE 2). Although the picture bears witness to an early departure from sexual stereotypes, the issue itself contained no discussion whatever of Beethoven's masculinity or of new approaches to his reception in popular music. The montage merely served as an eye-catcher for the question, "Why haven't women composed great music?" – a question debated by a feminist and a psychologist. Judith Rosen attributed the absence of a "female Bach" in music history to traditional gender roles, cultural habits, and social barriers, and pointed to exceptions from Francesca Caccini to Pauline Oliveros. Grace Rubin-Rabson, on the other hand, minimized the social obstacles and denied the compositional creativity of Clara Schumann while conceding to her a certain "biological creativity" (Clara Schumann gave birth to eight children). The psychologist replicated entrenched gender stereotypes by attributing a want of female creativity to a lack of inventiveness, intellect, and stamina. Although she did not invoke Beethoven as an example of male creativity, she resorted to lines of argument that had taken shape on his example (among others). "Masculinity" has often been employed as an analytical category in the reception of Beethoven. Eisler, to take an example, described Beethoven's music in 1927 as "manly even where it is tender, where it is intimate and soft," and his tenderness as never being "flaccid, amorphous, or decadent." Rolland summarily pronounced him "the most virile of musicians."[63]

The title page of *High Fidelity* prompted an early remonstration from a female composer. Pauline Oliveros had already questioned the standard heroic image of Beethoven in her theatrical works *Pieces of Eight* (1964), *Double Basses at Twenty Paces* (1968), and *Aeolian Partitions* (1969).[64] She responded to *High Fidelity*'s picture of Beethoven "in drag" with two actions. In one, she designed a series of postcards, together with Fluxus artist Alison Knowles, that fractured the image of the heroic masculine composer in ironic self-stagings. One picture shows Oliveros

63 Eisler, "Beethoven: Zu seinem 100. Todestage" (see note. 38), 44; Romain Rolland, *Beethoven: Les grandes époques créatrices*, 2nd edn. (Paris: Éditions du Sablier, 1928), 23.

64 Heidi Von Gunden, *The Music of Pauline Oliveros* (Metuchen: Scarecrow Press, 1983), 71–78.

herself seated in a garden, with Beethovenian scowl, alongside an equally earnest Beethoven made of paper maché; a caption reads "Beethoven was a Lesbian."[65] In another, an essay entitled "Divisions Underground," she countered the question posed in *High Fidelity* about the lack of great woman composers by asking a counter-question: why do men still ask the wrong questions?[66] Here she took up arguments from a *New York Times* article that she had published three years earlier with the title "And Don't Call Them 'Lady' Composers," in which she pointed to a number of terms that belittle women and assign them deprecating tags.[67]

The masculinity construct found its way into the theoretical discussion of Beethoven only around the turn of the millennium following a heated polemical debate sparked in the early 1990s by Susan McClary's description of the recapitulation in the opening movement of the Ninth as "one of the most horrifyingly violent episodes in the history of music." According to McClary, in the recapitulation the masculine persona refuses, with mighty detonations, to return to the original womb-like emptiness. Then, in a leaping conclusion, she construes this as "murderous rage."[68] Her argument draws basically on the dualistic categories, familiar since Adolph Bernhard Marx, of a "masculine" first theme and a "feminine" second theme in sonata-allegro form.[69] However, she gives "masculine" a negative connotation as "violent." The association of violence with Beethoven's music had already been made explicit in Stanley Kubrick's widely viewed film adaptation (1971) of Anthony Burgess's novel *A Clockwork Orange* (1962).[70] Following these controversies, however, several years had to elapse before the categories of gender and sexuality were called upon for an understanding of historical conditions. Regarding Beethoven, Sanna Pederson, writing in 2000, pointed to the connection between the composer's public position, the narrative of the heroic, and the masculinity construct.[71] Later she plausibly explained that the switch from a universal to a specifically masculine label was also amenable to historical verification. She thereby laid bare the reception-historical phenomenon that Beethoven was capable of "representing simultaneously the all-encompassing and the particular."[72]

The identification and study of ideas attributed to Beethoven – ideas that have dominated the interpretation of his life and music in the twentieth century – have led to a wild journey through a welter of ideological shortcuts and distortions in his reception. They reveal that the attributed meanings are subject to the currents of the day, for they are linked to conflicting ideological value systems. They function as delimitation mechanisms by including and excluding various broadly conceived groups of people, ranging from specific nations and genders to a universal commonality. At the same time, they have an inbred ambiguity that permits wholly conflicting interpretations and appropriations, and thereby seems to suppress specific ideological co-optations of the past. This resistance has given rise to the many appropriations of, say, the Ninth Symphony at the hands of totalitarian régimes and democratic alliances of all stripes,[73] driving the phenomenon to new flowerings, over and over again.

Although ideological misuse during the wars of the first half of the twentieth century led to a downturn in ideational interpretations among many postwar composers and theorists, the trend in music publications, marketing strategies, and cultural policies seems, in the long run, to be fully intact. When the

65 Louise Gray, "Beethoven Was A Lesbian," *The Wire* (December 2016), published online at www.thewire.co.uk/in-writing/essays/pauline-oliveros-louise-gray (accessed 20 November 2019).

66 Pauline Oliveros, "Divisions Underground" [1973], in idem, *Software for People: Collected Writings 1963–80* (Baltimore: Smith Publications, 1984), 97–111.

67 Pauline Oliveros, "And Don't Call Them 'Lady' Composers" [1970], in ibid., 47–51, esp. 47–48. See also Dörte Schmidt, "Bonn Feier: Die Repräsentation der Kultur in der Beethoven-Stadt und das Projekt der Komponistin Pauline Oliveros 1977," in *Feste – Opern – Prozessionen: Musik als kulturelle Repräsentation*, Jahrbuch Musik und Gender, vol. 1, ed. Katharina Hottmann and Christine Siegert (Hildesheim: Georg Olms, 2008), 131–49, esp. 141.

68 Susan McClary, "Getting Down Off the Beanstalk: The Presence of a Woman's Voice in Janika Vandervelde's *Genesis II*," in idem, *Feminine Endings: Music, Gender, and Sexuality* (Minneapolis: University of Minnesota Press, 1991), 112–31, esp. 128. On the first version, in which McClary construes the ending as "throttling murderous rage of a rapist incapable of attaining release," see Esteban Buch's essay in this volume, 143–56, esp. 150–51.

69 See Albrecht Riethmüller, "Wunschbild: Beethoven als Chauvinist," *Archiv für Musikwissenschaft* 58 (2001): 91–109, esp. 95–96.

70 According to Beatrix Borchard, McClary's interpretation was prompted by the film; see "Beethoven: Männlichkeitskonstruktionen im Bereich der Musik," in *Kunst, Geschlecht, Politik: Geschlechterentwürfe in der Kunst des Kaiserreichs und der Weimarer Republik*, ed. Martina Kessel (Frankfurt: Campus, 2005), 65–83, esp. 82.

71 See Sanna Pederson, "Beethoven and Masculinity," in *Beethoven and his World*, ed. Scott Burnham and Michael P. Steinberg, (Princeton: Princeton University Press, 2000), 313–31.

72 Sanna Pederson, "Beethoven und Männlichkeit im Kontext der Revolution von 1848/49," in *Der "männliche" und der "weibliche" Beethoven: Bericht über den Internationalen musikwissenschaftlichen Kongress vom 31. Oktober bis 4. November 2001 an der Universität der Künste Berlin*, ed. Cornelia Bartsch, Beatrix Borchard, and Rainer Cadenbach (Bonn: Beethoven-Haus, 2003), 21–31, esp. 22.

73 Slavoj Žižek demonstrated this "universal adaptability" in an impressive list of its appropriations. See Sophie Fiennes and Slavoj Žižek's documentary film *The Pervert's Guide to Ideology – What is Ideology?* (UK and Ireland: Blinder Films, 2012), 00:18:30–00:22:50.

Berlin Philharmonic opened the season in New York's Carnegie Hall in October 2001, following the attacks on the World Trade Center, they summarily replaced Webern, Wagner, and Mahler with Beethoven in order to convey the "musical statement" of a composer motivated by grand ideals and a firm faith in liberty.[74] The German composer and music critic Arno Lücker, in an otherwise uncommonly neutral bar-by-bar analysis of the C minor Piano Sonata, op. 111, explained its dotted rhythms and its reference to the music of the French Revolution by speaking of the "political struggle for freedom of the individual," calling it "far and away Beethoven's most important personal and artistic theme."[75] When the Ninth was performed in Hamburg's Elbphilharmonie during the G20 summit of July 2017 (at the request of Angela Merkel),[76] it was meant once again to proclaim a "brotherhood of man," though, to be sure, it also laid bare the German roots of the European national anthem. And in the Beethoven anniversary of 2020 the message of a "harmonious unity between mankind and nature" in the *Pastoral* served as an admonition to protect the environment.[77] Some ideological aberrations may have vanished in the collective self-regulation of Beethoven's ideational reception, but the basic ethical constants endure.

74 Anthony Tommasini, "As Ever in a Crisis, Beethoven Reigns," *The New York Times* (5 October 2001): E1, online at www.nytimes.com/2001/10/05/movies/critic-s-notebook-as-ever-in-a-crisis-beethoven-reigns.html (accessed 20 November 2019).

75 Arno Lücker, "op. 111 – Eine Analyse in 335 Teilen," in *Bad Blog of Musick*, https://blogs.nmz.de/badblog/2016/01/29/op-111-eine-analyse-in-335-teilen-takt-2 (accessed 20 November 2019).

76 The concert was given in the Elbphilharmonie on 7 July 2017. The Philharmonic State Chorus of Hamburg and the Hamburg State Opera Chorus performed under the baton of Kent Nagano with solo vocalists Christiane Karg, Okka von der Damerau, Klaus Florian Vogt, and Franz-Josef Selig. See rf/bb (ndr), "Elbphilharmonie stimmt G20-Teilnehmer mit Beethoven ein," in *Deutsche Welle* (DW), 7 July 2017, www.dw.com/de/elbphilharmonie-stimmt-g20-teilnehmer-mit-beethoven-ein/a-39578750 (accessed 20 November 2019).

77 "The Pastoral Project: Beethoven loved nature – we love it, too!", published online at https://pastoralproject.org/project-information (accessed 20 November 2019).

Anton Webern
Diary Entry
(1904)

On 6 November 1904, twenty-year-old Anton Webern (1883–1945) entered the Great Auditorium of Vienna's Musikverein to hear the first subscription concert of the Vienna Philharmonic's 1904–05 season. The program, conducted by Felix Mottl, featured Wolfgang Amadeus Mozart's "Prague" Symphony (K. 504), Hans Pfitzner's Scherzo for Orchestra, and Ludwig van Beethoven's Third Symphony, the *Eroica* (op. 55). The concert had been sold out for days and was awaited with excitement, for the Philharmonic had been forced to play under various guest conductors following the resignations of their regular conductors Gustav Mahler (in 1901) and Joseph Hellmesberger Jr. (in 1903). Mottl had made his début with the Philharmonic just a few months earlier in Salzburg and was preceded by a sterling reputation. The noonday concert on 6 November solidified that reputation, particularly through his reading of the *Eroica:* Julius Korngold found the performance "superb," and Mottl was "repeatedly called back at the end by storms of applause."[1]

Webern, too, was probably among those who "called" for the conductor, for the concert inspired him to write an entry in his diary (SEE PLATE 1).[2] Although he makes no mention of Mottl, he would hardly have waxed so rapturous and flamboyant if the performance had been mediocre or poor. His diary entry exudes an absolute veneration and idealization of Beethoven that impressively reflect his youthful élan while typifying the general view of Beethoven at the *fin de siècle.* Here he invokes imagery that portrays Beethoven as a hero, genius, deity, consoler, man of solitude, and role model. This imagery was so widespread at the time that no single source can be found for Webern's vision of Beethoven, although it bears analogies to the symbolic burden of Max Klinger's Beethoven monument and Gustav Klimt's Beethoven frieze, both displayed at the Vienna Secession from April to June 1902.[3]

The diary entry has an astonishing structural rigor. It begins with a Beethoven quotation that Webern chose as a fitting motto for the *Eroica,*[4] followed by a concise programmatic précis of the symphony ("From sorrow and suffering..."). Webern then reflects on his own past and future reception of Beethoven's music ("ever-greater clarity"), which, in a further section, leads to the desire for a modern music based on Beethoven's historical model but analogous to the contemporary painting of Giovanni Segantini ("I long for ..."). The entry ends with another motto. These five sections are tightly interlocked by means of four key concepts – strength, truth, longing, and solitude – that function as connecting links between the sections. Webern considered the first two of these concepts to be qualities inherent in Beethoven's music, with truth being particularly central, as it forms the *telos* of the two sections following the motto. In this way, his own process of reception ("ever-greater clarity") resembles the program of the *Eroica* itself in its symbolic thrust, and amounts to an increase in knowledge. Thus, just as Webern "searches for truth," he longs for a contemporary artist, a "Beethoven of our times." To achieve that truth, an artist must pursue a life "in solitude," as also expressed in the Hebbel quotation at the end of the entry.

1 J.K. [Julius Korngold], "Philharmonisches Konzert," *Neue Freie Presse,* no. 14442 (7 November 1904): 9–10, at 10.

2 Anton Webern, Diary 1 (Anton Webern Collection, PSS). Published in Anton Webern, "Drei frühe Tagebücher," ed. Barbara Schingnitz, in *Der junge Webern: Texte und Kontexte,* ed. Thomas Ahrend and Matthias Schmidt (Vienna: Lafite, 2015), 217–324, at 254 (diary entry) and 303 (commentary).

3 See e.g. the review of the Secession Exhibition by W., "Die Beethoven-Woche," *Neue Freie Presse,* no. 13525 (20 April 1902): 2–4, at 4, which refers to Beethoven as a "god," a "hero," and a "man who renounced the world," and assigns him the attributes of "strength" and "lenience."

4 The quotation stems from Beethoven's letter to Nikolaus Zmeskall (c. 1798). Webern may have taken it from Friedrich Kerst's *Beethoven im eigenen Wort* (Berlin: Schuster, 1904), 136, which appeared in autumn 1904. According to his own library catalogue (Anton Webern Collection, PSS), he owned a copy of the book.

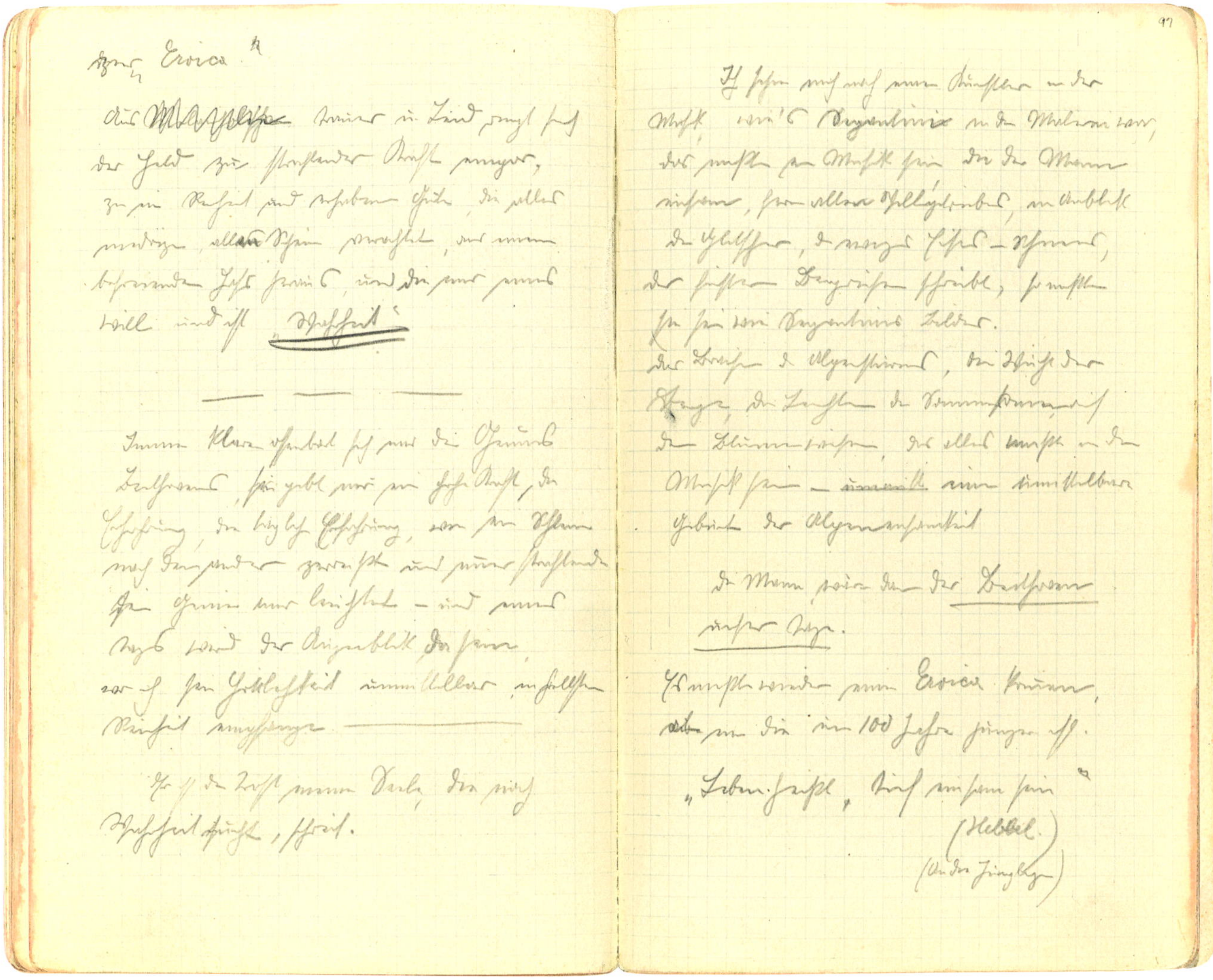

PLATE 1
Anton Webern, Diary 1 (c. 1900–06). Entry of or after 6 November 1904, pp. 96–97
(ANTON WEBERN COLLECTION, PSS)

TRANSLATION

["Power is the moral principle of those who excel others, and it is also mine." That would be the best motto] for the "Eroica."

From sorrow and suffering, the hero struggles upward to radiant strength, to a purity and sublime excellence that despises all lowness, all illusion, from a liberating hatred. It wants only one thing, and is "truth."

——— ——— ———

Beethoven's genius reveals itself to me with ever-greater clarity; he gives me great strength, experience, the daily experience as one veil after another is torn away and his genius illuminates me with growing radiance. And one day the moment will come when I receive his divinity directly in utmost purity ————

He is the comfort of my soul, which searches and cries out for truth.

I long for an artist in music as Segantini was in painting; it would have to be a music that he writes in solitude, far from the turmoil of the world, in the face of glaciers, of eternal ice and snow, of dark titanic mountains; it would have to be like Segantini's paintings.

The roaring of the alpine storm, the vigil of the mountains, the glow of the summer sun upon the flowering meadows: all of that would have to be in the music – an immediate birth of alpine solitude[.]

That man would then be the Beethoven of our times.

Another Eroica must come, but one that is 100 years younger.

"To live is to be profoundly solitary"
(Hebbel.)
(An die Jünglinge)

PLATE 2
Photograph from an unidentified newspaper showing the Schwarzspanierhaus (House of the Black-Robed Spaniards), the building in which Beethoven died, scheduled for demolition (c. November 1903)
(ANTON WEBERN COLLECTION, PSS)

That Webern situates this life in the mountains is specifically motivated by his own affinity to mountain landscapes and the enthusiasm he felt at the time for the paintings of Segantini.[5] Yet the connection between Beethoven and mountains was a widespread notion at the time and was frequently drawn upon to symbolize Beethoven's sublimity and grandeur. Wagner used it in his Beethoven essay to illuminate "the true nature of music in general (by which we understood Beethoven's music in particular)," referring among other things to the image of a "high valley in Uri" traversed "in sublime solitude" while hearing the echo of a "jubilant cry of a shepherd."[6] And Felix Weingartner introduced his book *The Symphony Since Beethoven* with a description of a "tremendous group of mountains" and its "snow-covered peak" to convey the unattainability of Beethoven's achievement.[7]

For all its structural density, Webern's diary entry is marked by a relatively simple dualism of values: the negative concepts of "sorrow and suffering," "lowness," and "illusion" are contrasted with "radiant strength," "sublime excellence," "purity," and "truth"; and (alpine) "solitude" has its antithesis in "the turmoil of the world." Yet the contrast is not only static; it is caught in a dynamic flux: just as the hero "struggles upward" and Webern sees the genius "with ever-greater clarity" and "growing radiance," his quest and longing are directed toward a higher plane. This is no less apparent in the *topos* of truth laid bare – a *topos* that Webern implicitly employs by invoking the image of the torn veils that ultimately liberate the eye for knowledge and discovery. In this dynamism of values, Webern reveals a sentimental awareness dominated by the sense of a fractured reality – by inadequacy – and therefore aspiring toward ideals in order to overcome that inadequacy. In this light, the concept of truth has a key function, being less a propositional truth (which is why Webern need not define it) than a cultural value, and thus just such an ideal. The immediacy with which Webern grasps it shows how deeply he was rooted in nineteenth-century idealism, and how completely untouched he was by the fundamental skepticism with which post-Enlightenment modernism confronted truth. Friedrich

5 See the articles by Andrea Gottdang, Thomas Ahrend, Felix Meyer, Matthias Schmidt, and especially Markus Böggemann in *Anton Webern und Giovanni Segantini*, a special issue of *Musiktheorie* 30, no. 4 (2015). Especially revealing of the connection between Beethoven and mountain symbolism is Webern's letter of 29 July 1905 to Heinrich Jalowetz in Anton Webern, *Briefe an Heinrich Jalowetz*, ed. Ernst Lichtenhahn (Mainz: Schott, 1999), 114.

6 *Richard Wagner's* Beethoven *(1870)*, trans. Roger Allen (Woodbridge: Boydell, 2014), 97 and 67.

7 Felix Weingartner, "The Symphony Since Beethoven" [1897], trans. H. M. Schott, in *Weingartner on Music & Conducting: Three Essays by Felix Weingartner* (New York: Dover, 1969), 235–304, at 245.

Nietzsche, to choose an example, denied that "truth remains truth when the veils are withdrawn," thereby questioning the categorical nature formerly associated with it. Nietzsche has lost confidence in absolute truth, as Webern sees it, and dismisses the "will to truth" or the "love of truth" as mere "youthful madness."[8]

Webern deeply admired Beethoven's music to the end of his days. His diary entry is one of the most striking signs of this, but certainly not the only one. Unlike his lectures of the 1930s, when his rapture gave way to sober observation,[9] he referred to a concert of the Ninth Symphony in 1903 as "the most solemn hour" of his life.[10] And in a letter of 1911 to Alban Berg he reflected on Christmas as the celebration of a night "on which a great man was born," prompting him to ask rhetorically, "Should one not so celebrate Beethoven's birthday in this way?"[11] Finally, a document of a special kind, preserved among Webern's papers, is a newspaper photograph of the house in which Beethoven died (SEE PLATE 2). Though undated, it probably appeared in November 1903, when plans were made public to tear down the Schwarzspanierhaus (House of the Black-Robed Spaniards) for a new building – plans that were eventually carried out. But the special value of this document resides not only in the fact that he wanted to preserve the image of a symbolic memorial site as it was about to disappear, but also that the demolition took place literally before his very eyes: ever since moving to Vienna in autumn 1902 to study musicology, he lived opposite the Schwarzspanierhaus – namely, in the building shown at the right edge of the photograph.

Simon Obert

8 Friedrich Nietzsche, *The Gay Science: With a Prelude in Rhymes and an Appendix of Songs*, trans. Walter Kaufmann (New York: Vintage Books, 1974), 38.

9 In his lectures of the early 1930s, Beethoven represents the pinnacle in the evolution of form; see Anton Webern, *The Path to the New Music*, ed. Willi Reich, trans. Leo Black (Bryn Mawr: Theodor Presser Company, 1963), e.g. 30 and 33. His subsequent lectures on musical form (1934–38) are based almost exclusively on Beethoven's piano sonatas; see Anton Webern, *Über musikalische Formen: Aus den Vortragsmitschriften von Ludwig Zenk, Siegfried Oehlgiesser, Rudolf Schopf und Erna Apostel*, ed. Neil Boynton (Mainz: Schott, 2002).

10 Webern, "Drei frühe Tagebücher" (see note 2), 238.

11 Anton Webern, letter to Alban Berg, 21 December 1911, in Kathryn Puffet and Barbara Schingnitz, *Three Men of Letters: Arnold Schönberg, Alban Berg and Anton Webern, 1906–1921* (Vienna: Hollitzer, 2020), 143. Webern also seems to have pursued this idea in later life. Frederick Deutsch Dorian records an almost identical remark from him in a conducting course from the early 1920s; see Frederick Deutsch Dorian, "Webern als Lehrer," *Melos* 27 (1960): 101–06, esp. 101.

Charles Ives *Concord Sonata* (c. 1915–19)

After his death, Beethoven's fame spread as rapidly in the United States as it did in Europe, thanks in particular to the newly founded philharmonic societies and their orchestras. For example, the New York Philharmonic Society, founded in 1842, gave no fewer than seventeen performances of Beethoven symphonies in its first twenty-eight concerts, and Beethoven was cultivated with similar alacrity in Boston.[1] Also active in Boston and environs were Margaret Fuller and John Sullivan Dwight, who dealt at length with Beethoven in their periodicals *The Dial* (1840–44), *The Harbinger* (1845–49), and *Dwight's Journal of Music* (1852–81). Fuller and Dwight belonged to the inner circle of New England Transcendentalism, a philosophical and literary movement centered on Ralph Waldo Emerson, informed by German Idealism, and sustained by a staunch impetus for social reform. They admired Beethoven with almost cultish devotion and interpreted his music very much in the spirit of Transcendentalist thought. Fuller particularly emphasized his forays into new, uncharted regions of feeling and expression, while Dwight saw in his music not least a utopian element, "a presentiment of coming social harmony."[2]

Around the mid-nineteenth century the veneration of Beethoven reached such a pitch that he soon became the measure of all things among musicians and audiences alike. It is thus no coincidence that the name of Beethoven adorns the proscenium of Boston Symphony Hall, inaugurated in 1900 (SEE PLATE 1), whereas the other medallions affixed to the galleries were left blank. Even in such times of crisis as the First World War, when public opinion took a sharp anti-German turn, the prestige of Beethoven, who was widely viewed as a universal artist transcending his era and nationality, was hardly tarnished. Evidence of this can be seen not least in a famous "twinned work" of American music: Charles Ives's so-called *Concord Sonata* (his Piano Sonata No. 2), composed largely between 1915 and 1919, and the associated volume *Essays Before a Sonata* (1919), in which he portrayed the protagonists of Transcendentalism active in Concord, Massachusetts (besides Emerson these included Nathaniel Hawthorne, Bronson Alcott and his second-oldest daughter Luisa May, and Henry David Thoreau).[3] Both works, self-published in 1920, contain multiple references to Beethoven. In the epilogue to the *Essays,* for example, Ives (1874–1954) praised Beethoven's music as an art that strives for truth and is thus entirely beholden to "substance," whereas he criticized Richard Strauss, probably his most famous contemporary, for being chiefly interested in "manner," i.e. the devices of musical representation. From this Ives concluded that "This choice tells why Beethoven is always modern and Strauss always medieval."[4] Further, in the main section of the essays he expressed his conviction that Emerson, in his best moments, came as close to the divine as Beethoven,[5] this being, to his mind, the highest imaginable praise he could bestow on the poet-philosopher.

Far more important than the textual references in the Essays are, however, the musical allusions to Beethoven in the *Concord Sonata*. Indeed, large stretches of Ives's sonata, written in a sort of free tonality, are pervaded with highly recognizable melodic *object trouvés,* including, besides scraps of church

1 For a discussion of the reception of Beethoven in the United States see Michael Broyles, *Beethoven in America* (Bloomington: Indiana University Press, 2011).

2 John Sullivan Dwight, "Music Review: Music in Boston during the Past Winter. No. IV", *The Harbinger* 1/12 (30 August 1845): 194.

3 The *Concord Sonata* arose over a long period of time and is partly based on sketches that date back to the year 1907. See Geoffrey Block, *Charles Ives: Concord Sonata* (Cambridge: Cambridge University Press, 1996), 20–27. In contrast, *Essays Before a Sonata* was written in relatively short order in 1919.

4 Quoted from Charles Ives, "Epilogue" in idem, *Essays Before a Sonata, and Other Writings*, ed. Howard Boatwright (New York: W.W. Norton, 1962), 83.

5 Ibid., 30.

PLATE 1
The Beethoven medallion in Symphony Hall, Boston
Photograph by Len Levasseur
LEN LEVASSEUR, THE NEO PRESS, BY KIND PERMISSION

hymns and folk tunes, the opening motif of Beethoven's Fifth Symphony. These quotation-like elements function like signposts partitioning the sonata's musical train of thought, which proceeds by free association rather than by schoolbook logic and is not always easy to follow. The integrative impact of these melodic elements is particularly noticeable in the case of those motifs that appear in more than one movement. One such cyclic element is the Beethoven motif.

Ives's use of this motif is highly ambiguous. Two of the church hymns employed in the sonata – "Martyn" by Simeon B. Marsh (1834) and "Missionary Chant" by Heinrich Christoph Zeuner (1832) – likewise begin with repeated notes followed by a descending third,[6] making it at least theoretically conceivable that Ives merely quoted Beethoven "indirectly" (i.e. via Marsh or Zeuner). An assumption along these lines is quickly dispelled, however, by a perusal of the *Essays,* where Ives explicitly mentions the opening motif of Beethoven's Fifth and makes it clear that he regards it as a musical analogy to Emerson's spiritual message: as a symbol of "the soul of humanity knocking at the door of the divine mysteries, radiant in the faith that it *will* be opened – and the human become the divine!"[7]

Apart from this "intertextual" ambiguity, the four-note motif in the *Concord Sonata* is noteworthy in that it appears not only in isolation, but woven increasingly tightly with other quotations and motifs into a longer melodic entity as the movements proceed. This entity, known in the Ives literature as the "human faith" melody[8] owing to a relevant remark from the composer, has a four-part design (SEE EXAMPLE 1, P. 72).

The melody is already present in the sonata's first two movements ("Emerson" and "Hawthorne"), where, however, it is buried beneath other musical events within the multi-layered piano texture. It then appears very clearly and in compact form in the third movement ("The Alcotts"): most distinctly at its end, as can be seen from a copy of the first edition shown here (SEE PLATE 2, P. 73). This statement of the "human faith" theme could hardly be more urgent. Nevertheless, in the final movement ("Thoreau"), Ives manages to enhance it one more notch by having the melody step outside the piano texture, as it were, and entrusting it to Thoreau's instrument, the flute (albeit *ad libitum*).[9]

Ives's combination of the Beethoven motif with other motivic elements demonstrates in miniature (i.e. on the level of the "human faith" melody) an equality of highbrow and lowbrow, of élite and quotidian, that informs the work as a whole, with its alternation of contrasting musical types and stylistic

6 For the melodies quoted by Ives see Clayton W. Henderson, *The Charles Ives Tunebook* (Bloomington: Indiana University Press, 2nd edn. 2008), esp. 55–56 and 58–59. A good discussion of Ives's treatment of these melodies can be found in J. Peter Burkholder, *All Made of Tunes: Charles Ives and the Uses of Musical Borrowing* (New Haven: Yale University Press, 1995), 350–57.
7 Ives, *Essays Before a Sonata* (see note 4), 36.
8 Ibid., 47.
9 See Felix Meyer, *"The Art of Speaking Extravagantly": Eine vergleichende Studie der* Concord Sonata *und der* Essays Before a Sonata *von Charles Ives* (Berne: Paul Haupt, 1991), 180–87.

EXAMPLE 1
Charles Ives, Piano Sonata No. 2 ("Concord, Mass., 1840–60") (c. 1915–19), movt. 3 ("The Alcotts"), "human faith" melody (see Plate 2, systems 4–5)

levels. Emerson had demanded this same equality for literature seventy years earlier.[10] As rapturously as Ives honored Beethoven in his *Essays Before a Sonata* and the *Concord Sonata,* and as urgently as he invoked his great predecessor precisely in the above passage from "The Alcotts" (he claimed that he wanted to capture the historically dubious scene in which Beth Alcott, the third-oldest daughter of Bronson Alcott, tried her hand at Beethoven's Fifth on the family spinet[11]), Ives nevertheless was little concerned with exclusively invoking the European tradition of art music and its outstanding representative, Beethoven. Instead, he pursued an inclusive, multi-perspective approach to composition which most of his contemporaries found bewildering but whose impact on music history would prove all the more pervasive after his death – and completely so in post-modernism.

Felix Meyer

10 A concise account of this connection by Wolfgang Rathert can be found in Wolfgang Rathert and Berndt Ostendorf, *Musik der USA: Kultur- und musikgeschichtliche Streifzüge* (Hofheim: Wolke, 2018), 282–94, esp. 290.

11 Ives, *Essays Before a Sonata* (see note 4), 47. Kyle Gann casts doubt on the historical veracity of this scene in his comprehensive study *Charles Ives's* Concord: *Essays after a Sonata* (Urbana: University of Illinois Press, 2017), 214–15.

PLATE 2

Charles Ives, Piano Sonata No. 2 ("Concord, Mass., 1840–60") (c. 1915–19). First edition (Redding, CT: C.E. Ives, 1920), movt. 3 ("The Alcotts"), p. 57

(ELLIOTT CARTER COLLECTION, PSS)

Ivan Wyschnegradsky "The Life of Beethoven" (1918)

Ivan Wyschnegradsky (1893–1979), a pioneer of microtonal music, grew up in his native St. Petersburg but spent most of his life in Paris, where he settled in 1920 to explore with several piano manufacturers the possibility of building a quarter-tone piano. Although he evidently did not intend at first to settle there permanently,[1] he remained in the French capital for the rest of his days, with few interruptions. Little is known about his life in pre-1920 St. Petersburg. We know the dates of his education: from 1911 to 1915 he studied harmony and composition privately with Nikolai Sokolov, a professor of composition at St. Petersburg Conservatory; and at the same time he took courses in mathematics and philosophy at the university, where he also read law on a regular basis from 1912 to 1917. But during these years he also underwent two spiritual experiences that he later referred to as formative for his life.[2] The first gave rise to a key composition, *La Journée de l'existence*, an oratorio for narrator, chorus, and orchestra based on a text from his own pen. After the second he began to introduce his ideas on quarter-tone music into his own compositions. Yet the extent to which these experiences represent *ex post facto* stylizations is an open question. He claimed that they began respectively on 25 October 1916 and 25 October 1918. If the exact two-year interval separating these dates is enough to raise eyebrows, they appear in a special light when we consider that the October Revolution in Russia began exactly midway between them on 25 October 1917.

The Revolution was particularly significant for Wyschnegradsky, for although he was born into the grand bourgeoisie (his father was a bank director and his grandfather the tsar's minister of finance from 1887 to 1892), he viewed Communism in a positive light, as he later emphasized on many occasions.[3] This attitude is particularly apparent in his song cycle *L'Évangile rouge* for bass-baritone and piano, op. 8 (1918–19), a setting of thirteen poems by Vasily Knyazev. The texts may in part be called agitation poetry; the first, for example, reads: "Who is for the reds – to me! / Who hates the war of the rich – towards me! / Who has no fear of tribulation – forward! / Who awaits the fatal storm – forward! / Child of liberty – here!"[4] And in 1919 he was employed at a research institute founded in the wake of the organization of the new Soviet state – namely, a laboratory for musical acoustics headed by the organist and musicologist Jacques Handschin and the physicist Valentin Kovalenkov. The laboratory was subordinate to the music division (headed by Arthur Lourié) of Anatoly Lunacharsky's Commissariat of Enlightenment.[5]

Nonetheless, one year after the Revolution Wyschnegradsky also produced an eleven-page manuscript entitled "The Life of Beethoven." It falls into three sections, beginning with a continuous list of years from 1770 to 1827, into which he entered the most important events in the composer's life. This is followed by three pages on which he jotted down his thoughts on Beethoven's life, works, and social context, and finally by a catalogue of works in which he wrote out the opus numbers from 1 to 138 and supplied most of them with titles and dates.

1 See Lucile Gayden, *Ivan Wyschnegradsky* (Frankfurt am Main: Belaieff, 1973), 13.

2 See Pascale Criton's introduction in Ivan Wyschnegradsky, *Libération du son: Écrits 1916–1979*, ed. Pascale Criton (Lyon: Symétrie, 2013), 20–32.

3 See Juan Allende-Blin, "Ein Gespräch mit Ivan Wyschnegradsky," in *Aleksandr Skrjabin und die Skrjabinisten*, ed. Heinz-Klaus Metzger and Rainer Riehn (Munich: Edition Text + Kritik, 1983), 103–22, esp. 104–05.

4 *L'Évangile rouge*, op. 8, is published in *Les cahiers du CIREM* 14–15 (1990), special issue *Révolution(s) politique et musique*, 187–223. The English translation is adapted from the version in the booklet of the CD *L'Évangile rouge (The Red Gospel)* (Montréal: Societé nouvelle d'enregistrement, 1999, SNE-647-CD), 4.

5 See Janna Kniazeva, *Jacques Handschin in Russland: Die neu aufgefundenen Texte* (Basel: Schwabe, 2011), 202–05. As early as 1925 Handschin had pointed to Wyschnegradsky's involvement in the project; see his article "Akustisches aus Rußland," in *Gedenkschrift Jacques Handschin: Aufsätze und Bibliographie*, ed. Basel chapter of the Schweizerische Musikforschende Gesellschaft, compiled by Hans Oesch (Berne: Haupt, 1957), 249–62, at 252.

PLATE 1
Ivan Wyschnegradsky, "Zhizn' Betkhovena" (The Life of Beethoven) (1918). Handwritten notes, p. 3
(IVAN WYSCHNEGRADSKY COLLECTION, PSS)

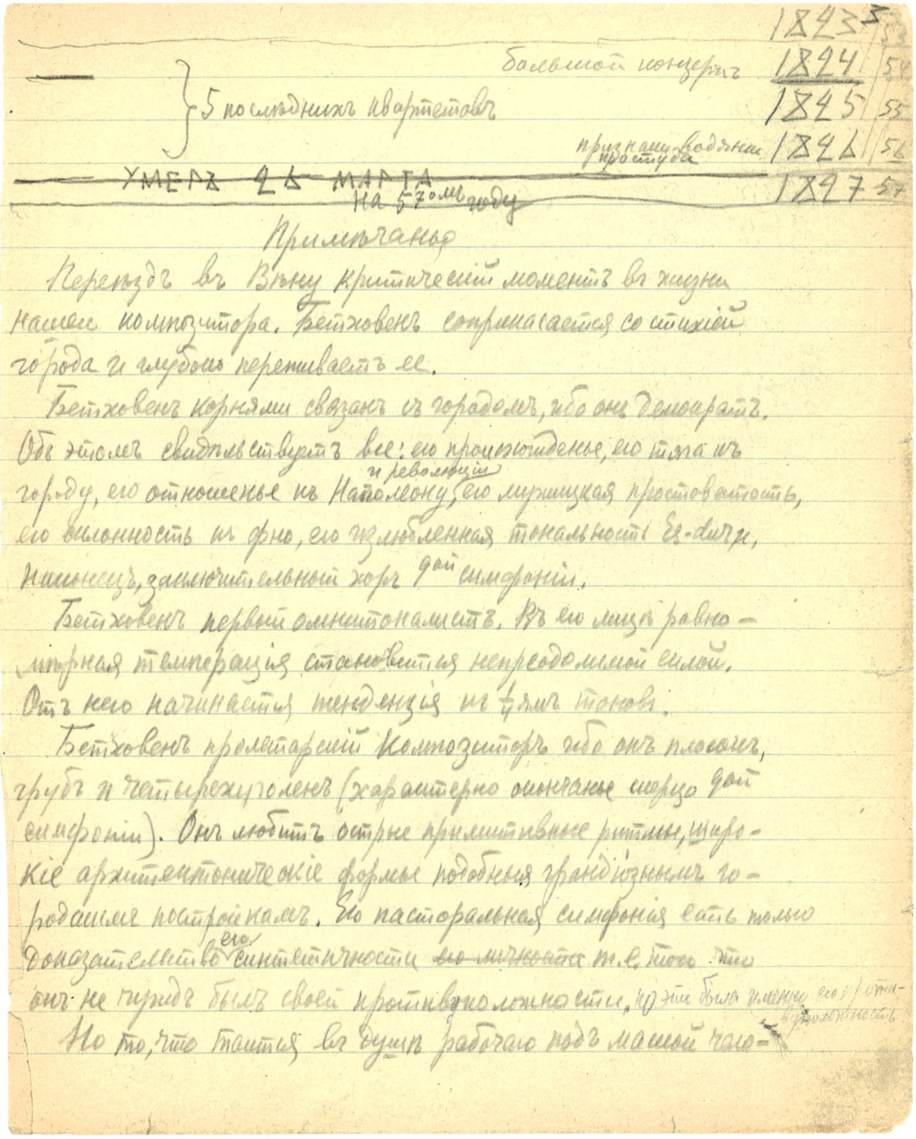

TRANSLATION OF DOCUMENT REPRODUCED
(J. BRADFORD ROBINSON AND ANDREAS WEHRMEYER)

1823/53
Great concert 1824/54
} Last five quartets 1825/55
Recognition, edema, catarrh 1826/56
DIES ON 26 MARCH in his 57th year 1827/57

Notes

The move to Vienna was a critical moment in the life of our composer. Beethoven came into contact with the urban element and experienced it deeply.

Beethoven is firmly rooted in the city, for he is a democrat. Everything testifies to this: his origins, his inclination toward the city, his relation to Napoleon and revolution, his rustic simplicity, his inclination toward the piano, his favorite key of E-flat major, and lastly the final chorus of the 9th Symphony.

Beethoven was the first omnitonic composer. Equal temperament became an irresistible force within him. The trend toward quarter-tones began with him.

Beethoven is a proletarian composer because he is plain, coarse, and angular (as characterized by the end of the Scherzo in the 9th Symphony). He likes crisp, primitive rhythms, broad architectural forms resembling grandiose urban buildings. The "Pastoral" Symphony is only further proof of this synthesis in ~~his personality~~ – that is, proof that the opposite was not unknown to him, but that it was precisely the opposite.

But what lurks in the soul of the worker beneath the mask of the man-machine is fierce rage. So, too, with Beethoven.

Of particular interest are Wyschnegradsky's notes in the middle section (see its first page (PLATE 1, P. 75) with translation). Apart from the third paragraph, where he advances the thesis that the evolution toward quarter-tone music began with Beethoven, his skeletal comments are mainly concerned with construing Beethoven as a democrat, a proletarian composer, and an ally of the present-day worker. Evidence for Beethoven's democratic convictions, he maintains, are his "origins," his "inclination toward the city" (the site of the new democratic bourgeoisie), and his "relation to Napoleon and revolution." The "proletarian composer," he maintains, is manifest in musical qualities that he defines as simplicity of structure and grandeur of form – qualities, it may be concluded, that make Beethoven's music accessible to the working class. To explain Beethoven's alliance with the workers, Wyschnegradsky argues that they inhabit the same emotional domain: "rage." Therein, he continues, lies a certain limitation. But he also portrays Beethoven as "part of mankind's future," by which, as befitted the circumstances of his time, he meant the classless society of Communism. As Wyschnegradsky bases these pronouncements on the "scherzos and finales" of the symphonies without further elaboration, it is safe to conclude that he had in mind their power, "oriented on the masses,"[6] and the utopia of universal brotherhood expressed in the finale of the Ninth, this probably being one of his basic tenets. In a diary entry from these days he refers to the word *frères* (brothers) in the Ninth as an overarching verity and the only conceivable first word.[7]

Wyschnegradsky's observations clearly fall beneath the banner of the new social system. But what could their purpose have been? The idea that they originated as notes for a lecture is most unlikely, for the tabular biography and the catalogue of works, both of which aim at completeness, are too detailed for use in a lecture. They more likely arose in connection with a book project. The newly formed Soviet Union stood in great need of educational programs and materials to disseminate the new social order in all realms of life. Indeed, the activities undertaken in this regard were enormous; "in the Russia of the Bolsheviks," a contemporary observer tells us, they "are arising daily [...]. The books that are printed run into gigantic editions of two or three hundred thousand."[8]

For several reasons, Beethoven functioned as a role model in the context of these activities. For one thing, he had lived in an age of social upheaval similar to that experienced by early twentieth-century Russia. More than that, his music was identified with the French Revolution; this made it "closely related to the world-view of the revolutionary proletariat" of today. At the same time it bore no symptoms of the decadent individualism of the late-bourgeois era,[9] and could therefore be smoothly integrated into the newly constituted musical life as a "good" tradition. But for another thing, when it came to the creation of a specifically proletarian music, hopes were set on a "new musician of Beethoven's stamp."[10] The young Soviet Union faced the problem that it had created a proletarian society but had no genuinely proletarian art at its command. It had not yet entered the "epoch of new culture," to quote Leon Trotsky's sober assessment, but "only the entrance to it." The task therefore resided in taking "possession, politically, of the most important elements of the old culture, to such an extent, at least, as to be able to pave the way for a new culture."[11] Wyschnegradsky's notes on Beethoven, even if the circumstances of their origin remain obscure, were clearly devoted to this task.

Simon Obert

6 Anatoly Lunacharsky, "Die Bedeutung der Musik Chopins für die Menschheitskultur" [1910], in idem, *Musik und Revolution: Schriften zur Musik*, ed. and trans. Guido Bimberg (Leipzig: Reclam, 1985), 57–69, at 60.

7 Ivan Wyschnegradsky, "Sur l'essence du Surart" [1917], in idem, *Libération du son* (see note 2), 74–85, at 82.

8 Allan Wallenius, "Culture under the Soviets," *Soviet Russia: Official Organ of the Russian Soviet Government Bureau* 1/22 (1 November 1919): 13–15, at 13. See also Karl Laux, *Die Musik in Russland und in der Sowjetunion* (Berlin: Henschel, 1958), 321.

9 Anatoly Lunacharsky, "Was ist aktuell an Beethoven?" [1927], in idem, *Musik und Revolution* (see note 6), 199–208, at 207–08 and 203–4. See also Amy Nelson, *Music for the Revolution: Musicians and Power in Early Soviet Russia* (University Park: Pennsylvania State University Press, 2004), 110.

10 Anatoly Lunacharsky, "Musik und Revolution" [1926], in idem, *Musik und Revolution* (see note 6), 141–50, at 147.

11 Leon Trotsky, *Literature and Revolution* [1923], ed. William Keach, trans. Rose Strunsky (Chicago: Haymarket Books, 2005), 159.

Richard Strauss *Metamorphosen* (1944–45)

One of the ever-present yet ever-varying problems of musicology, besides the relation between composers and their works, is the nexus between artistic creation, aesthetics, and reception history. No one who takes scholarly freedom seriously will play these concepts against each other, but will combine them as legitimate viewpoints and employ them in different ways to confront problems of music history. Music, its study, and its criticism can be embroiled in or stand above encrypted politics, and there are both inherent and transcendent types of contextualization. In this light, Richard Strauss's *Metamorphosen*, a "study for twenty-three solo strings," is an interesting case in many respects.

Strauss dismissed *Metamorphosen* as a "wrist exercise" or "scribble," composed for his posthumous papers following the completion of his historically significant oeuvre with *Capriccio* (premièred in 1942). Exactly which genre or aesthetic it belongs to – whether it is a "study" (to quote its subtitle) or a musical confession (as in the ending reproduced here) – may seem irrelevant. But in fact it is very relevant, as is the question of whether the piece is absolute or program music. Paradoxes abound in the rich welter of features that constitute *Metamorphosen*, allowing us to conclude that it is absolute and programmatic in equal measure.

In summer 1944 Richard Strauss (1864–1949) received a commission for a new work from Paul Sacher, the conductor of the Zurich Collegium Musicum. At the time, he was already planning to write a piece for strings. His sketches for this "Adagio for Strings" suffered many interruptions and dragged on for a fairly long period. By late March 1945 the sketches had been followed by a draft short score, and then by a full score, completed in Garmisch on 12 April 1945. An earlier problem in the work's genesis has been clarified: chronologically, the sketch "Trauer um München" (Mourning for Munich), though motivically related to the theme of the "study," is not a precursor but a consequence of *Metamorphosen*. It forms a middle section of the heavily revised and unpublished memorial waltz "Munich" of 1939, into which it was inserted as a triple-meter *minore* section under the heading "in memoriam" following the city's aerial bombardment.[1]

A much more famous and controversial "In memoriam" appears at the end of *Metamorphosen*, where cellos and basses quote the Funeral March from Beethoven's *Eroica* Symphony in the original key of C minor and double note values (SEE PLATE 1, P. 78). Who or what is the object of this commemoration and (a related question) the "festeggiare il sovvernire di un grand Uomo" of the *Eroica*? The author left no words on the subject. Critics, interpreters, and scholars are called upon to concoct answers, as has happened abundantly over the seventy-five years of the work's reception history. All of their proposals can draw on longstanding traditions and should not be summarily dismissed from today's perspective.

Here we will not delve into fundamental questions regarding the relationship of poetics to practice, or the concepts of "heroism" and "grandeur."[2] Instead, let us examine an early incident in the work's reception history. It should be borne in mind that potential conflicts arising from a work written

1 See Timothy Jackson, "The Metamorphosis of the *Metamorphosen:* New Analytical and Source-Critical Discoveries," in *Richard Strauss: New Perspectives on the Composer and His Work*, ed. Bryan Gilliam (Durham: Duke University Press, 1992), 193–242; Birgit Lodes, "Richard Strauss' Skizzen zu den 'Metamorphosen' und ihre Beziehung zu 'Trauer um München,'" *Die Musikforschung* 47 (1994): 234–52; and idem, "Eine 'Urfassung' der Metamorphosen von Richard Strauss?" *Musica* 48 (1994): 275–79.

2 Just how disparate the pictures portrayed by musicology can be when confronted with such an ideologically charged case becomes evident when we compare Laurenz Lütteken's inaugural lecture (2001) with the arguments advanced by Albrecht Riethmüller, who views Strauss's *Eroica* quotation as a "musico-semantic trick." See Laurenz Lütteken, *"Eine 3000jährige Kulturentwicklung abgeschlossen": Biographie und Geschichte in den Metamorphosen von Richard Strauss* (Winterthur: Amadeus, 2005), and Michael Walter and Albrecht Riethmüller, "Richard Strauss – Vier letzte Jahre: Ein Gespräch," in *Deutsche Leitkultur Musik? Zur Musikgeschichte nach dem Holocaust*, ed. Albrecht Riethmüller (Stuttgart: Steiner, 2006), 37–44, at 39.

50
sehr langsam
In memoriam!
dim.
pp

PLATE 1 (OPPOSITE)
Richard Strauss, *Metamorphosen: Study for Twenty-Three Solo Strings* (1944-45). 2nd full score fair copy, with conductor's markings by Paul Sacher, p. 50
(PAUL SACHER COLLECTON, PSS)

in the final stage of the Third Reich – including its "In memoriam!" – will depend on the critic's vantage point. The work received its première in Zurich on 25 January 1946 in multilingual Switzerland, a "neutral" country during the war. The following autumn, a controversy arose when two newspapers republished, in German translation, a polemical article against the first Dutch performance of *Metamorphosen*. The conductor Curt Rudolf Mengelberg, it claimed, had forced the audience "to celebrate the loving memory of the very man in whose name, and on whose orders, the slaughter took place."[3] This thesis, that the composer's "In memoriam" referred to Adolf Hitler[4] (a Hitler interpretation as a synecdoche for Strauss's entanglement with the Nazi régime would have been more to the point), was roundly rejected by the editor of the *Schweizerische Musikzeitung*, Willi Schuh: "The words 'in memoriam!' mean 'in memory of Beethoven!' The note refers quite obviously to the quotation alone, not to the entire work. That this purely musical fact should be twisted into a political weapon is beyond comprehension."[5] But music and politics cannot be so easily separated, particularly as Schuh, Strauss's chosen biographer and the projected author of "Contributions to a World History of Music," had received the following lines in a letter sent to him on 20 May 1946:

"When the book can be published is a second question; for today, after all, there is a danger that the author [i.e. Schuh] will be torn apart, quartered, and broken on the wheel by every cultural historian, university professor, the Jewish press, and all the Teutonic patriots who hope for a restoration of the 'German hegemon,' a return of Barbarossa from Kyffhäuser and of Hitler from the bunker in the Reich Chancellery, following a new war between America and Russia, if he has the courage to write that political Germany *had* to be destroyed once it had fulfilled its world mission: the creation and consummation of German music."[6]

As an example of "aesthetic fundamentalism," this horrifying thought far eclipses Karlheinz Stockhausen's admiration for the terrorist attack on the World Trade Center.[7] Whether in opposition or in agreement, destructive politico-military nationalism is as unacceptable today as the triumphant artistic nationalism of a musical "world mission."

Can the title of *Metamorphosen* be validated by hermeneutics and music analysis? Three works of literature stood godfather within Strauss's cultural horizon: Goethe's poem *The Metamorphosis of Plants* (an essay in natural philosophy), Apuleius's novel *Metamorphoses, or The Golden Ass* (with its narrative leaps), and above all Ovid's verse poem *Metamorphoses*, the myths of which transform transient human beings into the telos of permanent entities. The same transformation takes place in Strauss's composition: following a long process, as monochrome in its string timbre as it is dazzling in its harmonic textures, the work comes to an end, in accordance with a heavily modified sonata form,[8] by revealing an affinity between two figures – a melody from the opening in the upper voice (from m. 9), contrapuntally intertwined with the Beethoven quotation in the bass. It is as if a profound expression of mourning were being elevated into a monument in notes in the manner of a literary conceit.

No solution can be expected to the "In memoriam" problem, and as a result many questions are left unanswered. Strauss's "study" is performed, researched, and criticized all over the world. Its emotive content, as intended by its creator, was neither a final word nor a final sound. To be sure, *Metamorphosen* remains controversial as a document on an individual or on a state of affairs, but its sounds unfold with a ravishing beauty transcending the context of its origins.

Hermann Danuser

3 Matthijs Vermeulen, "Ein doppelter Skandal: Das Concertgebouw gedenkt Hitlers," *National-Zeitung*, no. 493 (Basel, 25/26 October 1947; abridged in *St. Galler Tagblatt*, no. 508 (30 October 1947). Vermeulen's article was first published in *De Groene Amsterdamer* on 11 October 1947.

4 That the link between the funeral march and Hitler was not fabricated out of thin air can be seen in the fact that it was broadcast following the announcement of his death on 30 April 1945. See Hans-Joachim Hinrichsen, "'Seid umschlungen, Millionen': Die Beethoven-Rezeption," in *Beethoven Handbuch*, ed. Sven Hiemke (Kassel: Bärenreiter; Stuttgart: Metzler, 2009), 567–609, at 592.

5 Willi Schuh, "Greuelmärchen um Richard Strauss' 'Metamorphosen,'" *Schweizerische Musikzeitung* 87 (1947): 437–38, at 438. See also idem, "Epilog zu 'Greuelmärchen um Richard Strauss' 'Metamorphosen,'" ibid.: 455–56.

6 "Wann es [das Buch] erscheinen kann, ist eine zweite Frage, da heute immerhin die Gefahr besteht, daß sein Autor [Schuh] von allen Culturhistorikern, Universitätsprofessoren, der jüdischen Presse sowohl wie von allen germanischen Patrioten, die nach einem neuen Krieg zwischen Amerika und Rußland die Wiederkehr der 'Deutschen Weltmacht' und die Rückkehr Barbarossa's aus dem Kyffhäuser und Hitlers aus dem Bunker der Reichskanzlei erhoffen – zerrissen, gevierteilt, gerädert werde, wenn er den Mut hat zu schreiben, daß das politische Deutschland zerstört werden *mußte*, nachdem es seine Weltmission: die Erschaffung und Vollendung der deutschen Musik erfüllt hatte." Richard Strauss, letter of 20 May 1946 to Willi Schuh, in Richard Strauss, *Briefwechsel mit Willi Schuh* (Zurich: Atlantis, 1969), 89.

7 See Hermann Danuser, *Weltanschauungsmusik* (Schliengen: Argus, 2009), 486–87.

8 See Hermann Danuser, "Über Richard Strauss' 'Metamorphosen'"[1983], in idem, *Gesammelte Vorträge und Aufsätze*, ed. Hans-Joachim Hinrichsen, Christian Schaper, and Laure Spaltenstein, vol. 4 (Schliengen: Argus, 2014), 258–72; Birgit Lodes, "Richard Strauss' Skizzen zu den 'Metamorphosen'" (see note 1); Jens-Peter Schütte, "Das instrumentale Spätwerk," in *Richard Strauss Handbuch*, ed. Walter Werbeck (Stuttgart: Metzler; Kassel: Bärenreiter, 2014), 463–98; also Stefan Keym, "Ausklang oder offenes Ende? Dramaturgien der Schlussgestaltung in den Tondichtungen von Richard Strauss und ihr historischer Kontext," in *Richard Strauss: Der Komponist und sein Werk: Überlieferung, Interpretation, Rezeption: Bericht über das internationale Symposium zum 150. Geburtstag, München, 26.–28. Juni 2014*, ed. Sebastian Bolz, Adrian Kech, and Hartmut Schick (Munich: Allitera, 2017), 167–89.

Rolf Liebermann *Leonore 40/45* (1951–52)

As the title implies, the opera *Leonore 40/45*, by the Swiss composer Rolf Liebermann (1910–99) on a libretto by the German culture impresario Heinrich Strobel (1898–1970), reimagines *Fidelio* for the postwar era. The work loosely traces the plot of Beethoven's opera using a listener-friendly dodecaphonic musical language. The world première in Basel on 26 March 1952 brought together musical luminaries from all over Europe, and the work was received with ovations.[1] Critical reception was mixed. Strobel's witty bilingual (French-German) libretto was universally admired, but Liebermann's music was deemed to be too ponderous for the text. A critic for the Basel *National-Zeitung* found: "Twelve-tone sledgehammers are used to swat flies; the music drags down the repartee."[2]

The opera's plot takes place during the German occupation of Paris and the subsequent liberation. In order to deflect any troublesome memories the audience might have had of this time period, *Leonore 40/45* takes the story of the brave woman from the French Revolutionary drama and turns it into a harmless comedy. As the character of narrator / guardian angel, Monsieur Émile, proclaims in the Vorspiel, "Emotion and agitation will be avoided at all costs."[3] Human foibles will be presented in a sympathetic way. The "moral" of the opera is the precept that people of different nationalities are still fundamentally alike. War is never portrayed as resulting from human agency; it's just something that "happens." Our young heroes, the sensitive oboe-playing German soldier Alfred (who "never fired a shot"), and the *charmante* Parisienne Huguette, ignore the war and occupation as much as possible to focus on their love. Even though it was surely Strobel's and Liebermann's intention to divert the audience rather than tug at their heartstrings, the moral stance advocated by the work, and particularly the role of Beethoven's music as valorizing the German occupier-hero, remains problematic.

Page 23 from Liebermann's autograph score (SEE PLATE 1) shows a key moment in the Vorspiel. It is July 1939, and Alfred and his father are listening to a radio broadcast of *Fidelio,* which is interrupted by an announcement about the impending mobilization of the German army. Liebermann's score indicates the precise passage in Beethoven's opera in the Peters vocal score of *Fidelio,* and notates the exact moment of the interruption. We hear the climactic moment of the opera, starting with the second trumpet call announcing the arrival of the minister who will free Florestan from his unjust imprisonment, and continuing with the quartet, "Es schlägt der Rache Stunde." Alfred's father complains, "They *would* have to interrupt the beautiful Fidelio quartet again!"[4]

Here the well-worn trope of beautiful music overcoming ugly politics rears its head for the first of many times in the opera. Listeners are urged to recall a time before the war, when Beethoven could still be understood as a composer of humane and heroic works, and had not become the German nationalist hero in the cultural politics of the Third Reich. In a sleight of hand typical of the postwar "Stunde Null" (Zero Hour) attitude, pre- and postwar concepts of Beethoven are explicitly linked in this scene, while conveniently skipping over the time in between.

PLATE 1 (OPPOSITE)
Rolf Liebermann, *Leonore 40/45,* opera semiseria (1951–52). Full score fair copy of version 1, Prelude, p. 23
(ROLF LIEBERMANN COLLECTION, PSS)

1 See O.M. [Otto Maag], "Leonore 40/45," *National-Zeitung*, no. 143, 26 March 1952.

2 "Es wird mit Zwölftonkanonen nach Spatzen geschossen, die Musik hängt sich als Schwergewicht an die leichte Konversation." Ibid.

3 "Rührung und Erschütterung werden tunlich vermieden." Libretto by Heinrich Strobel, *Leonore 40/45: Opera semiseria in einem Vorspiel und sieben Bildern (zwei Akte)* (Vienna: Universal Edition, 1952), 5.

4 "Jetzt müssen sie das schöne Fidelio-Quartett wieder unterbrechen!" Ibid., 7. Liebermann's choice is ironic, since this quartet, "Es schlägt der Rache Stunde," a tumultuous, fast-paced number punctuated with *sforzandi*, is powerful but not "schön" – that would be the iconic quartet from the first act ("Mir ist so wunderbar").

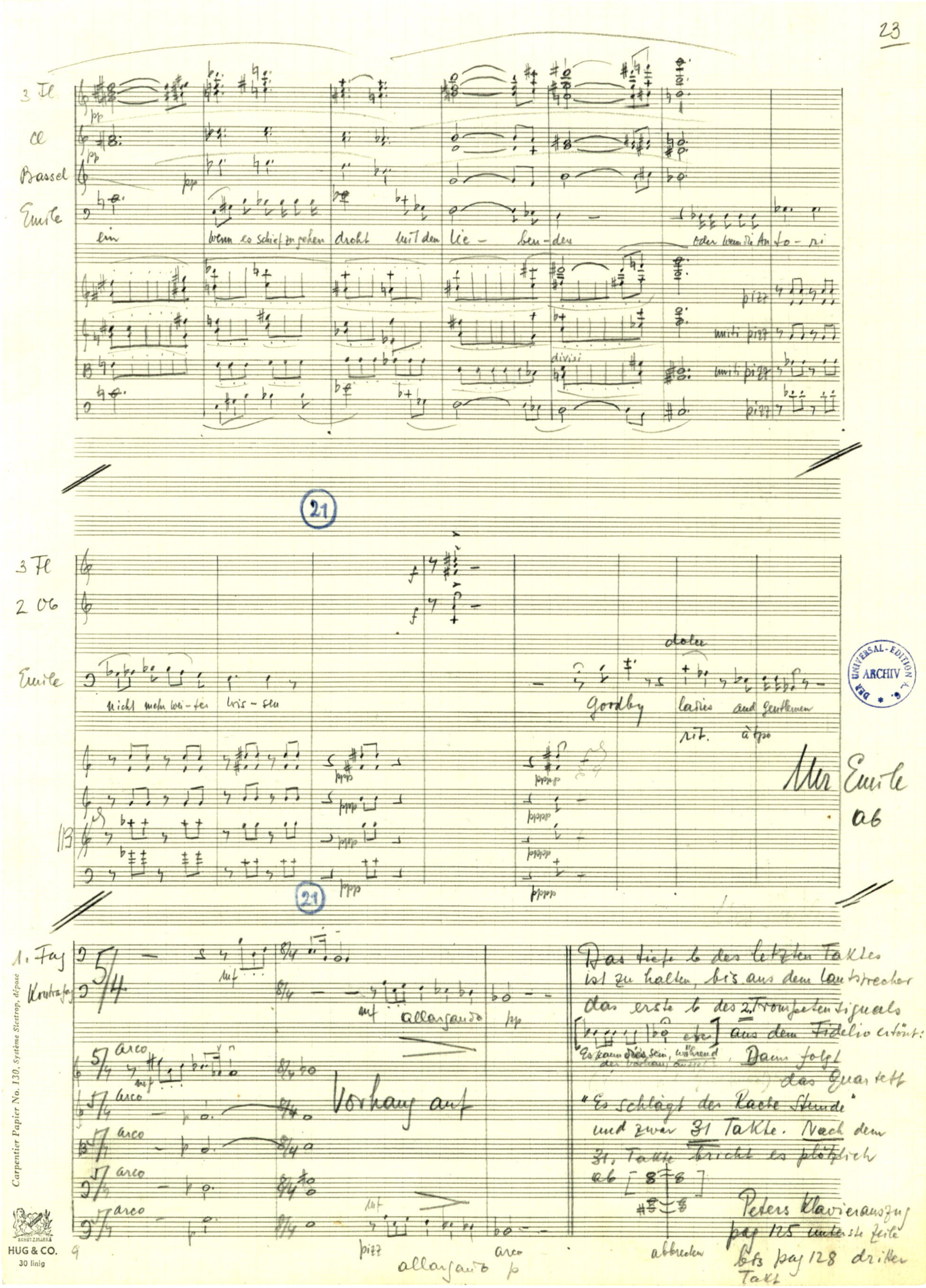
23
3 Fl
Cl
Emile
2 Ob
1. Fag
Kontrafag
Vorhang auf
arco
pizz
Das tiefe b des letzten Taktes ist zu halten, bis aus dem Lautsprecher das erste b des 2. Trompetensignals
aus dem Fidelio ertönt:
Dann folgt das Quartett
"Es schlägt der Rache Stunde" und zwar 31 Takte. Nach dem 31. Takte bricht es plötzlich ab
Peters Klavierauszug pag 125 unterste Zeile bis pag 128 dritter Takt
ARCHIV
Carpentier Papier No. 130, Système Sicotrop, déposé
HUG & CO.
30 linig

PLATE 2
Rolf Liebermann, *Leonore 40/45*, opera semiseria (1951–52). Printed edition of version 1 with handwritten corrections for version 2, Finale, p. 16
(ROLF LIEBERMANN COLLECTION, PSS)

Alfred and Huguette are brought together by their shared love of music, which conveniently smooths over any moral quandaries that might arise from such a relationship. The couple clearly represent Germany and France, and their love stands in for the anodyne wish that people would not hate each other.[5]

Through various plot twists, the couple get back together, and in the last scene they marry. In the revised version of the finale, a chorus of bureaucrats squabbles over technicalities as they try – in vain – to prevent the couple's wedding[6] (SEE PLATE 2). Here Liebermann re-uses the music from a comic scene in the first act in which modern music ("dodecaphonie") is caricatured as "cacaphonie." But the bureaucrats' objection is not musical, but rather political. The couple cannot be married, they insist, because neither of them has been denazified. Aside from the somewhat forced symmetry – actually only one of them would require denazification – the more disturbing point is that those who wish to force a reckoning with the past are depicted as dull, vindictive bureaucrats who sing in a crude parody of twelve-tone music. There is a contradiction here. Whereas Liebermann's modern musical idiom would seem to place the work in a postwar, progressive space that is opposed to Fascist

5 As Huguette puts it in the 5th Bild, "Es muß endlich Schluß sein mit dem Haß zwischen unseren Völkern – und Schluß mit den Kriegen. Was Alfred und mir gelang, muß auch im Großen gelingen." Ibid., 30.

6 Hans Curjel noted that the finale was revised after the Basel première, and that the new version was first performed in Cologne in autumn 1952. See Everett Helm et al., "Current Chronicle," *The Musical Quarterly* 39, no. 2 (1953): 241–75, esp. 273. While the libretto contains the original version, the revised version is preserved in the Universal Edition piano-vocal score of 1952.

cultural values, the musical parallelism in this scene sets up a strange equivalency between Philistines who hate modern music and those willing to come to terms with the past.[7]

The opera concludes with a fugue (à la *Don Giovanni* or *Falstaff*) in which the characters step out of the plot and intone, apparently without irony, the moral "All is for the best in the best of all possible worlds."[8] The fugue subject and much of the material is taken from the overture, implying a return in the plot to the situation before the war. It gives the audience the same comfort: we can just rewind the clock and go back to a time when people loved music and each other and there was no political discord.

The plot's message that the two main characters are equivalent erases any sense of moral responsibility for the war. The Beethoven associations in particular are used to support and ennoble the German character, Alfred, who stands in for the unjustly imprisoned Florestan. But unlike in *Fidelio,* in *Leonore 40/45* the male characters Alfred and Monsieur Émile drive the action. Whereas Beethoven's and Sonnleithner's Leonore takes one life-threatening risk after another in order to rescue her captive husband, Huguette does not take much initiative.[9] The plot depicts the lovers as equals, as if they existed in a "neutral" postwar world, but the power dynamic between the couple seems instead to reflect that of the German occupation of France.

Leonore 40/45 attempts to retell Beethoven's drama of liberation for an audience eager to recover the legacy of German music while leaving behind the politics of the recent German catastrophe.[10] The difficulty, indeed the impossibility, of threading this needle makes for a deeply problematic work, as Simeon Thompson has pointed out.[11] *Leonore 40/45* can therefore be seen as part of the larger project of attempting to reclaim Beethoven's "universal" and humane message in the spirit of a newly united Europe.

This message did not resonate everywhere. While *Leonore 40/45* enjoyed critical success in Cologne, Münster, and some other German theaters, there were boos and protests in Berlin. In Milan, quite remarkably, "the audience remained completely indifferent," and got up to leave at the end of the performance without any applause at all.[12] It is not clear why these audiences objected to the opera. Possibly they didn't like the staging, the performance, or the modern idiom of the music. But it is also possible that, especially in Italy, the opera's rosy depiction of the German occupation of Paris was distasteful to the partisani who had fought the German army in the bloody conclusion to the war. Instead of seeing this Beethovenian opera as a parable of universal humanity and European unity,[13] some audiences might have taken offense at the somewhat forced and light-hearted attempt to erase the memory of Germany's violent past.

Anne C. Shreffler

7 Michael Custodis and Friedrich Geiger point out that the conventional historiographical division between the persecuted advocates of modern music and Nazi traditionalists needs to be questioned anyway, especially with regard to the early postwar years. See their *Netzwerke der Entnazifizierung: Kontinuitäten im deutschen Musikleben am Beispiel von Werner Egk,* Hilde und Heinrich Strobel (Münster: Waxmann, 2013), 12.

8 "Alles wendet sich zum Guten in der besten aller Welten," Strobel, *Leonore 40/45* libretto (see note 3), 43. The quotation is from Voltaire's *Candide,* in which the French philosopher satirizes Leibniz's optimism, as Simeon Thompson has noted; see his "Beethoven und der Zweite Weltkrieg in der künstlerischen Reflexion der Nachkriegszeit: Stanley Kubricks *A Clockwork Orange* und Rolf Liebermanns *Leonore 40/45,*" in *Rund um Beethoven: Interpretationsforschung heute,* ed. Thomas Gartmann and Daniel Allenbach (Schliengen: Argus, 2019), 456–64, esp. 460.

9 As Willi Schuh put it in his review, the plot procedes "ohne daß der charmanten Heldin allzu großer Heroismus zugemutet zu werden braucht." -uh, "Leonore 40/45: Uraufführung von Rolf Liebermanns Oper im Stadttheater Basel," *Neue Zürcher Zeitung,* no. 676, 28 March 1952.

10 As Emily Richmond Pollock notes, "*Fidelio* became a recurring motif in the programming of postwar German opera houses, as Beethoven was constructed as a universally 'good' part of the German national identity that had persisted through and inherently resisted the Third Reich's appropriation of German music." See her *Opera after the Zero Hour: The Problem of Tradition and the Possibility of Renewal in Postwar West Germany* (Oxford: Oxford University Press, 2019), 28–29.

11 Thompson, "Beethoven und der Zweite Weltkrieg" (see note 8), 463.

12 "On m'a raconté qu'à la première représentation, comme du reste, à la dernière à laquelle j'assistais, le public est resté totalement indifférent, et à la fin du spectacle, chacun s'est levé, est parti, sans rien manifester." A.A-R., "Milan: Deux premières à la Scala," *Schweizerische Musikzeitung* 94, no. 5 (1954): 196–97, esp. 196.

13 Karl Heinz Ruppel reported on the Milan performance: "Quite apart from the basic mistrust with which the La Scala audience confronts contemporary music, neither the human destinies of the main characters [...], who begin to fall in love during the occupation of Paris and overcome every obstacle to find each other, nor the humanitarian, pro-European idea documented in the plot was able to win their approval." ("Weder das menschliche Geschick der Hauptfiguren [...], die einander während der Besetzung von Paris zu lieben beginnen und über alle Hindernisse hinweg einander finden, noch der humanitäre, europafreundliche Gedanke, der sich in dieser Bühnenhandlung dokumentiert, vermochte – ganz abgesehen von dem prinzipiellen Mißtrauen, mit dem es Werken der zeitgenössischen Musik begegnet – das Scala-Publikum zu gewinnen.") Ruppel, "Die Oper und die Welt von gestern: Ein Beitrag zur Soziologie des italienischen Opernpublikums," *Melos* 21, no. 2 (1954): 53–56, at 55.

George Rochberg
"Passions According to the Twentieth Century" (1967)

The 1960s were, as is generally known, a time of massive upheavals in almost every area of politics, society, and culture. But even in this decade of turmoil, few composers were as radical in their realignment as George Rochberg (1918–2005). After a rather slow beginning to his career, in the course of the 1950s he emerged as one of the most capable American twelve-tone composers of his generation. But instead of proceeding along the "modernist path," e.g. by expanding or modifying twelve-note technique, in the early 1960s he increasingly turned his back on the contemporary avant-garde's mentality of progress and adopted a pluralistic concept in which the sounds of the present enter into direct dialogue with music of the past. Much has been written (and conjectured) about the reasons for this change: deep-seated personal setbacks (particularly the death of his son in 1964) probably played a role, as did the wish, typical of its time, to overcome the dominant postwar mentality of progress (Rochberg called it "technocratic") in favor of a more "humanistic" view of art.[1] Yet this view did not suddenly appear on Rochberg's horizon; it had deep roots in much earlier events, especially the traumatic war experiences that the young draftee of 1942 had amassed on the European front in 1944 and 1945.[2]

The goal to which Rochberg aspired in the 1960s was to create music as an *ars combinatoria* in which a very wide range of techniques, stylistic resources, and musical idioms, past and present, were meant to coexist and interact.[3] This idea was based on a circular concept of time that was contrary to the prevailing teleological mentality. In his essay "No Center," a loose series of aphorisms and maxims published in 1969, he described it as follows: "I stand in a circle of time, not on a line. 360 degrees of past, present, and future. All around me. I can look in any direction I want to."[4] In this way he argued for maximum freedom in the choice of his artistic bearings and points of departure. And as we know from other passages in the same essay, he also parted ways with his avant-garde colleagues, opposing their faith in (alleged) rationality and historicity and taking the composer's personal sensibility as the guide to artistic activity: "Sensory order takes precedence over external logic and methodology. He [the composer] stands unprotected before the winds of change. He stands only on what he has come to love. He is what he loves."[5]

It comes as no surprise, then, that Beethoven's music looms large in Rochberg's "combinatorial art": for Beethoven's works were the very embodiment of the traditional concert repertoire with which Rochberg had grown up and to which he remained attached to the end of his days. He was also especially fond of discussing them in his theoretical writings, such as his posthumously published treatise on classical and extended tonality.[6] Not least of all, he made use of Beethoven's music in many ways in his own compositions. The spectrum ranges from brief quotations that function, so to speak, as goads to further development in his own idiom (e.g. in nos. 7 and 21 of the *Caprice Variations* for solo violin, composed in 1970, where the initial sparks come from short snippets of movement 3 of Beethoven's op. 74 String Quartet and

1 See *inter alia* Alan Gillmor, "The Apostasy of George Rochberg," *Intersections* 29, no. 1 (2009): 32–48.

2 Recently Rochberg's war experiences and their implications have been thoroughly examined by Amy Lynn Wlodarski in *George Rochberg, American Composer: Personal Trauma and Artistic Creativity* (Rochester: University of Rochester Press, 2019).

3 On the evolution of this ideal in Rochberg see ibid., 68–69. On Rochberg's polystylism in its international context see David Metzer, *Quotation and Cultural Meaning in Twentieth-Century Music* (Cambridge: Cambridge University Press, 2003), 113–28.

4 George Rochberg, "No Center" [1969], in idem, *The Aesthetics of Survival: A Composer's View of Twentieth-Century Music*, rev. edn. (Ann Arbor: University of Michigan Press, 2004), 129–34, at 132.

5 Ibid., 134.

6 George Rochberg, *A Dance of Polar Opposites: The Continuing Transformation of Our Musical Language*, ed. Jeremy Gill (Rochester: University of Rochester Press, 2012).

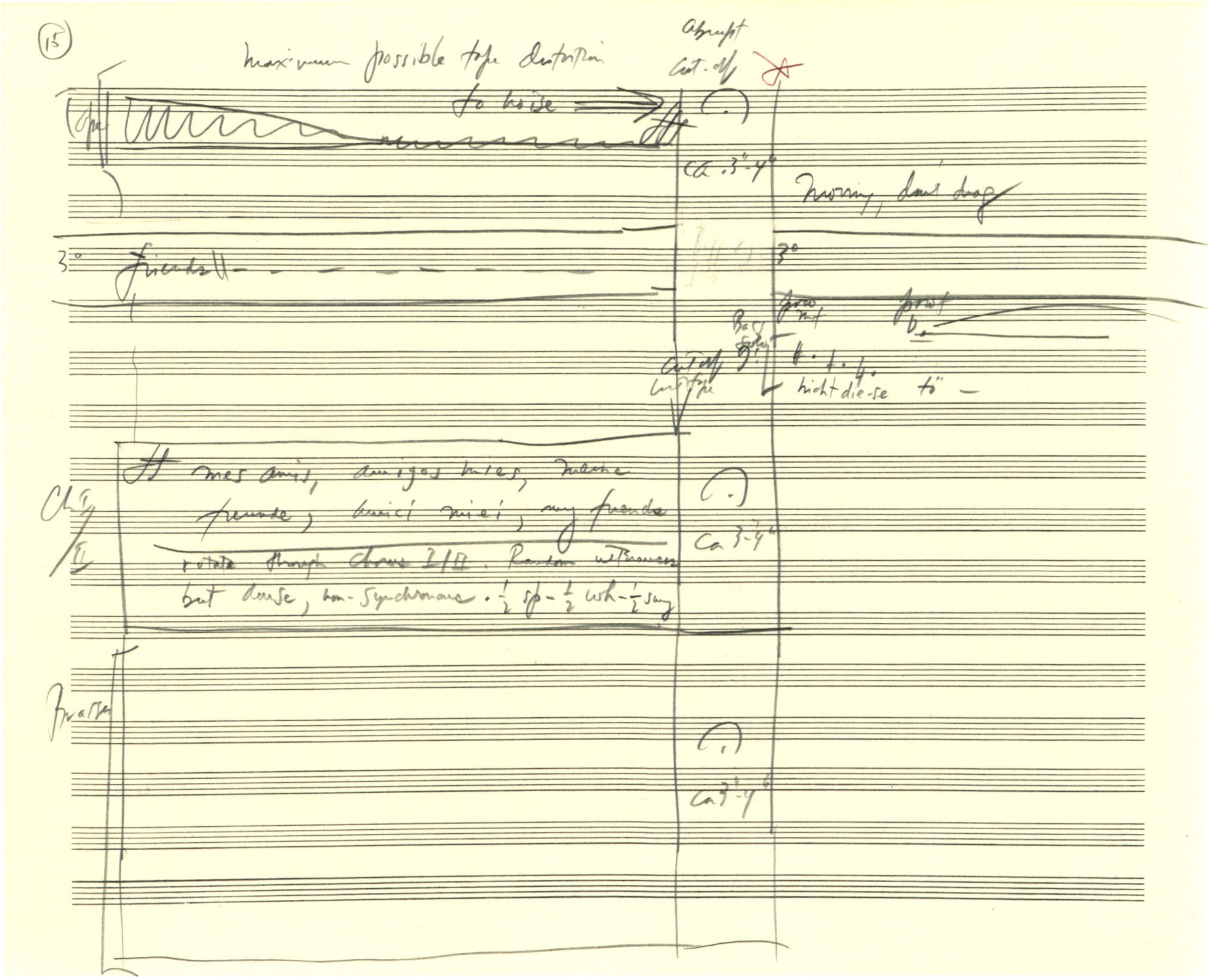

PLATE 1
George Rochberg (1918–2005), "Passions According to the Twentieth Century" for solo voices, chorus, jazz quintet, wind instruments, percussion, piano, and tape (1967). Draft score, movt 3, p. 15
(GEORGE ROCHBERG COLLECTION, PSS)

the finale of the Seventh Symphony) to a sort of "*faux* Beethoven" (as in the third movement of his String Quartet No. 3, 1971–72, which stands in marked contrast to the style of the work's other movements).[7]

A different and darker side of Rochberg's invocation of Beethoven comes to the fore in "Passions According to the Twentieth Century," an unpublished composition completed in the spring of 1967. This large-scale stage work for actors, dancers, speakers, singers, chorus, orchestra, and prerecorded tape emerged from an even more monumental plan and paved the way to the closely related (both in expression and technique) Third Symphony of 1969. In both pieces Rochberg taps a vast arsenal of theatrical, textual, and musical sources in order to construct from the chosen materials a gigantic polystylistic collage whose sharp splices are meant to highlight the "unrestrained and perpetual violence of man which [...] in the twentieth century has reached peaks of incredible intensity and horror."[8] "Passions," which is structured as a series of (plot-driven) "scenes" and (more meditative) "passions," places its focus on two widely separate chapters in the persecution of the Jews: Herod's Massacre of the Innocents, and the Holocaust. This was the first time that Rochberg, who now included his own Jewish identity within his purview, explicitly took up this human tragedy in his music, although Jewish themes and events had occasionally given him artistic inspiration in the past.[9]

When conceiving "Passions," it quickly transpired that Beethoven's music would play a major role. For Rochberg, this was predestined, not only because of its attractiveness as compositional raw material, but equally because hardly any other music embodied a humanistic message that had been so execrably trampled upon in recent history, especially during the Holocaust. As he noted in the sketches for "Passions," "The master of Bonn's realm has gone up in the smoke of Auschwitz. How can I say with him *Freude, schöner Götterfunken, Tochter aus Elysium* ... I can return no longer to my Elysium."[10] It was precisely this thought that he translated into music, using truncated and distorted Beethoven quotations. Perhaps the most glaring example of such a disruption occurs at that passage in the final section of "Passions" in which a tape recording of the double fugue from the finale of Beethoven's Ninth is, after four bars, increasingly overmodulated to produce maximum distortion, sustained for roughly ten seconds at quadruple *forte* (SEE PLATE 1, P. 85). The destruction of the Beethovenian utopia, compressed in the double fugue by the superposition of the "Freude" and "Millionen" themes, is thus re-enacted with almost blatant brutalism.

Nonetheless, the impression conveyed by the passage is double-edged, if not to say ambivalent. For during this process of sonic extirpation, and especially in its immediate aftermath, Beethoven's words "O Freunde, nicht diese Töne" are recited or sung in several languages; and, given Rochberg's withdrawal from the avant-garde at that time, it is hard to resist viewing this quotation as an aesthetic warning, particularly as later, in his posthumously published autobiography, he interprets it in precisely this sense (although, perhaps as a precaution, he does so in a series of rhetorical questions):

"*Nicht diese Töne*. Not these sounds. What sounds is he (Beethoven) talking about? The sounds that destroy peace and harmony, the sounds that bring disruption, pain, unhappiness, sadness, depression? Was this a prophetic insight into the darkness yet to break loose in the twentieth century and wreak havoc in music? Was this a foretelling, however shadowy and vague, of serialism's and aleatory's sinking into the wastes of indeterminateness?"[11]

7 See Felix Meyer, "'Everything we love belongs to us': George Rochberg's Adoption of Tonality," in *Tonality since 1950*, ed. Felix Wörner, Ullrich Scheideler, and Philip Rupprecht (Stuttgart: Steiner, 2017), 153–65.

8 George Rochberg, Introductory remarks to "Passions According to the Twentieth Century;" quoted from Joan DeVee Dixon, *George Rochberg: A Bio-Bibliographic Guide to His Life and Works* (Stuyvesant: Pendragon, 1992), 109–12, at 109.

9 See Wlodarski, *Rochberg* (see note 2), 100–19.

10 George Rochberg, textual sketches for "Passions According to the Twentieth Century," George Rochberg Collection, PSS. Quoted here from Wlodarski, *Rochberg* (see note 2), 91.

11 George Rochberg, *Five Lines, Four Spaces: The World of My Music*, ed. Gene Rochberg and Richard Griscom (Urbana: University of Illinois Press, 2009), 164.

Viewed in this light, one of the problematic aspects of "Passions" is surely its intimation, beneath the banner of anti-humanism, of an analogy between the (objective) atrocities of a criminal régime and Rochberg's (subjective) rejection of the radical avant-garde. Was it perhaps for these reasons (and not merely the impracticability of this colossal work) that he withdrew the score and concentrated on the closely related but minimally less ambitious Symphony No. 3? Whatever the case, that work, too, was destined to remain unsuccessful: it is one of the few Rochberg works never performed again after its première in November 1970.

Felix Meyer

Helmut Lachenmann
Staub
(1985–87)

The Ninth Symphony plays an outsized role in studies of Beethoven reception as well as in culture at large. The larger the work became in the public mind, the more it shrank. By the mid-twentieth century, the work had been reduced to a monument (having long served as a metonym for artistic greatness), a slogan ("all men are brothers"), and a very well-known tune. Even before said tune became the official anthem of the European Union in 1985, the symphony's ubiquitous ritual commemorative function often deafened listeners to whatever genuine musical and metaphysical meaning the work once held.

The Ninth also presents a programming challenge, because of its length (not quite long enough for a full evening) and its unabashedly triumphal conclusion. One needs a shortish work to precede the symphony – apparently, nothing can come after it. Conductors including Erich Leinsdorf, Hans Zender, and Michael Gielen often programmed Arnold Schoenberg's *A Survivor from Warsaw* with the Ninth, as a corrective to Schiller's rosy message.[1]

When the German composer Helmut Lachenmann (b. 1935) was commissioned by the Southwest German Radio (Südwestfunk) Symphony Orchestra of Baden-Baden, under Gielen, their new chief conductor, to write a "prologue" to the Ninth for the fortieth anniversary of the orchestra's founding, it was perhaps inevitable that the Beethoven work, deployed in its ceremonial role, would clash with an avant-garde piece by a controversial composer of "Nicht-Musik" (non-music).[2] The circumstances surrounding the thwarted première are well known: the piece was removed from the program at the last minute, because some of the musicians felt that it was not appropriate for an anniversary celebration at which high-ranking political figures would be present.[3] As Alastair Williams has pointed out, "Ironically, this reactionary response did, at least, recognize that *Staub* challenges a set of conventions. What none of the protagonists in this dispute could have known at the time was that two years later the Ninth would become a symbol of German reunification."[4] The Saarland Radio Orchestra rescued the première, even performing it with the Ninth, on 19 December 1987.[5]

Like many other of Lachenmann's works of the 1970s and '80s (such as *Accanto*), *Staub* (Dust) is a product of the composer's increasingly productive relationship with musical tradition (rather than one of negation).[6] The well-known controversy surrounding *Staub*'s première long overshadowed the work itself, which represents a potent intervention against a stultified and routine Beethoven reception. It frees the monumental Ninth from its plaster cast, revealing the living, audible body beneath. *Staub* takes bits and pieces of Beethovenian rhetoric and gives them new meaning by placing them in an expansive sound world. Lachenmann's work engaged so deeply with its model that it was even to be called *Prolog*.[7] What might be misconstrued as a dismantling of the Ninth in fact offers the listener a new way of hearing, which, as the composer put it, "has overcome, but not forgotten, its philharmonic fixation."[8]

The first sketch page displayed (SEE PLATE 1A, P. 90) shows how Lachenmann recalled musical material from the Ninth while considering ways in which the familiar music could be estranged. The indication SWF (as the Südwest-

1 Gerhard R. Koch, "Im zweiten Anlauf: Helmut Lachenmanns 'Staub' / Uraufführung beim Saarländischen Rundfunk," *Frankfurter Allgemeine Zeitung*, 22 December 1987; reprinted under the title "Feststück der dritten Art: Lachenmann-Uraufführung in Saarbrücken," *MusikTexte* 23 (February 1988): 54.

2 Lachenmann used the phrase "Nicht-Musik" in his brief program note for *Staub;* see Helmut Lachenmann, *Musik als existentielle Erfahrung: Schriften 1966–1995*, ed. Josef Häusler, 2nd edn. (Wiesbaden: Breitkopf & Härtel, 2004), 398.

3 The orchestra was, however, willing to perform *Staub* later at the Donaueschingen Festival, a venue devoted to contemporary music. See Helmut Lachenmann and Hans Brender, "Nicht mit Beethoven und nicht vor Späth," in ibid., 186–90, esp. 187.

4 Alastair Williams, *Music in Germany since 1968* (Cambridge: Cambridge University Press, 2013), 105.

5 The SWF première was to have taken place in July, 1986. Koch, "Im zweiten Anlauf" / "Feststück der dritten Art" (see note 1).

6 See Rainer Nonnenmann, *Beethoven und Helmut Lachenmanns "Staub" für Orchester (1985/87)* (Saarbrücken: Pfau, 2000), 5.

7 Lachenmann "schrieb ein Stück, das auch in einigen kompositorischen Aspekten auf die Neunte Bezug nahm und entschieden sinnvoll 'Prolog' heißen sollte." Koch, "Im zweiten Anlauf" / "Feststück der dritten Art" (see note 1).

8 Sounds, Lachenmann writes, thus become "neu transparent für ein Hören, welches seine philharmonische Bindung überwunden, aber nicht vergessen hat." Lachenmann, *Musik als existentielle Erfahrung* (see note 2), 398.

funk Orchestra was then known) at the top left provides a temporary label for the project. The first verbal inscription is enigmatic: "alles in meine weiße Mauer" (everything into my white wall), which resonates with the phrase "weiße Wand" (white wall) notated halfway down the page. The second inscription, "Was ist körperlich an der Neunten?" (what is corporeal about the Ninth?) is followed by an abstracted notation in whole notes of the A–E fifths that open the first movement of the symphony. Then come bits of the first theme's rhythm and contour. In the middle third of the page, Lachenmann indicates "Material" in the left margin. Rhythmic sketches that present the characteristic dotted rhythm of the Scherzo are followed by the indication "Orgelpunkt" (pedal point) on the right. Below that, fragments of the famous "Freude" theme are notated, labeled "Melodie" and encircled.

The extent to which the musical material of the Ninth figured into Lachenmann's early plans for the work is striking. Starting from the question of the music's physicality, he then wrote out some of the work's most characteristic rhythmic and melodic shapes. This sketch also gives some clues as to how Lachenmann will reinterpret the Beethoven material. The words "Sopran Schrei" (soprano scream) in the lower middle of the page indicates a mood of anguish rather than optimism. (Presumably this would be an instrumental scream rather than a vocal one.) Near the bottom of the page, with "Streicher / aus dem Tonlosen / kommend / ins Tonlose gehend / darin ertrinkend" (strings / emerging / from tonelessness / going into tonelessness / drowning in it), Lachenmann indicates not only that his sound world will extend to the realm of the barely audible, but that the string sounds will be drawn back into silence. The word "Fenster" (window) immediately below could be a reminder that this extended sound palette can open a window and provide a fresh perspective on a familiar view.

On the opposite sketch page (SEE PLATE 1B, P. 91), entitled "Ableitungen" (derivations), Lachenmann plots out the kinds of densities he wants to include, with the indications "tonlos," "Cluster," and "2 Klang" (two sounds or 2-note chord), as well as descriptions of percussion sounds. He even fixes the total registral range of the composition, from lowest to highest notes, in a sketch marked "Ränder" (boundaries) to the left of the tenth and eleventh systems. At the bottom of the page, the composer recalls the extremes of "silence" and "scream" from the previous page: "Bitte um Stille" (plea for silence) and "Schrei nach Stille" (scream for silence). Here the notion of "drowning" in silence is reversed; one pleads and even screams for silence, but doesn't get it.

Most remarkably, this page again contains the "Freude" melody, notated this time in its entirety (starting in the eighth system). While it may seem puzzling that a composer would even go to the trouble of writing out this familiar tune, by doing so (in addition to emphasizing the physicality of writing) Lachenmann explicitly includes it in his musical material. On page 44 of the published score the composer notates a fragment of the "Freude" theme in an empty system between the percussion and string parts, and, although it is not played, its rhythm is echoed in the orchestra, as Rainer Nonnenmann has pointed out.[9] The sketch page begins with the inscription "Charakter: wie eine Ruine" (character: like a ruin). This is a perfect description of what Lachenmann does to the famous theme. A ruin is an authentic physical object, not a copy or restoration. Its original material, however glorious it may have been, has aged and disintegrated. In *Staub,* Lachenmann reveals not the polished simulacrum of the Ninth that we get from recordings (or ceremonial performances), but rather fragments of its original material, altered by time, in all their ruined beauty.

Anne C. Shreffler

9 Nonnenmann discusses several instances of Beethoven "quotations" in the piece. He notes that this particular passage consists of "vague, toneless, 'dusty' Beethoven mutations; rather than functioning as quotations, they remain virtually unrecognizable, even to listeners who have pinpointed them in the score." ("[...] verschwommene und tonlos 'verstaubte' Beethovenmutationen, die nicht als Zitate fungieren und dem Hörer selbst dann so gut wie unkenntlich bleiben, wenn er sie zuvor in der Partitur ausfindig gemacht hat.") Nonnenmann, *Beethoven und Helmut Lachenmanns "Staub"* (see note 6), 21.

PLATES 1A AND 1B
Helmut Lachenmann, *Staub* for orchestra (1985–87). Sketches, 2 pages
(HELMUT LACHENMANN COLLECTION, PSS)

3

STRATEGIES OF REFERENCE

Simone Hohmaier

"You can only lose against Beethoven"?[1]

Modes of Reception in Twentieth- and Twenty-First-Century Composition

In memoriam Rainer Cadenbach

Some 150 years lie between Johannes Brahms's quip to conductor Hermann Levi – "You can't have any idea what it's like always to hear such a giant marching behind you!"[2] – and John Adams's confession: "Having Beethoven in the car while you are driving is exhilarating and terrifying and very humbling."[3] And yet, Franz Schubert's famous question notwithstanding ("[W]ho can do anything after Beethoven?"[4]), generations of composers have done one thing above all else: they have composed music, even and especially if it meant engaging with Beethoven. The reasons why his music has been so uniquely important to subsequent generations is neatly summarized by Claus-Steffen Mahnkopf: "In each of his major works, Beethoven invents new *categories* of music altogether. We find novel and previously unknown procedures and approaches whose ground-breaking qualities came to fruition only in the heyday of modern music [...]. There is hardly anything that Beethoven hasn't already considered, hardly any problems whose solution his music hasn't already prefigured."[5]

If Beethoven can function as a point of reference on such a scale for almost any form of composition in the twentieth and twenty-first centuries, the range of strategies for referring to his music is virtually limitless. Almost every compositional technique could be shown in one way or another to derive from Beethoven, and the only way to refer to him explicitly would be through titles, explanatory notes, documented quotations, or the like. Beethoven is omnipresent, all-powerful, almost inescapable.[6] To quote Steffen Schleiermacher, any attempt to approach a "great composer from the past is always a difficult business. Today, if you want to rise above blatant quotation and avoid the absurd temptation to compose

1 Steffen Schleiermacher, "Ein Skandal – heute? Zu meinem Orchesterstück 'Bann. Bewegung – mit Beethovens Erster,'" *MusikTexte* 145 (May 2015): 39.
2 Quoted from Max Kalbeck, *Johannes Brahms*, vol. 1, no. 1 (Berlin: Deutsche Brahms-Gesellschaft, 1912), 165.
3 "John Adams on 'Absolute Jest'" (for string quartet and orchestra), 2012, www.youtube.com/watch?v=h5bETcC1lFk (accessed 28 May 2020).
4 Otto Erich Deutsch, *Schubert: Memoirs by his Friends*, trans. Rosamond Ley and John Nowell (London: Black, 1958), 128.
5 "In jedem Hauptwerk erfindet Beethoven *Kategorien* von Musik überhaupt. Neuartige und bis dahin unbekannte Verfahrens- und Denkweisen treten auf, deren zukunftsweisende Eigenschaften erst in der Hochphase der neuen Musik zur Blüte kommen [...]. Es gibt kaum etwas, was nicht von Beethoven bereits bedacht, kaum etwas, dessen Lösung nicht bei ihm vorgezeichnet ist." Claus-Steffen Mahnkopf, *Kritik der neuen Musik: Entwurf einer Musik des 21. Jahrhunderts* (Kassel: Bärenreiter, 1998), 34–35.
6 My material is thus almost limitless. To date I have researched more than 600 compositions unambiguously related to Beethoven in the twentieth and twenty-first centuries alone – and this does not include *250 Piano Pieces for Beethoven*, edited in ten volumes by Susanne Kessel and Nikolas Sideris (London: Editions Musica Ferrum, 2015–20), hereafter abbreviated as *250 PPfB*. I am unfortunately forced to restrict myself to a few trends from the wealth of strategies with which composers have deliberately engaged with Beethoven. Thick monographs could be devoted solely to works dealing with aspects of his life (such as his deafness), or to arrangements and paraphrases of his works, or to the myriad sets of variations.

'… in the style of …', you quickly reach your limits as a composer. […] On the other hand, perhaps the most honest way of approaching the great composer – simply writing the best piece you can and dedicating it to him – is unavailable owing to the danger of arbitrariness. So how to proceed?"[7]

Prologue and Preludes

Is it a mitigating or an aggravating factor when a commission for a new work causes a composer to engage with Beethoven, something all composers must probably do anyway? Whatever the case, any commission to confront a particular piece to be performed at the same concert will require an explicit reference to Beethoven capable of being discussed in the program booklet. It will generally involve musical allusions and quotations, borrowings of material or structural concepts, or simply a sonic preparation for the work referenced. Most compositions intended to function as prologues to a Beethoven symphony are devoted to the Ninth. There may well be pragmatic reasons for this, but one reason is surely the multilayered social, symbolic, and composition-historical significance of the Ninth as being one of those works "in which bourgeois musical culture recognised the idea of itself in music."[8] But the Ninth may also function as nothing more than an empty symbolic vessel capable of being filled with arbitrary contents, thereby allowing it to define historical elements as such in a "post-historical world" and to project them emotionally to a worldwide audience.[9] That said, it is less the finale of the Ninth, with its "Ode to Joy," that has kindled the interest of composers than the opening of the first movement, with its string tremolandos and its descending fourths and fifths. The manner in which composers have dealt with this material varies widely. The ending of Rodion Shchedrin's *Praeludium* for orchestra (1999), for example, with its descending fifths and tritones above a cushion of triplet fifths, prepares the opening of the Ninth. Henri Dutilleux, in contrast, takes up the descending fifths and fourths at the very beginning of his *Pièce sans titre ("Muss es sein?")* of 2000 and fetches them into the present by adding an interior tritone. Here the musically inconsequential subtitle *Muss es sein?* may refer to the difficult task of writing a prologue to the Ninth at all. It was a task that Friedrich Cerha initially turned down, only to concede that, against his will, "the symphony's opening haunted my brain in the days that followed." The material began to reconstitute itself in his imagination and "to proliferate like a mycelium."[10] His *Paraphrase on the Beginning of Beethoven's Ninth Symphony* (2010) first takes up the work's opening by allowing descending fourths to resound like a carillon above a sustained string sonority. Soon the fourths actually do begin to proliferate, mutating into different but likewise "present-day" intervals in a large-scale escalation congealing at times into dodecaphony.

Two series of commissions, one issued by Riccardo Chailly for the Leipzig Gewandhaus Orchestra and another by Mariss Jansons for the Bavarian Radio Symphony Orchestra, have led to pieces that accompany other Beethoven symphonies. Steffen Schleiermacher's *Bann. Bewegung – mit Beethovens Erster* (2010) draws mainly on a pair of antitheses that he discovered in his own engagement with Beethoven, and in Beethoven's music itself. He has, he explained, "always been held spellbound, and moved, by the First Symphony in particular. Especially

7 "Eine musikalische Annäherung an einen großen Komponisten der Vergangenheit ist stets eine schwierige Sache. Will man sich über das plumpe Zitieren erheben und erliegt nicht dem widersinnigen Wunsch, 'im Stile von …' zu komponieren, gelangt man als heutiger Komponist schnell an Grenzen. […] Andererseits ist der Weg, einfach ein bestmögliches Stück zu komponieren und dann dies dem großen Komponisten zu widmen zwar vielleicht die ehrlichste Art der Annäherung, verschlossen aber wegen der Gefahr von Beliebigkeit. Wie sich also verhalten?" Schleiermacher, "Ein Skandal – heute?" (see note 1), 39.

8 Carl Dahlhaus, "New Music and the problem of musical genre," in idem, *Schoenberg and the New Music: Essays*, trans. Derrick Puffett and Alfred Clayton (Cambridge: Cambridge University Press, 1988), 32–44, at 36.

9 See Alexander Rehding, *Beethoven's Symphony No. 9* (New York: Oxford University Press, 2018), 32ff., and Slavoj Žižek's characterization of the Ninth as "an empty container open to all possible meanings" in the film *The Pervert's Guide to Ideology* (2012), excerpt available at www.youtube.com/watch?v=XM9erS90gTE (accessed 28 May 2020).

10 Friedrich Cerha, quoted from the booklet for *Edition Gewandhausorchester*, CD 4: *Ludwig van Beethoven, Friedrich Cerha*, VKJK1317 ([Altenburg]: querstand, 2014), 13. Introductory text also published on the DVD-ROM Friedrich Cerha, ed. Joachim Diederichs (Vienna: Lafite, 2018), 123.

by its opening movement." There, he continues, he found "this strange opposition between immobility and motion, even in the details. It's there in the very first theme appearing after the introduction."[11] He confronts the First Symphony with a structural mirror inversion: where the former opens with a dissonance unusual for its era, *Bann. Bewegung* begins with a pure C-major triad, namely, the one at the end of the first movement. Schleiermacher's work thrives almost exclusively on the above-mentioned antithesis between immobility (*Bann*) and motion (*Bewegung*) and their mediation: the first four chords, despite their high energy level, remain rooted to the spot.

Johannes Maria Staud takes a quite similar approach to the First Symphony in *Maniai* (2011) by constructing two antithetical moods (*furioso – grazioso*) based on Beethoven's use of contrast, that is, the contrast of "absolute delicacy alongside absolute savagery of the sort that no one before or after him was able to depict."[12] Knowing that his piece would be heard after the First in the concert, Staud took up the kinetic patterns of its finale and turned "Beethoven's rising cascades" upside down with descending, non-transposing, microtonally inflected scales (some of the notes are out of tune) and motivically succinct figures in contrary motion. In short, Beethoven's symphonies can lead to quite comparable approaches even in composers with very different styles.

Collage and Remix

At the beginning of Reiner Bredemeyer's orchestral piece *Bagatellen für B.* (1970), the opening chords of the *Eroica* initially lead the listener onto the wrong track by invoking one of Beethoven's greatest creations in the "heroic style" only to immediately follow it with one of the late bagatelles and with Bredemeyer's own music, consisting mainly of clusters, glissandos, and sustained sonorities.[13] As the interpolated passages remain intact and the cuts audible, *Bagatellen* forms an almost ideal-typical collage of three contrasting layers of material.

Perhaps the first Beethoven adaptation from this generic field of endeavor is a hybrid of collage and remix. However, it exists only in Stefan Wolpe's memories of his experiments with record players in the early 1920s, memories handed down in his "Lecture on Dada" (1962): "I had eight gramophones, record players, at my disposal. [...] Here you have only certain speeds [...] but there you could play a Beethoven symphony very, very slow, and very quick at the same time that you could mix it with a popular tune."[14] In other words, Wolpe combined various Beethoven recordings into a collage. However, regulating the speed of a record player entailed not only reducing or accelerating the tempo, but also altering pitch and timbre, and thus altering significantly the substance of the original, an intervention made possible by a new technological medium.

Karlheinz Stockhausen's *Stockhoven-Beethausen Opus 1970* also occupies an intermediate area between collage and remix by employing real instruments with predefined actions on the one hand, and arrangements and superpositions of Beethoven fragments in collage on the other. This area is a genre in which "everything can become anything" and every combination is "only a temporary stabilization before being dissected as raw material for something entirely different."[15]

11 Schleiermacher, "Ein Skandal – heute?" (see note 1), 39.

12 Johannes Maria Staud, quoted from Sybille Kayser, "Reflections: Die Auftragskompositionen zu Beethovens Symphonie," CD booklet for *Beethoven – The Symphonies and Reflections,* Mariss Jansons and the Bavarian Radio Symphony Orchestra, BR Klassik 900119 (Munich: BR Klassik, 2013), n. p.

13 Discussion of *Bagatellen für B.* in Nina Noeske, *Musikalische Dekonstruktion: Neue Instrumentalmusik in der DDR* (Cologne: Böhlau, 2007), 147–67.

14 Stefan Wolpe, "Lecture on Dada," in idem, *Das Ganze ist überall: Vorträge über Musik 1940–1962,* ed. Thomas Phleps (Saarbrücken: Pfau, 2011), 150–64, at 155. I wish to thank Heidy Zimmermann and Michelle Ziegler for drawing my attention to Wolpe's experiment.

15 Felix Stalder, "Neun Thesen zur Remix-Kultur" [2009], at https://irights.info/wp-content/uploads/fileadmin/texte/material/Stalder_Remixing.pdf, p. 17 (accessed 28 May 2020).

Stockhausen's starting point was the concept he explored in *Kurzwellen* (1968), "which, without mediation, uses unpredictable musical events received on short-wave radios as material for development." He then proposed to "simulate the improbable 'special case' in which, wherever we turn, Beethoven's music is playing from all the short-wave receivers."[16] Instead of such receivers, each of the four players has a tape recorder that allows him or her to play a continuous stream of Beethoven fragments, electronically manipulated, by switching on a loudspeaker. As underlying material, he excerpted passages from every genre and every period of Beethoven's career.[17] Although recognizable scraps of Beethoven (often head motifs) crop up time and again, their fragmentary character, schematic arrangement, and distortion render them basically unplaceable without outside help, and certainly not recognizable in the dramaturgical sequence divined by Winrich Hopp (from the early works to the late ones, and from small to monumental forms). Instead, what we hear is the aura of Beethoven's music.[18]

Many remix compositions of more recent date, although situated in art music, work with techniques borrowed from pop music, especially Techno. The pioneer in this area would seem to be Pierre Henry, who composed a classical tape collage as early as 1979 with his *La dixième symphonie: Hommage à Beethoven*. Here he viewed Beethoven's music as "concrete" sounds and treated it accordingly.[19] In contrast, Malte Giesen, in his *Trio (with remixed surface of Beethoven)* of 2014, employed quasi-analog and electronic remix techniques. In the scherzo from Beethoven's String Trio, op. 9, no. 3, he discovered forerunners of techniques applied particularly in pop music, such as scratching, looping, and shuffling, and felt called upon to employ DJ techniques in order to extract "loops and shuffles and short distortions and stumbles that Beethoven had already built into the musical structure, but which we might not hear that way at all today."[20] Beginning acoustically with the real sound of Beethoven's trio and an exact quotation from the opening of its scherzo, Giesen already takes the repeated notes in bar 4 as the basis of an analog loop.[21] The tonal repetition is extended to all instruments and expanded into quadruplets by altering the rhythm, and a prerecorded "fast loop" is added to the sound. In the second run, he inserts a C-minor loop already at the end of Beethoven's bar 7. At the first melodic culmination of the original (m. 11 in Beethoven), the climactic character is reinforced with an aggressive prerecorded synthetic sound. This not only interrupts the flow of the music, it also disturbs (and destroys) the lightness of the original, which, in Giesen's eyes, "stands in a tradition of entertainment music."[22]

Recomposition

Faced with a new commission, Michael Gordon asked himself what would happen if a modern-day composer were to use Beethoven material without being aware of it. He took aim at Beethoven's Seventh Symphony, choosing a characteristic feature from each movement in order to create something new from them. The result was *Rewriting Beethoven's Seventh Symphony* (2006). That Beethoven's "brutish and loud" music was an inspiration to him is already evident in the material he selected from the opening movement: the "huge barbaric opening chords,"[23] meaning the first four chords of the Seventh, are repeated many times (without the oboe melody)

16 Karlheinz Stockhausen, "Kurzwellen mit Beethoven Opus 1970," in idem, *Texte zur Musik 1963–1970*, vol. 3: *Einführungen und Projekte, Kurse, Sendungen, Standpunkte, Nebennoten*, ed. Dieter Schnebel (Cologne: DuMont, 1971), 121–22, at 121.

17 See Winrich Hopp, *Kurzwellen von Karlheinz Stockhausen: Konzeption und musikalische Poiesis* (Mainz: Schott, 1998), 263–415.

18 The aura of both composers – Beethoven and Stockhausen – seems to exert a special magnetism. Bassam Halaka, in his remix *StockhovenBeethausen elektronisch* (2015), combines excerpts from Beethoven's First to Fifth Symphonies with Stockhausen's electronic music. These two "musical giants" also meet in Martin Christoph Redel's *Begegnung – Rheinische Bagatelle* (in *250 PPfB*, vol. 3, 153), where passages from movements 1 and 4 of the *Eroica* are combined with a characteristic four-note chord from Stockhausen's work.

19 A new version dates from 1987, and in 1998 Henry reworked the piece into *Xe Symphonie Remix*. The early version of *Dixième symphonie* was performed live for the first time with three orchestral groups in 2019.

20 Quoted from Thomas Groetz, "Popkultur in der Neuen Musik: Nichts als Trash?," *Positionen* 119 (May 2019): 20–30, at 26–27.

21 Other composers of Beethoven remixes using loops include Bernhard Lang, in *Monadologie XXXIV: Loops for Ludvik* (with a reference to the Third Piano Concerto, op. 37), and Christoph Maria Wagner, in a remix of the Fifth Symphony (*remiX III*) and another of the "Ode to Joy" (*remiX XIII*, in *250 PPfB*, vol. 6).

22 Quoted from Groetz, "Popkultur in der Neuen Musik" (see note 20), 27.

23 Michael Gordon, "Rewriting Beethoven's 7th Symphony UK Premiere" [2006], at https://michaelgordonmusic.com/news/rewriting-beethovens-7th-symphony-uk-premiere (accessed 28 May 2020).

EXAMPLE 1
Ludwig van Beethoven, *Diabelli Variations* for piano, op. 120 (1819–23), No. 33, mm. 1–8

EXAMPLE 2
Claus-Steffen Mahnkopf, *Beethoven-Kommentar* for piano (2004), mm. 1–8

and subjected to transformation by having certain groups of instruments execute downward glissandos. Beginning with the seventh repetition, the low strings reach out for a grand counter-gesture and execute a slow upwards glissando. This becomes increasingly dominant until the chords are omitted entirely, only to return in rhythmically and harmonically agile form with echoes of pop idioms. Here the musical development so characteristic of Beethoven's music is wholly redefined and reduced to gradual change in contrary motion.

When Claus-Steffen Mahnkopf was asked to "write a contemporary variation of the Diabelli waltz that Beethoven made famous," he decided to "behave a little bit like Beethoven by essentially ignoring the model."[24] This, however, is precisely what does *not* happen in his *Beethoven-Kommentar* (2004), for the motifs of the variation movement which Mahnkopf derives from the simplest imaginable material (the chromatic scale) are clearly borrowed from Beethoven's Variation 33 (SEE EXAMPLE 1, P. 101), namely, from its "dotted" rhythm, which is readily discernible to the listener though it looks highly complex on the printed page. Nor does Mahnkopf ignore the original as his piece progresses: the formal design of his "commentary" is almost classically subdivided into four-bar units, the types of motion underlying its contrasting sections are obviously taken from the original, and the dotted "descending" gesture of the opening is likewise recomposed, as are the many triplet figures (mm. 5–8) (SEE EXAMPLE 2, P. 101) and the interlocking quintuplet ninths (mm. 9–12).

Unlike collage and remix, recompositions of Beethoven's music such as Gordon's and Mahnkopf's use pre-existing material as a basis for a new development in which only partial aspects of the original are retained and remain recognizable (albeit not necessarily so).

Quotation and Allusion

Perhaps the most common strategy for engaging with Beethoven is quotation. It comes in an impressive variety of forms: a quotation can be used as a theme for variations, as a cantus firmus in a contrapuntal texture, as part of a collage, of a quodlibet, or of a remix, or in many other ways. The boundaries of these categories are often blurred, as are those between allusion and quotation. Is a repeated semitone neighbor-note motion a sufficiently clear reference to *Für Elise,* or do we need the complete first phrase up to the tonic? Are three short notes followed by a long one enough to conjure up the theme of Beethoven's Fifth, or do we need a combination of repeated notes and descending third?

"Muss es sein?": Popular and Avant-garde Beethoven "Hits" — Besides the various functions of quotations, one interesting aspect of Beethoven reception is the choice composers make among characteristic motifs and themes. Here we can descry two tendencies. The first is to quote popular motifs and themes, above all from *Für Elise,* the "Moonlight" Sonata, the opening of the Fifth, and the "Ode to Joy." The second is to clearly emphasize quotations from works regarded as landmarks of modernism, such as "Der schwer gefasste Entschluss" from the op. 135 String Quartet or the *Grosse Fuge* (op. 133).

24 Claus-Steffen Mahnkopf, "Beethoven-Kommentar" [2004], at http://www.clausteffenmahnkopf.de/work-details/beethoven-kommentar/?mode=nodes (accessed 28 May 2020).

Two of the myriad works that quote *Für Elise* are particularly remarkable in that they independently take up a feature apparently hidden "between the lines": the tango rhythm. Matt Herskowitz, in *Tango-Toccata on "Für Elise,"*[25] initially quotes the first eight bars of the original, without any changes, and then approaches a tango in the Andante, introducing an appropriate rhythmic accompaniment after a transition to the "Elise" theme in 2/4 time. Jürg Wyttenbach, in *Noch weisst du nicht, wess' Kind du bist* (1979), gets more quickly to the point: the "Elise" theme is first stated in the right hand, as in the original; then, when the first destination pitch A4 is reached, the accompaniment part is not only judiciously reharmonized but transformed rhythmically into a tango mode, with semitone progressions added where Beethoven's "accompaniment" falls silent. There now follow several variations on the theme, always as a tango, until the violin joins in and the tango is enriched with snatches of the Violin Concerto, the op. 111 Piano Sonata, and the song alluded to in the title: *An einen Säugling* (WoO 108). The concluding song of farewell, "Ade, Elise," has a fragmentary melody taken from Beethoven's *Adelaide*. Wyttenbach introduces it with the first notes of the *Tristan* Prelude, the *Tristan* chord itself occurring on the syllable "-li-" of the cambiata motif on E-li-se. Here, if not earlier, the reference reveals itself to be a satire (SEE EXAMPLE 3).

EXAMPLE 3
Jürg Wyttenbach, *Noch weisst du nicht, wess' Kind du bist: Tango-Collage nach Beethoven* for piano, violin and voice ad lib. (1977), mm. 97–101

But quotations can be more than just an intentional (more or less serious) tribute or a reference to an underlying program. They can also indicate the composer's self-definition and allegiance to tradition. This function is fulfilled mainly by quotations from Beethoven's late music. Dmitry Shostakovich, in his Eighth String Quartet, op. 110 (1960), pursues such a strategy of self-definition within a modernist tradition. The first-movement fugue already points to a late Beethoven work with its subject D-E♭-C-B ("d-(e)s-c-h" in German letter notation, standing for **D**mitri **Sch**ostakowitsch), namely, to the first movement of Beethoven's String Quartet in C-sharp minor, op. 131. In the fourth movement he also quotes a variant of the "Muss es sein" motto from Beethoven's final String Quartet, op. 135, still clearly recognizable in spite of the altered intervals. The subtle ploy of the first movement resides in the union of Shostakovich's musical signature (D-E♭-C-B) and a Beethovenian compositional device. It culminates at the end of the movement, when the question "Muss es sein?" receives a direct answer in the form of the signature motif, likewise stated "verbatim."

25 *250 PPfB*, vol. 5.

Two later composers perpetuated this Beethoven-Shostakovich connection through the use of quotations. Alfred Schnittke, in his Third String Quartet (1983), constructs a line of tradition spanning some 400 years by juxtaposing transformed quotations from Orlando di Lasso's *Stabat Mater*, Beethoven's *Grosse Fuge* (op. 133), and Shostakovich's signature motif (ultimately a transposition of the first four notes of the Beethoven quotation, with B♭-B-A♭-G becoming D-E♭-C-B) as the basis of all three movements and mediating between the conflicting styles. Similarly Nicolas Bacri, in his Fourth String Quartet (1989–95), combines the subject of the *Grosse Fuge* with a motif derived from Shostakovich's Fifteenth String Quartet. The wealth of contrasts in the *Grosse Fuge* arising from constantly alternating small-scale sections is driven to extremes in Bacri's work, namely, to a breathless succession of minuscule contrasting sections. Here the referential quotations from the *Grosse Fuge* function, so to speak, as reassurance and one-upmanship at the same time.

Characteristic Chords as Opening Gestures — Quotations need not always consist of motifs or themes; the use of chords and opening gestures is also very attractive, particularly in reference to Beethoven, provided that they are sufficiently characteristic for listeners to recognize. As the chords are usually tonal, their specific quality lies in the combination of instrumentation and gesture.

György Kurtág's great orchestral composition ΣΤΗΛΗ (*Stele*, 1994) begins with what sounds like a truly Beethovenian chord but isn't: with a "unison G from the beginning of the *Third Leonora Overture*" (op. 72b).[26] Kurtág recalls that the start of the creative process was focused on a single chord: "When Abbado asked for *Stele*, I did seriously consider writing an orchestral work that would consist of only a single chord."[27] Although the instrumentation is different, it essentially contributes to the recognizability of the unison pitch as a reference to Beethoven (especially the timpani stroke and the preponderance of flutes). Much like the chord in Gordon's *Rewriting Beethoven's Seventh Symphony*, here the unison is immediately blurred microtonally by means of tremolandos and a glissando in the trombones.

In much the same way, Mathias Spahlinger's *passage/paysage* for orchestra (1989–90) begins with a "battered big bang,"[28] namely, with the transformed first two chords of the *Eroica*. In this case, however, they fulfill an entirely different function than at the beginning of Bredemeyer's *Bagatellen für B.*, where they have the effect of a signal and play with generic and stylistic hierarchies by being contrasted with bagatelles. In Spahlinger's case, they form a point of departure for micro-development and nascent de-hierarchization. Yet the choice of the *Eroica* chords is by no means arbitrary: Spahlinger is convinced that composing can be semantic, even political (a conviction that connects him with the Beethoven references of Aribert Reimann and Helmut Lachenmann), and the two opening chords caused him to think "of the anecdote about Beethoven furiously ripping off the title page with the dedication to Napoleon. [...] That can perhaps be taken to mean: nothing should be established or institutionalized that is not open-ended, that does not strive toward its own self-dissolution. [...] There are no fixed shapes, only those in the process of emerging and those in the process of decaying."[29] Accordingly, the Beethoven chords are already caught in a transformative process from the moment they first appear.

26 György Kurtág, *Three Interviews and Ligeti Homages*, ed. Bálint András Varga (Rochester: University of Rochester Press, 2009), 50.

27 Ibid. Whether this chord idea was related to the opening of the *Leonore* Overture is open to doubt, but the composition's second idea also bore a relation to Beethoven: the other "idea that occurred to me was to write nine symphonies, each lasting a few seconds" (ibid.).

28 "'Das Thema des Stückes ist Entwicklung': Mathias Spahlinger über 'passage/paysage' im Gespräch mit Martina Seeber" [2018], *Berliner Festspiele Blog*, at https://blog.berlinerfestspiele.de/das-thema-des-stueckes-ist-entwicklung/ (accessed 28 May 2020).

29 "jeder [dachte] an die anekdote: beethoven reißt wutschnaubend das titelblatt mit der widmung für napoleon [...] herunter. und das kann vielleicht signalisieren: keine etablierung oder institutionalisierung soll sein, die nicht nach vorne offen ist, die nicht ihre selbstsaufhebung betreibt. [...] es gibt keine etablierten gestalten, sondern nur solche, die im begriff sind, zu entstehen und solche, die im begriff sind zu vergehen." Reinhard Oehlschlägel, "'alles aus allem entwickeln': mathias spahlinger im gespräch über 'passage/paysage' für großes Orchester," *MusikTexte* 39 (April 1991): 23–32, at 24–25.

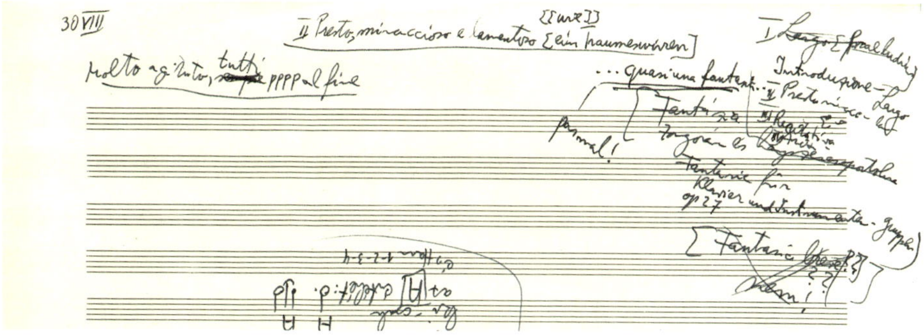

PLATE 1
György Kurtág, *...quasi una fantasia...* for piano and groups of instruments, op. 27, no. 1 (1987–88). Sketch
(GYÖRGY KURTÁG COLLECTION, PSS)

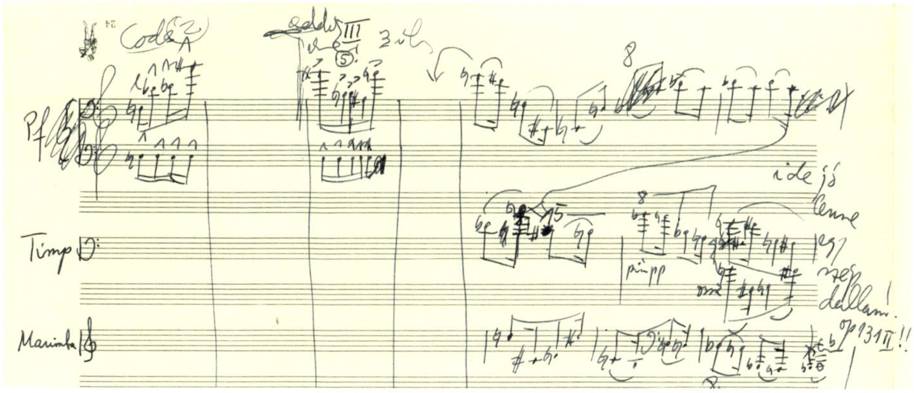

PLATE 2
György Kurtág, *...quasi una fantasia...* for piano and groups of instruments, op. 27, no. 1 (1987–88). Sketch
(GYÖRGY KURTÁG COLLECTION, PSS)

Titles and Headings — György Kurtág's compositional homages are typical of the way he treats the music of highly regarded predecessors: he isolates an element, illuminates it analytically from vantage points he considers important, exploits the possibilities it contains, and allows a concentrated essence to flow into the piece.[30] That said, his *(Hommage à Beethoven), Adagio cantabile*[31] is more than an exercise for the second movement of the *Pathétique* Sonata, op. 13, an exercise which, to quote the work's dedicatee Gergely Szokolay,[32] is aimed at training the dexterity necessary for playing this movement while keeping the hands quiet. Except for the steady eighth-note motion, the tonal material is wholly unrelated to Beethoven; it is restricted entirely to the white keys,[33] and the fingers move *legatissimo* in contrary motion within the space of open fifths, each time with a decreasing number of notes,[34] to be repeated *senza fine*. Nonetheless, the heading "Adagio cantabile" opens up a horizon of interpretation that goes far beyond the mere playing of the exercise, suggesting a melodic design resembling that of the slow movement of the *Pathétique*.

The title and opus number of Kurtág's *...quasi una fantasia...*, op. 27, no. 1, for piano and instrumental groups, obviously evoke Beethoven's two *quasi una fantasia* piano sonatas (op. 27).[35] That said, a sketch reveals that Beethoven's sonatas did not serve as a point of reference from the very start, for the title was only invented later after large parts of the music had already been composed. In dialogue with himself, Kurtág referred to the title *quasi una fantasia* with its enclosing ellipses as "pas mal!" (SEE PLATE 1). Nevertheless, Beethoven is present in this work, as he presumably was throughout the compositional process:[36] on a page for the coda of the second movement, alongside a sketch of bar 34, Kurtág wrote "ide jó lenne egy szép dallam op. 131 II" ("here a nice melody would be good op. 131, movt. 2") (SEE PLATE 2).

30 *Les Adieux* from *Játékok*, vol. 5, may have proceeded, in a manner typical of this composer, from an analysis of the Beethoven sonata. However, no such "missing link" has yet been unearthed among the materials of the Kurtág Collection.
31 *Játékok*, vol. 1.
32 See Gergely Szokolay, "Kurtág, as I Know Him," in *Centre and Periphery, Roots and Exile: Interpreting the Music of István Anhalt, György Kurtág and Sándor Veress*, ed. Friedemann Sallis, Robin Elliott, and Kenneth Gordon DeLong (Waterloo, Ontario: Wilfried Laurier University Press, 2009), 37–44.
33 Kurtág's Sketchbook f contains, on p. 7, an *ossia* variant with a general sharp key signature (György Kurtág Collection, PSS).
34 The systematic reduction in number of notes was not yet foreseen in an earlier variant. See Kurtág's Sketchbook 21, p. 43 (György Kurtág Collection, PSS).
35 They may also relate to Anton Webern's Variations, op. 27, in that one central structural element of Kurtág's op. 27 consists of what he himself calls the "diabolical leaps" that he found in the Webern work. To him, these leaps, used for the first time in *Bornemisza Péter mondásai*, op. 7, represented the "devil's visiting card." See Kurtág, *Three Interviews* (see note 26), 68–69.
36 Kurtág said, "Bartók's music is my mother-tongue, Beethoven's my grandmother-tongue." Quoted by Raphael Merlin, "Ewigkeits-Gestus," in *Für György Kurtág ...denn inniger ist, achtsamer auch...: Festschrift für György Kurtág*, ed. Hochschule für Musik Hanns Eisler (Berlin: Hochschule für Musik Hanns Eisler, 2015), 33.

EXAMPLE 4
Ludwig van Beethoven, String Quartet in B-flat major, op. 130 (1826), movt. 3, mm. 1–4

PLATE 3
Wolfgang Rihm, *Music for Three Strings* (1977), movt. 2, mm. 52–55. Full score fair copy

PLATE 4
Wolfgang Rihm, *Music for Three Strings* (1977), movt. 5, mm. 47–50. Full score fair copy

PLATE 5
Wolfgang Rihm, *Music for Three Strings* (1977), movt. 6, mm. 68–69. Full score fair copy

However, there is no "nice melody" following this remark, much less the one from the second movement of the op. 131 String Quartet, but only a short series of ninths in the harp, to be played *cantabile*. Even so, other components of *...quasi una fantasia...* can be related to Beethoven: the descending scales at the beginning are probably abstracted from that "primal musical comportment" which Kurtág had already become acquainted with as a child[37] (namely, from his mother's playing of Beethoven's F-minor Sonata, op. 2, no. 1) and which, incidentally, also follow directly upon the opening unison of Beethoven's Third *Leonore* Overture, to which Kurtág refers in *Stele*.[38]

Allusion — While most Beethoven quotations are easily recognizable as deliberate and intentional references, some composers work only with allusions to his music, with vague suggestions that merely adopt secondary aspects of the original or so severely transform it that it can only be surmised by the listener. In Wolfgang Rihm's *Music for Three Strings* of 1977 the Beethoven allusions are so tightly stitched into the compositional fabric that they convey the overriding impression of being genuine utterances from Rihm: they "would have had to be invented here if they hadn't already existed."[39] Rihm's trio begins with a chord at triple *forte* (the pitches E-F-A for the dedicatee Eva). After a third chord, an interval (a minor third) is gesturally highlighted in bar 11 for the first time. At this point it is still unable to raise claims to being an allusion, much less a quotation. Similarly, in bars 15–16, the reference to the opening of movement 3 of Beethoven's String Quartet op. 130 (SEE EXAMPLE 4) can only be guessed at. Not until the second movement does the origin of the material come more clearly to the fore (SEE PLATE 3).

Two of the many manifestations of this Beethoven material reveal with particular clarity how tightly the borrowed material is woven into Rihm's musical language, and what contrasting characters this material assumes in his hands: in movement 5 (*Canzona II*, mm. 47–50, SEE PLATE 4) the borrowed line turns into a cantilena, and in movement 7 (m. 69, SEE PLATE 5) it undergirds the highly expressive chordal climax of a passage of escalation.[40]

Compression, Expansion

While pitch and rhythm usually form the mainstay of quotations and allusions, several composers have taken it upon themselves to manipulate the temporal relations of Beethoven's music. Leif Inge, in *9 Beet Stretch* (2002), expands the Ninth Symphony to a duration of twenty-four hours using digital transformation procedures (granular synthesis) without distortions or pitch alterations. The piece was performed as a twenty-four-hour concert at which the classical concert infrastructure was replaced by rugs and cushions, thereby undermining the time-honored rites of a symphony concert. The presentation of the piece on the Internet additionally undermines the character of the performance as a unique event, for listeners can come and go at any time.[41]

An opposite strategy is the extreme compression of Beethoven's music. One example is Harald Muenz's *BeethovEnBloc* (2000), which takes the thirty-seven movements of the nine Beethoven symphonies as its material.[42] For

37 Kurtág, *Three Interviews* (see note 26), 8. A similar shape can be found *inter alia* in *Kis korál* (*Játékok*, vol. 1).

38 I wish to thank Péter Halász for drawing my attention to Kurtág's *Petite musique solennelle* (2015), which also begins with an allusion to Beethoven: all the instruments play a unison C, augmented by an F in the second run to create an open fifth, and tinged with chromaticism in the third run. Here, too, the "primal musical comportment" can be heard in the form of a descending line (mm. 14ff.), exposed as a solo. A note appended to the heading of the "Adagio molto" movement ("Si deve suonare tutto questo pezzo delicatissimamente [Beethoven, op. 27, no. 2, movt. 1]; con molto sentimento [Beethoven, op. 106, movt. 3]") is presumably a private message to the dedicatee, Pierre Boulez (a practice thoroughly typical of Kurtág), as is the allusion to Beethoven in the final bars, where Kurtág has written "Soll es sein?" beneath the last three chords.

39 Thus Wilhelm Killmayer regarding a comparable constellation in Rihm's Piano Piece No. 7. See "Zu Wolfgang Rihms Klavierstück Nr. 6 (*Bagatellen*)," *Melos* 51 (1992): 102–27, at 110.

40 See Reinhold Brinkmann, "Wirkungen Beethovens in der Kammermusik," in idem, *Vom Pfeifen und von alten Dampfmaschinen: Aufsätze zur Musik von Beethoven bis Rihm* (Vienna: Zsolnay, 2006), 32–72.

41 Leif Inge, *9 Beet Stretch*, at http://www.expandedfield.net/ (accessed 28 May 2020).

42 See the CD *Broken Beethoven in seven parts* (Istanbul: Müzik Hayvanı, 2012) (MH-G7-012). A complement to *BeethovEnBloc* is Muenz's *Beethovenamstück*, a semi-staged concept piece in which randomly selected Beethoven passages are played upside down (2015, *250 PPfB*, vol. 2).

each symphony, Muenz calculated a mean length for its movements and adjusted all the movements to fit that length, again without pitch alterations. For the next step, he calculated the mean duration of these superimposed forms in order to adjust them to a duration of 9 minutes and 26 seconds, using the same procedure, and again to superimpose them. Varied dynamics are not to be expected from this procedure: *BeethovEnBloc* remains at a constant *fortissimo*. The idea Muenz thus implemented – the simultaneity of all Beethoven symphonies – presumably derives from John Cage, who once said "he preferred to hear all Beethoven's symphonies simultaneously."[43] Peter Ablinger, too, wanted to "know what it sounds like."[44] In his *Weiss/Weisslich 22* (1996), he went one step further and compacted all nine Beethoven symphonies into the space of only 40 seconds. In his case, rather than calculating mean durations, he disected recordings of all the symphonies into 40-second snippets and piled them on top of each other. The same idea was taken yet another step further in Johannes Kreidler's *Compression Sound Art* (2009), in which all nine Beethoven symphonies were compressed to the performance duration of one second.[45] What all these attempts have in common is that, rather than yielding the essence of Beethoven's music, they congeal it into an alienated and no longer identifiable object. That such procedures so frequently focus on Beethoven probably has to do with his role as the most prominent representative of "opus music" and the concomitant need to question the "work" character of music altogether.

Beethoven as a Formal and Generic Paradigm

If Beethoven invented "new *categories* of music" with each major work,[46] his forms and genres – sonatas and variations on the one hand, concertos, symphonies, and string quartets on the other – are considered not only paradigmatic for his output in the awareness of the general public,[47] but evidently perfectly suitable for reference in a composition. In the twentieth century a movement in sonata form without a reference to Beethoven seemed well-nigh unthinkable.[48] But composers also felt challenged by his innovative species of variations, which burst the norms of their genre, especially in their stylistic variety and large-scale formal design. This has prompted composers to engage above all with the *Diabelli Variations* and to find solutions of their own.[49] One example is Frederic Rzewski's *The People United Will Never Be Defeated* (1975), a set of variations composed at the suggestion of the pianist Ursula Oppens, who incorporated the *Diabelli Variations* in her repertoire at the time. Like the Beethoven work, its thirty-six variations (including cadenza and reprise) on a popular theme (the Chilean protest song *El pueblo unido*) are a compendium of contemporary composing, from atonal, serialist-pointillist structures to jazz and blues. The piece has a rigorously structured form in which the first five of each six variations (in turn bundled into six groups) present styles and techniques of maximum diversity, which are then summarized in the sixth variation of each group. The sixth group repeats this relation on the level of the overall form.[50]

Of the countless compositional references to Beethoven's innovative cultivation of the symphony, string quartet, and concerto genres, Simon Steen-Andersen's *Piano Concerto* (2014) may serve as a representative example. It attempts nothing less than the rebirth of the piano concerto and the expansion of its classical

43 Alastair Williams, "Cage and Postmodernism," in *The Cambridge Companion to John Cage*, ed. David Nicholls (Cambridge: Cambridge University Press, 2002), 227–41, at 237.

44 Peter Ablinger, "Das Alte im Neuen: Über den Umgang mit musikalischer Weltliteratur in der Musik des 20. Jahrhunderts," radio lecture on Deutschlandsender Kultur (7 December 1991), at https://ablinger.mur.at/docs/altneu.pdf (accessed 16 September 2020).

45 An idea similarly expressed by Stockhausen (Beethoven's symphonies compressed to the duration of half a second) already in 1971; see his "Composing Statistically," in *Stockhausen on Music: Lectures and Interviews*, ed. Robin Maconie (London: Marion Boyars, 1991), 43–52, at 47. Kreidler produced further concentrates of *Für Elise*, the "Waldstein" Sonata (op. 53), the "Moonlight" Sonata (op. 27, no. 2), and the Sonata, op. 10, no. 1.

46 Mahnkopf, *Kritik der neuen Musik* (see note 5), 34.

47 See e.g. the emphasis placed on the symphony, piano sonata, and string quartet genres as well as sonata form in the German Wikipedia article "Ludwig van Beethoven," section "Bedeutung," at https://de.wikipedia.org/wiki/Ludwig_van_Beethoven#Bedeutung (accessed 3 January 2020).

48 Examples of explicit compositional engagement include the "Torso" movement from Jürg Baur's string quartet *Et respice finem* (1993) and Alfred Schnittke's Second Violin Sonata, subtitled "Quasi una sonata" (1968).

49 Worthy of mention above all others is Hans Zender's meta-variation *33 Veränderungen über 33 Veränderungen* (2010–19), which re-veals one-upmanship strategies on several levels. See also the contributions to *Diabelli 81: 17 Veränderungen über einen Walzer von Antonio Diabelli* (Vienna: Doblinger, 1983) and Otfried Büsing's *trentaquattro / ohne Diabelli*, which might be called a thirty-fourth Diabelli variation *ex negativo* consisting of the notes that do *not* occur in the upper voice of Diabelli's waltz (*250 PPfB*, vol. 4).

50 See Sandeep Bhagwati, "Von der Schönheit der Vielfalt in der Einheit: Notizen zu Frederic Rzewskis *The People United Will Never Be Defeated:* 36 Variationen über ein chilenisches Volkslied (1975)," *Melos* 51 (1992): 130–71.

instrumental forces by means of visual media. It begins with a concert grand piano projected onto a large screen. We then watch the piano falling in slow motion from the heights of a factory building and crashing to the ground, heavily damaged. Here the de(con)struction of the piano in the twentieth century is symbolically summed up within the space of a few seconds.[51] At the same time, this sublime moment is considerably stretched out, through the slow-motion video and a meticulous transcription of the sound track, into a highly complex orchestral sound.[52] Another media extension turns the piano concerto into a double concerto: projected onto a second surface is a video recording (controlled by a live pianist via a sampler) of the performer of the première, who recorded this second piano part beforehand on the heavily damaged instrument. In this staged apotheosis of the piano concerto, Beethoven serves as king's witness for the generic traditions of piano music altogether. First, we hear a brief allusion to the opening of Tchaikovsky's First Piano Concerto, played on the damaged piano in the video, with the initial chord microtonally inflected (i.e. out of tune; m. 694). Then come two allusions to Beethoven. The first is a microtonally altered transitional passage from the opening movement of the Piano Concerto, op. 15 (mm 458–65), marked "QUASI BEETHOVEN!" in the score (mm. 710–17). As in the Beethoven work, Steen-Andersen follows this passage (m. 718) with a cadenza representing the second Beethoven quotation. However, it is taken from the opening movement of the Piano Sonata, op. 101 (mm. 41–52), and entrusted initially to the battered piano in the video. The real instrument comes into play only at the lengthened repeat of this passage, where it appears with a transposed and disfigured version of the recapitulation from Beethoven's sonata in dialogue with its adversary in the video. Before (Beethoven's) quoted recapitulation, Steen-Andersen creates a media fracture by having the video pianist turn his head and, as the music falls silent, look into the camera, and thus into the audience, thereby indicating that the ensuing recapitulation is staged. The contrast between the furious timpani in the concerto quotation and the heartrendingly wretched sonata quotation also signifies that the genre cannot be reconstituted by merely reverting to the tradition that Beethoven has come to symbolize.

Stylistic Copy and De(con)struction

"When a composer makes use of existing material," Mauricio Kagel once opined in an interview, "a series of questions at once arise: serious homage or irony?"[53] Indeed, not all stylistic copies of Beethoven are meant to be read as satirical de(con)structions. A good many pieces of *Gebrauchsmusik* are specifically intent on producing a successful stylistic copy, and enjoy wide dissemination as a result. Günther von Noé's "Humorous Variations" on *Happy Birthday to You* and Peter Heidrich's *Happy Birthday Variations* are two favorite examples of this. Stylistic copies and parodies can also be intended as attempts to rescue Beethoven; Adorno, writing about the *Missa Solemnis,* already proposed "to alienate" the work, "in Brecht's terms [...]; to break through the aura of irrelevant worship which protectively surrounds it."[54]

To be sure, "to break through the aura of irrelevant worship" can be accomplished in many different ways. Mauricio Kagel's *Ludwig van* has been seen as just such an attempt; and Wolf Vostell, in the wake of the Fluxus movement,

51 See *inter alia* Gunnar Schmidt, *Klavierzerstörungen in Kunst und Popkultur* (Berlin: Reimer, 2013), and Stefan Drees, "'... and Destruction after all is a form of creation': Instrumentenzerstörung zwischen Theatralität und medialem Reenactment," *Neue Zeitschrift für Musik* 176, no. 2 (2015): 32–37. A piano "falling" from the ceiling is also a central object in Georg Nussbaumer's Beethoven-related installation *Zukunftsschrei(b)maschine* (2018), where it produces sounds reminiscent of the "Fate" motif from Beethoven's Fifth.

52 See Stefan Drees, "'Expanded music': Zur medialen Erweiterung von Körper und Klavier in Simon Steen-Andersens *Piano Concerto* (2014)," *Jahrbuch des Staatlichen Instituts für Musikforschung Preußischer Kulturbesitz 2017*, ed. Simone Hohmaier (Mainz: Schott, in press).

53 Taken from Mauricio Kagel's interview with Karl Faust in the liner notes to the LP *Ludwig van* (Hamburg: Deutsche Grammophon Gesellschaft, 1970) (DGG 2530 014).

54 Theodor W. Adorno, "Alienated Masterpiece: The *Missa Solemnis,*" in idem, *Essays on Music*, ed. Richard Leppert (Berkeley: University of California Press, 2002), 569–83, at 570.

deconstructed Beethoven in his action *Vietnam-Symphonie zum Beethoven-Jahr (1970)* by proclaiming railway travelers in Cologne Central Station to be performers for seventy-two hours and having them carry out such actions as cleaning a platform.[55] In contrast, Simon Steen-Andersen, in *In Spite Of, and Maybe Even Therefore* (2007), practiced destruction in a literal sense: here an amplified instrumental ensemble consisting of piano, contrabassoon, double bass, and piccolo noisily intones paradigmatic textures from "contemporary" music (glissandos, clusters) at quintuple *forte,* interspersed with lengthy pauses. During the pauses a flute, a horn, and a clarinet hint at fragments of traditional music, namely, from Beethoven's Bagatelle, op. 126, no. 5, which, however, is unrecognizable. The Beethoven fragments increase in length from one silence to the next, and the music is slowly reconstituted from fragments. At the same time, the material basis of this reconstruction is gradually removed in a literal sense of the term: the musicians disassemble their instruments in accordance with a pre-defined choreography. Yet they remain true to their task of restoring the musical cohesion and continue to play on their dismantled instruments. The reference to Beethoven, inaudible to the listener, is probably meant to be symbolic: here, as in *Piano Concerto,* he serves as an emblem for an irrecoverable past. With the loss of its material basis, the artistic "superstructure" can no longer function, and composition no longer means "building an instrument,"[56] but dismantling it.

Despite the surfeit of shopworn "Beethoven hits" (such as the "Ode to Joy") in the satires and de(con)structions of his music, it should not be forgotten that we are dealing with supreme compositional achievements and that everything might have turned out quite differently. This, in any case, is the idea behind Samuel Penderbayne's *Thank you for the struggle,*[57] which retraces a compositional process based on the material of the "Moonlight" Sonata – a process destined, as it were, to fail. A C-sharp minor chord, played *pianissimo,* first gives way to a cluster at triple *forte,* signalizing that the search for an appropriate expression is still unsuccessful. Furious clusters are heard "when the elements don't fit well with one another" – for example, when a passages marked "fantasia: molto rubato" experiments with the pitches of bars 32ff. from the "Moonlight" Sonata without producing a satisfactory result. Here it seems as if one actually can only lose against Beethoven. Given the right circumstances, however, it might simplify the composer's engagement with the titanic forebear: the composer can confidently lean back and "drink a decent glass of wine before the concert in order to await the defeat and face it with the necessary composure."[58]

55 Documentation in *Beethoven 1770–1970: 3. Dezember 1970 – 15. Januar 1971,* ed. Wolfgang Becker (Aachen: Neue Galerie, 1970). On Beethoven and Fluxus see *inter alia* Stefan Fricke, "Kämpfen gegen die Bürgermusik: Beethoven, Fluxus und anderes," *Neue Zeitschrift für Musik* 162, no. 4 (2001): 32–35.

56 Helmut Lachenmann, "Über das Komponieren," in idem, *Musik als existentielle Erfahrung: Schriften 1966–1995,* ed. Josef Häusler (Wiesbaden: Breitkopf & Härtel, 1996), 73–82, at 77.

57 *250 PPfB,* vol. 3.

58 Steffen Schleiermacher, quoted from Tom Service, "Riccardo Chailly on Beethoven: 'It's a long way from the First to the Ninth,'" *The Guardian* (25 October 2011), at www.theguardian.com/music/2011/oct/25/beethoven-cycle-riccardo-chailly (accessed 28 May 2020).

Béla Bartók
Piano Concerto No. 3
(1945)

Béla Bartók came into contact with Beethoven's piano sonatas already in his childhood as a highly gifted piano pupil. Later, having matured into a concert pianist, he programmed several of them in his recitals, and between 1909 and 1912 he prepared new practical editions of most of them (of twenty-five sonatas, to be precise) for the Budapest publishing house of Rózsavölgyi.[1] But it was not only Beethoven's piano music that attracted his lifelong interest: Beethoven's entire oeuvre was so important to him that in 1939, in an interview with Serge Moreux, he called him one of the three musical lodestars whose achievements had to be further pursued. Just as counterpoint had been renewed by Bach, he said, and just as harmony had been reimagined by Debussy, Beethoven had revolutionized the idea of form, thereby channeling music onto new paths.[2]

It thus comes as no surprise that Beethoven's music left unmistakable traces on Bartók's compositional output. In a good many cases, however, it is difficult to determine whether the traces are unconscious reminiscences or deliberate references. His string quartets, for example, reveal remarkable parallels to Beethoven's, in both their details and their overall evolution.[3] Furthermore, major thematic and structural aspects of the opening movement of his Sonata for Two Pianos and Percussion recall Beethoven's C-major Piano Sonata, op. 53 – the "Waldstein" Sonata.[4] But perhaps the most obvious and widely discussed example of such an intertextual reference occurs in the slow middle movement of the last work he was able to complete: the Third Piano Concerto of 1945.

Bartók composed this concerto at an extremely difficult period in his life. His career as a pianist had already come to a standstill in early 1943, both for reasons of health and from a lack of public interest; his works were rarely performed; and above all he was massively weakened by slowly advancing leukemia, which his doctors had long kept a secret from him. However, after a stay in a sanatorium in Saranac Lake, NY, beginning in late June 1945, his physical condition temporarily improved to the extent that between July and September 1945 he was able to write out his Third Piano Concerto, a work he had long planned for his wife Ditta Pásztory. All that was left incomplete was the orchestration of the last seventeen bars, a task undertaken after his death on 26 September 1945 by Tibor Serly. (Serly also prepared a performance version of the Viola Concerto, composed more or less at the same time but left in sketch form.)

All of this casts a special light on certain peculiarities of the Third Piano Concerto, and specifically on its slow second movement, the beginning of which is shown here in Bartók's autograph fair score (SEE PLATE 1, P. 112). The very fact that Bartók, an agnostic, headed the movement "Adagio religioso" already catches our eye. But the opening of the movement, clearly patterned after movement 3 of Beethoven's A-minor String Quartet, op. 132 (the *Heiliger Dankgesang*, or "Holy Song of Thanksgiving to the Deity by a Convalescent, in the Lydian Mode"), strongly suggests that the piece should be viewed as a personal confession, as an expression of gratitude following his (illusory) recovery from a critical illness. The parallel with the relevant passage in the Beethoven piece is all the more striking in that, in both cases, the "Holy Song of Thanksgiving" alternates with passages resembling a chorale (SEE EXAMPLE 1, P. 113):

1 A tabular overview of Bartók's work as an editor is provided by László Somfai's "Nineteenth-Century Ideas Developed in Bartók's Piano Notation, 1907–14," in *Music at the Turn of the Century: A 19th-Century Music Reader*, ed. Joseph Kerman (Berkeley: University of California Press, 1990), 181–99.

2 See Serge Moreux, *Béla Bartók: Leben, Werk, Stil*, trans. Ursula Müller (Zurich: Atlantis, 1950), 14.

3 See also János Kárpáti, *Bartók's Chamber Music* (Stuyvesant: Pendragon, 1994), chap. 1, "The Legacy of Beethoven," 21–30.

4 See in particular Michael Russ, "Bartók, Beethoven and the Sonata for Two Pianos and Percussion," *Journal of the Royal Musical Association* 137, no. 2 (2012): 307–49.

PLATE 1
Béla Bartok, Piano Concerto No. 3, BB 127 (1945), movt. 2, "Adagio religioso." Full score fair copy, p. 22
(BÉLA BARTÓK COLLECTION, PSS)

EXAMPLE 1
Ludwig van Beethoven, String Quartet in A minor, op. 132 (1825), movt. 3, mm. 1–8

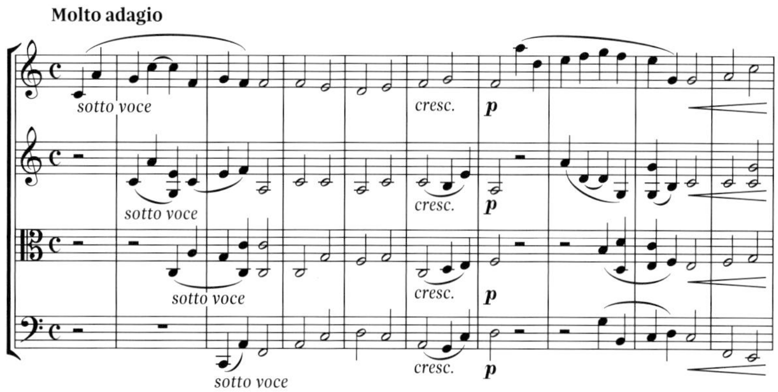

As in the Beethoven quartet, the music is interrupted five times by such chorale interludes. However, the contrast between the two textures is far greater in Bartók's work, owing to the alternation of orchestra and solo piano. (The continuity draft (SEE PLATE 2, P. 114) clearly shows that the chorale was conceived as a self-contained whole. The letters a), b), etc. signify the entrance of the *Dankgesang* passages.) While in the Beethoven quartet the opening section is followed by two trios, with the first headed "gathering new strength" (*neue Kraft schöpfend*), in Bartók's work it is succeeded by a (single) middle section of "nature music" that incorporates actual bird song.[5] Moreover, the final section is heavily dominated by the chorale, now stated by the orchestra and festooned with neo-baroque figuration in the piano. Here, at the very end of the movement, the Beethoven allusion appears one final time.

Yet this autobiographical interpretation of the movement (and even of the entire work) falls short of the mark. Not least of all, it ignores a stylistic or technical aspect: namely, that the concerto is pervaded by more or less abrupt juxtapositions of contrasting inflections or idioms. In this respect, and in a certain simplification of the compositional fabric, it reveals features typical of what both Theodor W. Adorno and Edward W. Said described as a "late style."[6] Bartók's homage to one of the last works by the very composer who sparked the discussion of late style embodies just such an inflection. Indeed, it might even be called a dual archaism, given that Beethoven himself resorted to an antiquated style. Precisely the "foreignness" of this allusion – a foreignness very much in keeping with Said's understanding of late style as an "ontological exile" – lends the autobiographical connotation a certain detachment, and hence qualification.

This is all the more clearly the case when we examine the placement of the formal types Bartók employed in the concerto's overall form. Roughly speaking, the three-movement work is symmetrically constructed: the two genuinely Bartókian outside movements (though ultimately inspired by Hungarian folk music) frame the tripartite middle movement (the "Adagio religioso"). In much the same way, the outer sections of that movement (the Beethoven allusion and the chorale passages) frame the central birdsong section. In this light, the concerto proceeds from "subjective" music (movement 1) via "mediated" music (opening of movement 2) to "objective" nature music and back again to its starting point. In the overall form, the nature music at the center of the "Adagio religioso" thus constitutes the heart of the concerto. More than that, as Wolfgang Rathert has pointed out, it forms the concerto's "structural and emotional linchpin," to which the "man-made music" relates as a sort of subordinate tier, or what might be called a *seconda pratica*.[7]

5 Jürgen Hunkemöller provides a formal analysis of the movement in his essay collection *Bauernmusik und Klangmagie: Bartók-Studien* (Hildesheim: Georg Olms, 2013), 151–56. On the "bird music" in the middle of the movement see Maria Anna Harley, "Birds in Concert: North American Birdsong in Bartók's Piano Concerto No. 3," *Tempo*, no. 189 (June 1994): 8–16.

6 See *inter alia* Theodor W. Adorno, *Beethoven: The Philosophy of Music: Fragments und Texts*, ed. Rolf Tiedemann, trans. Edmund Jephcott (Cambridge: Polity Press, 2002), 123–37 and 154–61; and Edward W. Said, *Late Style: Music and Literature Against the Grain*, ed. Michael Wood (New York: Pantheon, 2006).

7 Wolfgang Rathert, "Überlegungen zur Deutung des Adagio religioso im 3. Klavierkonzert von Béla Bartók," in *Musik und kulturelle Identität: Bericht über den XIII. Internationalen Kongress der Gesellschaft für Musikforschung Weimar 2004*, ed. Detlev Altenburg and Rainer Bayreuther (Kassel: Bärenreiter, 2012), vol. 2, 440–47, at 446.

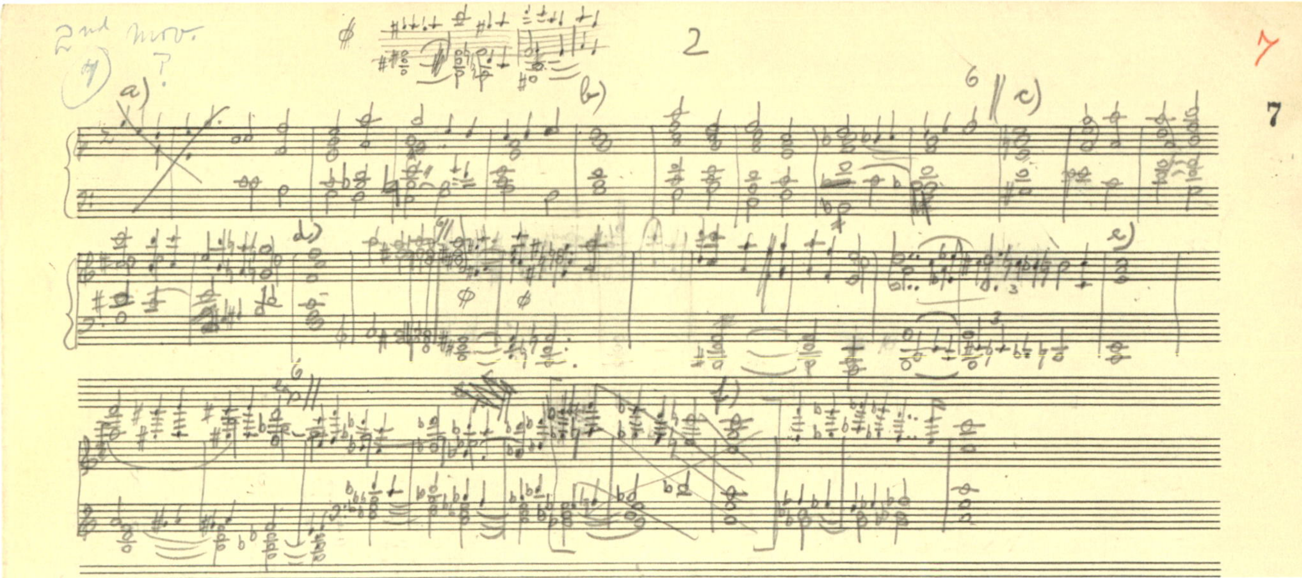

By implication, the Beethoven allusion or adaptation thus represents a sort of interim stage *en route* to the work's inmost core. But this in no way diminishes its importance. On the contrary: Bartók's deep admiration for Beethoven already finds expression in the fact that Beethoven is the only composer he honored by alluding to a specific piece. (His two other ideals, Bach and Debussy, are merely invoked in his general style.) And surely Bartók, despite what we said above, identified to a certain extent with Beethoven's *Dankgesang:* given his precarious health, it was anything but a foregone conclusion that he had gathered enough "new strength" to commit to paper a concerto of some twenty-five minutes' duration.

Felix Meyer

PLATE 2
Béla Bartok, Piano Concerto No. 3, BB 127 (1945), movt. 2, "Adagio religioso." Sketches, p. 7
(BÉLA BARTÓK COLLECTION, PSS)

Cristóbal Halffter String Quartet No. 2, *Mémoires 1970* (1970)

The career of Cristóbal Halffter, who was born in Madrid in 1930, has been shaped by a particular family constellation. His uncles Rodolfo (1900–1987) and Ernesto (1905–1989) were both highly esteemed composers in the Ibero-Mexican music scene; yet his grandfather moved to Madrid from the East Prussian city of Königsberg (now Kaliningrad) only in 1890, and the boy spent part of his school years in the town of Velbert in Westphalia, where his father was a factory director from 1936 and 1939. Given this background, Halffter has always seen himself as a builder of cultural bridges. His musical talents became evident in early childhood, and he had completed his studies at Madrid Conservatory already by the age of twenty-one. (In 1964 he became the Conservatory's director, only to resign two years later in protest at the political circumstances in Spain.) His concern was not only to define the identity of Spanish modernism within the musical culture of Europe and the West (in the broadest sense), but also to overcome the stubborn ideological divide between "periphery" and "center." Consequently, the relationship between the stylistic worlds of his era and historical references to the past plays a crucial role in his highly varied musical idiom and his complex dramaturgical strategies.

Despite the increasingly decentralizing aesthetic tendencies in twentieth-century music history (at least in the West), many composers, regardless of their avant-garde or conservative leanings, felt called upon to take up the challenge of the supreme genre of instrumental music: the string quartet. Halffter was no different; on the contrary, the string quartet looms large in his oeuvre, which covers every major genre, including electronic and political music. To date he has produced ten string quartets, dating from 1955 to 2018. On the one hand they display the breadth and complexity of his compositional technique; on the other, they form a coherent body, owing to the common aesthetic questions they pose. In this way, not only did Halffter use the string quartet to define his position in contemporary music (as well as his relationship to tradition), he also entrusted it again and again with highly personal experiences, so that the works take on the character of diaries. The first path allowed him to try out experimental and independent approaches; the second places his quartets in an evolutionary line extending from late Beethoven and Schubert via Smetana, Janáček, and Bartók to the present day.

Halffter's Second Quartet, subtitled *Mémoires 1970*, lucidly reflects the state of post-serial composition in the 1960s and the altered view of music history among its proponents. As the subtitle implies, it deals with memories, whether stored in collective cultural consciousness or harboring (auto-) biographical connotations. The piece originated to satisfy a commission from America, namely, from the Elizabeth Sprague Coolidge Foundation, which has promoted the composition and performance of contemporary music since 1925. For the 1970 Beethoven Bicentennial, the Foundation commissioned relevant pieces of chamber music from Halffter and other distinguished composers, including Milton Babbitt, George Crumb, and Luigi Dallapiccola. Halffter chose the quartet format and referred specifically to Beethoven's final String Quartet in F major, op. 135, published in the year of his death (1827).

EXAMPLE 1 (FAR LEFT)
Ludwig van Beethoven, String Quartet in F major, op. 135 (1826) 3rd mvt. mm. 5–6

EXAMPLE 2 (LEFT)
Cristóbal Halffter, String Quartet No. 2, *Mémoires 1970* (1970), mm. 36–39

EXAMPLE 3
Ludwig van Beethoven, String Quartet in F major, op. 135 (1826) 1st mvt., mm. 145–49

EXAMPLE 4
Cristóbal Halffter, String Quartet No. 2, *Mémoires 1970* (1970), mm. 53–57

EXAMPLE 5
Ludwig van Beethoven, String Quartet in F major, op. 135 (1826) 4th mvt., mm. 73–76 and 103–08

EXAMPLE 6
Cristóbal Halffter, String Quartet No. 2, *Mémoires 1970* (1970), mm. 184–93

It is a work whose intricate construction is concealed behind a "semblance of simplicity,"[1] and whose finale is headed by a puzzling instance of eye music, the nine-note motto "Muss es sein? Es muss sein! Es muss sein!" (Must it be? It must be! It must be!). Halffter decided to extract four excerpts from movements 1, 3, and 4. However, they occur in reverse order, and he avoided quoting from the scherzo, a movement referred to by Theodor W. Adorno as a "danse macabre."[2]

First we hear the main theme of the slow movement (mm. 5–6 in Beethoven, mm. 36–39 in Halffter), then an excerpt from the opening movement (mm. 145–49 in Beethoven, mm. 53–57 in Halffter), and finally two fragments from the finale (mm. 73–76 and 103–08 in Beethoven, mm. 184–93 in Halffter). Contrary to our initial impression, the quotations are not precise borrowings but subtly reshaped reminiscences. The first (SEE PLATE 1, P. 118) seems like a verbatim reiteration of the main theme of the slow movement, artfully designed by Beethoven as a cross between ternary form and a set of variations (SEE EXAMPLES 1 AND 2). But the meter is changed from 6/8 to 4/4 and the durations are doubled from eighth notes to quarter notes, dislocating the points of emphasis and the phrase structure, while the pitch content and key of the theme (or, more precisely, its immediate repetition) remain unchanged. On closer inspection, however, we note that the motion of the viola part (mm. 37–38 in Halffter) is made to correspond to the variant in Beethoven's reprise (m. 35) through the interpolation of a passing E♭, thereby placing it in direct contrary motion to the first violin. The second quotation (SEE EXAMPLES 3 AND 4) is taken from the recapitulation in the opening movement. First we hear the original borrowing of a motivic complex from the concluding group, which combines a lively triplet figure in unison rhythm and partly inverted pitch content with an expressive melodic idea in the first violin. But hardly has this idea been stated than it fades away in chromatic distortion. The third field of quotations (SEE EXAMPLES 5 AND 6) begins with an imitative stretto of the emblematic "Es muss sein" motto at the end of the exposition, emphasized in the manner of a fanfare (mm. 73–76). This is immediately followed by the D minor episode from the first section of the development (mm. 103–08) as an elliptic montage, with the whirling second motivic unit from the main theme now enlarged into a doleful, funereally tinged melody with suggestions of canonic imitation among cello, viola, and first violin. Halffter halves the original durations from quarter notes to eighth notes in the first part of the quotation (mm. 184–87) and from quarter notes to sixteenths in the second part (mm. 188–93). This arithmetic acceleration breaks off with the fragmentary return of the "Es muss sein" motif in the viola, now truncated to just two notes and given an aura of resignation and despair.

In a highly symbolic fashion, Halffter takes up the thread of Beethoven's music as a sort of phantasm. But ghostly and innovative compositional and performative techniques and programmatic elements crop up also in his own music, as witness *Oda par felicitar a un amigo,* written one year earlier. In this sense *Mémoires 1970,* at once an obeisance to Beethoven's genius and a protest at his mystical deification,[3] becomes a self-referential utterance. The device of explicit quotation, rather than foreshadowing postmodernism, serves as a means of probing the dialectic between proximity and distance, between what is one's own and what comes from elsewhere. Beginning in the 1960s the American composer George Rochberg, in works such as *Music for the Magic Theater,* had critiqued the serialists' faith in progress by obsessively mimicking classical music and then allowing it to devolve all the more painfully into disillusion and decay. In contrast, Halffter allows the past to emerge almost

1 Friedhelm Krummacher, "Streichquartett F-Dur op. 135," in *Beethoven: Interpretationen seiner Werke,* ed. Albrecht Riethmüller, Carl Dahlhaus, and Alexander L. Ringer (Laaber: Laaber, 1996), vol. 2, 347–64, at 349.

2 Theodor W. Adorno, *Beethoven: The Philosophy of Music: Fragments und Texts,* ed. Rolf Tiedemann, trans. Edmund Jephcott (Cambridge: Polity Press, 2002), 191.

3 See Cristobál Halffter, "Selbstbildnis II," in *Donaueschinger Musiktage 1971,* program book (Donaueschingen: Gesellschaft der Musikfreunde, 1971), 30–31, at 31: "The score [...] contains various Beethoven motifs that fit well into the entirety of my work. Their purpose is both to honor this extraordinary composer and to protest against his mystification." ("Die Partitur [...] enthält verschiedene Motive von Beethoven, die sich gut in die Gesamtheit meines Werkes einfügen. Sie sind sowohl als Ehrung für diesen außergewöhnlichen Komponisten wie auch als Protest gegen seine Mystifizierung gedacht.") Halffter's *Planto por las víctimas de la violencia* for chamber ensemble and electronic manipulation was premièred in Donaueschingen on 17 October 1971.

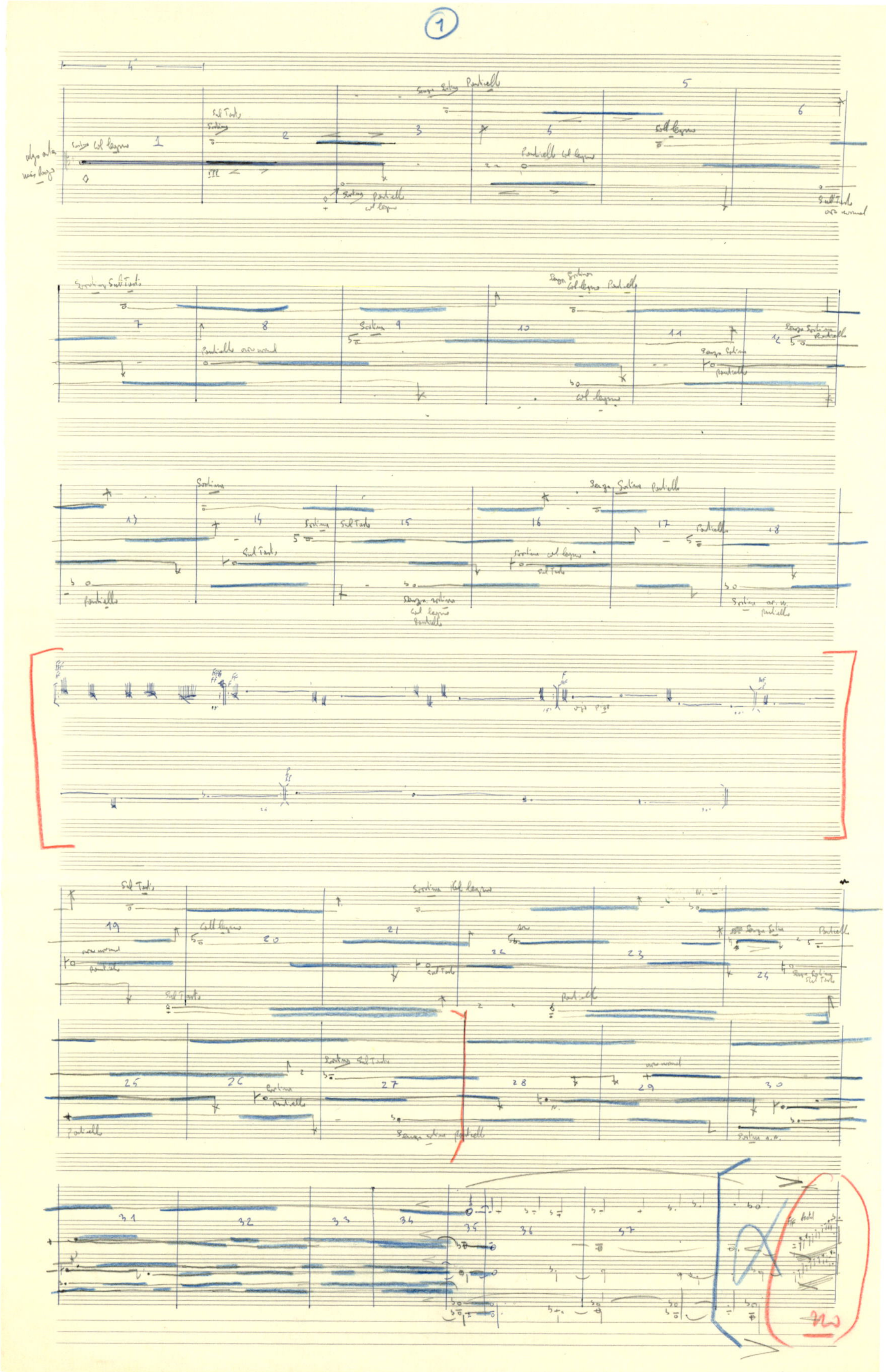

PLATE 1 (OPPOSITE)
Cristóbal Halffter, String Quartet No. 2, *Mémoires 1970* (1970). Draft score, p. 1
(CRISTÓBAL HALFFTER COLLECTION, PSS)

organically from his own radical language, poised on the verge of silence, and lets it return to itself. The boundary between these two dimensions is permeable, but also enigmatic.

The Second Quartet was premièred at the Library of Congress in Washington, DC, by the Claremont Quartet on 31 October 1970. In 1974–75 Halffter returned to it and prepared a version for twelve strings, which he published under the title *Pourquoi*. As the word lacks its usual question mark, the meaning of the title remains in a state of limbo similar to that of the question-and-answer game in Beethoven's motto. (Halffter himself said of the title that it alludes to the fundamental problem of the ability of art to communicate within the triangular relationship between composer, performer, and listener.[4]) Moreover, in *Pourquoi*, the second and third borrowings occur later than in the string quartet, now with the aleatoric passages expanded.[5]

Almost thirty years later, in 2007, Halffter returned yet again to Beethoven in his Seventh String Quartet, *Espacios de silencio*. It is surely no coincidence that the number seven has a dual function here: the work has seven sections that elide to form a single large-scale movement. As a model he took Beethoven's C-sharp minor Quartet, op. 131, whose expressive intensity and cyclic thematic design have given it a towering position in the history of the string quartet. Richard Wagner construed it as the metaphorical traversal of a day in Beethoven's life.[6] Halffter reacted to Wagner's interpretation by prefixing his quartet with some lines of verse by the fifteenth-century Spanish poet Jorge Manrique, invoking the path of the soul, the transfiguration of the past, the inexorability of death, and the ultimate implosion of past, present, and future. Unlike Luigi Nono's string quartet *Fragmente – Stille, An Diotima* (1979–80), whose Hölderlin passages, though printed in the score, are accessible only to the performers, Halffter asks that the audience be informed of Manrique's verses and the quartet's formal structure in the program notes. Once again his object is to convey a collective social and historical experience that likewise represents a confrontation between past (the poem) and present (the music). In the Seventh Quartet, too, Halffter's musical language is extremely challenging and demanding. Imbued with the traumatic experiences of the twentieth century, it ends in the very silence that formed the point of departure for *Mémoires 1970*.

Wolfgang Rathert

4 See Hubert Daschner, *Spanische Musik auf der Höhe ihrer Zeit: Cristóbal Halffter* (Saarbrücken: Pfau, 2000), 135.

5 See also Germán Gan Quesada's comments in his thesis "La cita musical en la obra de Cristóbal Halffter (1970–2000): Estrategias formales y funciones estéticas" (Universidad de Granada, 2002), 57–63.

6 See *Richard Wagner's* Beethoven *(1870)*, trans. Roger Allen (Woodbridge: Boydell, 2014), 121–22.

Dieter Schnebel
Beethoven-Symphonie
(1985)

Thanks to his books *Denkbare Musik: Schriften 1952–1972* and *MO-NO: Musik zum Lesen*,[1] the composer-theologian Dieter Schnebel (1930–2018) became one of Europe's very first metamusicians under the banner of John Cage's "experimental music."[2] In early 1970 he joined other critically minded colleagues by contributing an article on Beethoven's handling of musical material to the slender miscellany *Beethoven '70*.[3] This article, later expanded and reissued in *Denkbare Musik*, discusses the piano sonatas opp. 7 and 110 in a rough-hewn comparison between early Beethoven, an adherent of the French Revolution, and late Beethoven, who acted "regressively" by reacting toward the outside world with "ideologization." He noticed an interaction between the latest developments in composition, traceable back to Beethoven, and the current view of Beethoven himself: "The experiences stimulated by Beethoven" in present-day composition, he observed, "impinge upon him, altering for example the presentation of his works, which, being heard in a new way, also appear in a new guise." The "retaining and releasing" of musical processes as practiced by more recent composers (such as Cage) have now "infected Beethoven."

It was with these goals of hearing "in a new way" and "in a new guise" in mind that Schnebel arranged the opening movement of the Fifth Symphony to create his *Beethoven-Symphonie* for chamber ensemble (1985), thereby completing the series of five arrangements that he later titled *Re-Visions I*.[4] Conventional terms are thrown off balance: Is this "infection" of a Beethovenian magnum opus a "re-production," and in that case the task of the performer, as Hans von Bülow would have argued? Or is it a critique of sonic structures fossilized in the work's performance history? Or a delayed reaction to the Beethoven ideology of the Third Reich and its subliminal prolongation in a divided Germany? Or the intervention of a post-modern intellectual under the influence of negative anthropology?

One underlying idea of this *Re-Vision* resides in the interaction between meter and rhythm: Beethoven's "Allegro con brio," in 2/4 meter, has been transformed into a "Schwungvoll [buoyant] (tempo 1)" in 5/8 meter beginning with a dotted quarter-note in the strings. This prevents the famous, semantically charged "Fate motif" of three upbeat eighths from being perceivable as an upbeat at all (SEE PLATE 1). Every listener will substitute the eighth-note motif, for it is rooted in the deep memory of musical culture. But other elements are added as well. For one thing, the B♭4 in the horn alters the ambiguous tonality of the opening (C minor vs. E-flat major) into a "false" certainty by allowing the symphony to begin in E-flat major. For another, the percussion employed at the beginning of the motto, "Pa (stiff paper or plastic)," indicates that noise plays a more extended and semantically charged role in the arrangement than in the original. Schnebel exploits various ways of grouping the notes of a 5/8 bar (first theme, mm. 1ff.: 2+3; second theme, mm. 63ff.: 3+2) to project different kinds of cross-rhythmic destabilization. At the repeat of the exposition, however, he restores the duple meter and adds the dominating sound of a xylophone to the events, as he notes in a sketch of the

1 Dieter Schnebel, *Denkbare Musik: Schriften 1952–1972*, ed. Hans Rudolf Zeller (Cologne: DuMont, 1972); and idem, *MO-NO: Musik zum Lesen* (Cologne: DuMont, 1969). *MO-NO* emerged from Schnebel's work *ki-no: Nachtmusik für Projektoren und Hörer* (1963–67).

2 Of the two premises I apply for "metamusic," Schnebel attaches primary importance to the first: the equal stature of the four forms of the musicological concept of text (sound, notation, verbal language, image). See Hermann Danuser, *Metamusik* (Schliengen: Argus, 2017), 24–30.

3 Dieter Schnebel, "Das angegriffene Material: Zur Gestaltung bei Beethoven," in *Beethoven '70* (Frankfurt am Main: Fischer, 1970), 45–55. Enlarged in Schnebel, *Denkbare Musik* (see note 1), 130–38, quotations below at 137.

4 Two years earlier, in 1983, I examined the four preceding arrangements (Webern, Bach, Schubert, and Wagner), asking how they might be interpreted in the history of composition. See Hermann Danuser, "Aktualisierende Interpretation – ein Spiegel der Kompositionsgeschichte? Zu den Be-arbeitungen Dieter Schnebels" (1986), in idem, *Gesammelte Vorträge und Aufsätze*, ed. Hans-Joachim Hinrichsen, Christian Schaper, and Laure Spaltenstein (Schliengen: Argus, 2014), vol. 4, 273–85. *Beethoven-Symphonie* was premièred in Essen on 14 April 1988, with Alexander Schwinck conducting the Folkwang Chamber Orchestra.

PLATE 1

Dieter Schnebel, *Beethoven-Symphonie* for chamber ensemble (1985). Full score fair copy, p. [1]

(DIETER SCHNEBEL COLLECTION, PSS)
BY KIND PERMISSION OF SCHOTT MUSIC, MAINZ

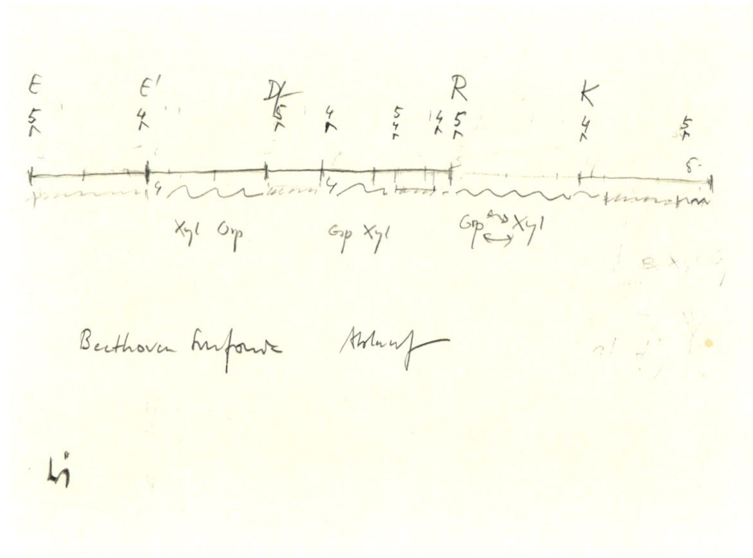

PLATE 2
Dieter Schnebel, *Beethoven-Symphonie* for chamber ensemble (1985). Sketch
(DIETER SCHNEBEL COLLECTION, PSS)

movement's formal layout, as well as in the expansion of part of the development section ("E" = exposition, "Df" = development, "R" = recapitulation, and "K" = coda; SEE PLATE 2).[5]

Elsewhere Schnebel wrote "Adapt musical characters." Here he distinguishes three types: "Sharpening processes (mainly rhythmic devices)," "Softening processes (mainly sonic)," and "Multiplication processes."[6] In fact, the piece is dominated by expression marks to indicate textures that are thinned, thickened, softened ("tender and cantabile," m. 66), or mechanized ("hammering – like work," m. 6 of the recapitulation).

The choice of the Fifth Symphony as the auditory arena of a *Re-Vision* may be related to Schnebel's turn to psychoanalysis and a book cited in his Beethoven article of 1970,[7] a book that attaches central importance to the concept of fate (*Schicksal*). Decades later, in 2001, Schnebel himself took up this approach in a lecture.[8] It crops up again in his final composition, *(BSH) Schicksalslied: Beethoven – Hölderlin* (2017), in which he combines works of towering importance to musical and literary history by two artists born in the same year and both enamored of revolution. In Beethoven's case these were the Fifth Symphony, the "Appassionata" Sonata, and the String Quartet, op. 135 (as well as biographical sources), in Hölderlin's case the eponymous poem and excerpts from the novel *Hyperion*.

The work's "epilogue" touches on the ending of that novel. A contralto and a narrator simultaneously deliver the words "Leben ewig einig glühend All" and "Schicksal Glück" (sung) and "Beethoven Hölderlin nächstens mehr" (spoken). In the very last bar, Schnebel bids farewell with the Latin and Greek words "trans" and "meta." Barely half a year after the work's dedication ("For Grit | 'as thanks and promise' | 6 December 2017"), the author of *Glossolalie* died in Berlin on Whitsunday, 20 May 2018. His *Schicksalslied*, a work commissioned by the Bonn Beethovenfest, received its posthumous première there four months later.

Hermann Danuser

5 Bars 125 to 178 of Beethoven's score are first converted from duple meter to 5/8 meter (2+3). Then, beginning in m. 179, they are given a varied repeat in a duple meter (2+2) with the sound of a vibraphone predominant. This expands the form of the *Re-Vision* compared to the original, so that the "development section" now seems partly analogous to the "exposition." Following this interpolated section, *Beethoven-Symphonie* presents the remainder of Beethoven's original development and retransition (mm. 179–248) while restoring the uneven meter (at first 3+2, later 2+3).

6 "Musikalische Charaktere bearbeiten": "Schärfungsprozesse (hauptsächlich rhythmische Mittel)," "Aufweichungsprozesse (hauptsächlich klanglich)," and "Multiplikationsprozesse." Dieter Schnebel, "Bearbeitungen," textual manuscript, one page (Dieter Schnebel Collection, PSS), with further comments not cited here. The three main terms are underlined.

7 Editha and Richard Sterba, *Beethoven und sein Neffe: Tragödie eines Genies: Eine psychoanalytische Studie* (Munich: Szczesny, 1964).

8 A typescript in the Dieter Schnebel Collection (PSS) bears the title "Der schwer gefaßte Entschluß" and a subtitle that translates as "Musical and Psychoanalytical Thoughts on Beethoven and his Final Quartet." The first two sections were published as "Mutter-Vater: Musik- und psychoanalytische Überlegungen zu Beethoven," in *Der "männliche" und der "weibliche" Beethoven: Bericht über den Internationalen musikwissenschaftlichen Kongress vom 31. Oktober bis 4. November 2001*, ed. Cornelia Bartsch, Beatrix Borchard, and Rainer Cadenbach (Bonn: Beethoven-Haus, 2003), 163–71. The third section on op. 135, in which Schnebel interprets Beethoven's motto "Muss es sein?" and the response "Es muss sein!" in relation to his nephew's fateful suicide attempt, was omitted from the publication.

Aribert Reimann
Nahe Ferne
(2002–03)

In the works of the Berlin composer-pianist Aribert Reimann (b. 1936) reflections on music history form a counterweight to the visceral emotional force of his worlds of sound. The second son of the organist and church musician Wolfgang Reimann (a pupil of Max Reger in Leipzig) and the concert and opera singer Irmgard Reimann, he grew up in artistically stimulating surroundings. Thanks to the professional work of his parents (both also taught at the Berlin-Charlottenburg Academy of Music) and his own activities as a boy soprano and piano accompanist for his mother, he became familiar at an early age with the seminal works of music history, from the Baroque era to the present day. He received formative musical experiences as the "Yea-Sayer" in Kurt Weill's school opera *Der Jasager* and as the soloist in the "Et incarnatus" of Mozart's great C minor Mass (K. 427). Reimann's initial essays in composition, including a setting of Lenau, date from 1946. His comprehensive command of the musician's craft and the standard repertoire was acquired as a vocal coach at the Berlin City Opera, as a student of Ernst Pepping, Friedrich Hartig, and Boris Blacher at the Berlin Musikhochschule, and through his longstanding collaboration with singers of the stature of Elisabeth Grümmer, Ernst Haefliger, and Dietrich Fischer-Dieskau.

Reimann's artistic signature was already clearly manifest in the first works he presented to the public in the late 1950s: settings of Gabriela Mistral and Paul Celan. Here he combined the essential, albeit antithetical positions of contemporary music, namely, the expressive density of the Viennese School and the pinpoint concision of the New Music of the 1920s, conveyed to him via Blacher and Stravinsky. This internal tension found expression in melodic and linear forces constantly taken to extremes. In the course of his artistic development Reimann explored and refined this tension in the central genres of music theatre, instrumental and sacred music and, above all, art song. More than any other composer of his generation, he opened up new realms of expression to the idea of "musical lyricism."[1] Part of this same process was an increasingly deep study of the classical-romantic canon, whether through arrangements of entire works, as in *"... oder soll es Tod bedeuten?": Eight Songs and a Fragment by Felix Mendelssohn Bartholdy after Poems by Heinrich Heine* for soprano and string quartet, connected by six intermezzos (1996), or through variations on existing works or themes, as in *Metamorphoses on a Minuet by Franz Schubert (D. 600)* for ten instruments (1997) and *Seven Fragments in memoriam Robert Schumann* for orchestra (1988). True, in these works Reimann also responded to the return to tradition by the postwar avant-garde and the 'New Tonality' generation, as represented by Dieter Schnebel's *Re-Visions* and various complexes of orchestral works by Wolfgang Rihm. Nevertheless, his approach was (and still is) neither deconstructivist nor purely intertextual in its alignment. Rather, he seeks an exegesis in notes that redefines, over and over again, the relation between nearness and distance in a dialogue with the past.

Reimann's engagement with Beethoven, both as a performer and as a composer, must be viewed in this context. For example, he often performed the song cycle *An die ferne Geliebte*, op. 98, with Ernst Haefliger, and the

1 See Ellen Freyberg, *"Es sind noch Lieder zu singen jenseits der Menschen": Studien zur musikalischen Lyrik Aribert Reimanns* (Hofheim: Wolke 2019).

pianistic and compositional challenges of his Variations for Piano (1979) take up the demanding thread of the *Diabelli Variations*, op. 120. In conversation he claimed that although he admired Beethoven's power of expression, he felt much closer to the language of his beloved Mozart. At root, Reimann's musical thought is lyrical and governed by melody, and thus stands opposed to Beethoven's predominant emphasis on the instrumental. Precisely this ambiguity forms the precondition for his orchestral work *Nahe Ferne* (Near Distance), commissioned by the Bonn Beethovenfest and premièred in Bonn by Jonathan Nott and the Bamberg Symphony on 12 October 2003. (The 2002 Festival commemorated the 175th anniversary of Beethoven's death and adopted, from Franz Grillparzer's funeral oration, the motto "You have not lost him but won him.") As his point of departure Reimann chose the Piano Piece in B-flat major, WoO 60, composed in 1818 for the Polish pianist Maria Szymanowska (1789–1831) and published six years later in a supplement to the *Berliner Allgemeine Musikalische Zeitung* with the title *Dernière pensée musicale de Louis van Beethoven*. This little piece, described by Adolph Bernhard Marx as a "boldly scribbled conundrum,"[2] stands at the outset of Beethoven's so-called late period. Theo Hirsbrunner refers to it as "one of the most extraordinary things Beethoven ever wrote," owing to the manner in which rhythm and harmony are held "continuously in abeyance": "It seems as if born of a single instant, a playfully improvised whim, a hesitant search for and, in the end, a lucky discovery of a certain unity, but one whose fabric remains fragile."[3] At the same time, the choice of key (B-flat major) and its origins at the same time as the "Hammerklavier" Sonata may well imply that we are dealing here with an encrypted self-portrait or an interior landscape in which stability (the preservation of the tonal framework) and fragility (the surprising yet covertly logical harmonic twists) strike a precarious balance.

Fragmentation and improvisatory gesture on the one hand, rigorous exploitation of the skeletal, almost trivial thematic substance on the other: these served as ideal starting points for Reimann's own procedures. He transformed the thirty-nine-bar "bagatelle" of some ninety seconds' duration into a fourteen-minute fresco for full orchestra with nine elided movements. Of the features of Beethoven's original, he was probably most stimulated by the growing chromaticism of the thematic material, including a use of enharmonic equivalence rarely encountered in Beethoven. The growing chromaticism increasingly deforms an initially compact diatonic cadential formula and finally dissolves it contrapuntally in a sort of fugato. The original piece admits interpretation as an extremely compact three-part sonata form, an abstract symmetrical structure, or a written-out dominant-to-tonic tension.[4] Reimann at once magnifies and radicalizes it by tripling its tripartite form (9 = 3 × 3), thereby placing it, so to speak, under a microscope. Fittingly, the theme is heard not at the beginning, but only in the fourth movement, where it is finally disclosed in the woodwinds (SEE PLATE 1). Drawing on Reimann's familiar surrealist aesthetic, we might even call it a purposeful disfiguration. In dialectical terms, the shock element is now assigned to the appearance of the original in the form of sonic islands and dreamlike reminiscences within Reimann's dissonant, churning, but frequently delicate stream of sound. It is no accident that *Nahe Ferne* has a close inner rapport with the orchestral work *Spiralat halom* (Dream Spirals), which originated at the same time.

Reimann evidently felt so inspired by this task that he took the (for him) unusual step of writing a detailed commentary to *Nahe Ferne*. Here he spoke of "disturbances," a "structural collapse," and "superimpositions" that constantly evaporate. This refers not only to the internal musical processes, but equally to

PLATE 1 (OPPOSITE)
Aribert Reimann, *Nahe Ferne: Moments for Ludwig van Beethoven's Piano Piece in B-flat major, WoO 60* for orchestra (2002–03). Full score fair copy, p. 16
(ARIBERT REIMANN COLLECTION, PSS) BY KIND PERMISSION OF SCHOTT MUSIC, MAINZ

2 Adolph Bernhard Marx, *Ludwig van Beethoven: Leben und Schaffen*, Erster Theil, 3rd edn., ed. Gustav Behncke (Berlin: Otto Janke, 1875), 75.

3 "[…] etwas vom Außerordentlichsten, was Beethoven geschrieben hat. […] Sowohl rhythmisch als auch harmonisch bleibt das Stück in der Schwebe; es wirkt ganz wie aus dem Augenblick geboren, eine Laune der spielerischen Improvisation, ein zögerndes Suchen und am Schluß ein glückliches Finden einer gewissen Geschlossenheit, deren Gefüge aber zerbrechlich bleibt." Theo Hirsbrunner, "Klavierstück B-Dur WoO 60," in *Beethoven: Interpretationen seiner Werke*, ed. Albrecht Riethmüller, Carl Dahlhaus, and Alexander L. Ringer, 2nd edn. (Laaber: Laaber, 1996), vol. 2, 441–42.

4 Exhaustive discussion in Anselm Gerhard, "'Ein kühn hingeworfenes Räthselwort': Das Klavierstück WoO 60 und die Voraussetzungen von Beethovens 'Spätstil,'" *Musiktheorie* 12 (1997): 217–34.

16
IV
Picc.
Fl.
Ob.
EH.
Kl.
Fg.
Kb.
p sempre

the basic artistic task of generating the aesthetic present from the past. At the end of his commentary he explains, in technical terms, how he implemented this using contrapuntal devices of mirror reflection:

"Toward the end of the movement [no. 8] we briefly hear, in the high strings (and in transposition), the mirror reflection of the reprise of Beethoven's theme from bars 26 to 29, together with the original form of the theme in trumpet and horn. The last four notes in the violin harmonics lead into piece no. 9, and thus back to the beginning of no. 1. [...] The game is interrupted again and again by violin and viola harmonics from no. 1 (now isolated and no longer as a chordal sonority), by quotations of the theme from the reprise, by a chord in the harp (the basic form and mirror reflection of the penultimate chord of the piano piece), and by figures and pizzicatos in the cellos and double basses (original and mirror reflection of bars 30 to 32, 35, and 36). The flutes, having arrived in the high register, lead to the concluding section, now followed only by the final two notes of the high string harmonics, at first shifted from the distant past to the near present with their nine-note material, then vanishing into a distant future."[5]

Although *Nahe Ferne* has a *de facto* ending, its potential continues: the piece and its ambiguous title thus point to a "distant future" that can be interpreted auto-poetically as the mission of art *per se*. The earnestness that Reimann brought to bear on the "Titan" Beethoven (without allowing himself to be crushed by the weight of his oeuvre and its subsequent impact) were again put on display ten years later, this time in the twelve-minute *Prologue to Beethoven's Ninth Symphony* for chorus and string orchestra. Here he employed the verses from Schiller's "Ode to Joy" that Beethoven chose not to set, ending with the line "Even the dead shall live." By employing an apocalyptic image alluding to the Book of Revelation, Reimann not only created another subliminal tie to the basic themes underlying his own work, but also, in a critical spirit, opened up the Beethoven myth for the present day.

Wolfgang Rathert

5 "Gegen Ende des [achten] Satzes hört man (in einer Transposition) kurz in den hohen Streichern zweimal die Spiegelung der Reprise des Beethoven-Themas der Takte 26 bis 29, zusammen mit dem Thema in Originalgestalt in Trompete und Horn. Die letzten vier Töne in den Flageoletts der Violen leiten über in das neunte Stück und damit zurück in den Anfang des ersten Stückes [...]. Unterbrochen wird das Spiel immer wieder von den Flageolett-Tönen der Violinen und Violen, jetzt einzeln und nicht mehr als Zusammenklang, aus dem ersten Stück, von Zitaten des Themas aus der Reprise, von einem Akkord in der Harfe (Grundgestalt und Spiegelung des vorletzten Akkordes des Klavierstückes), von Figuren und Pizzicati in Violoncelli und Kontrabässen (Original und Spiegelung der Takte 30 bis 32, 35 und 36). Die Flöten, jetzt in der hohen Lage angekommen, führen zum Abschluß, nur noch gefolgt von den letzten zwei Tönen der hohen Streicherflageoletts: zu Beginn mit ihrem Neuntonmaterial aus vergangener Ferne ins Nahe gerückt, in zukünftige Ferne entschwindend." The text, originally reproduced in the program booklet of the concert on 12 October 2003, has been published on the Schott web site at https://de.schott-music.com/shop/nahe-ferne-no175466.html (accessed 27 March 2020).

Jürg Wyttenbach
Completed Sketches for the Piano Sonata, op. 109 (2005–06)

When Jürg Wyttenbach (b. 1935) included his completions of the sketches for op. 109 in a lecture-recital on Beethoven's late piano sonatas, he dispelled the notion that he was pretending to solve compositional problems that the great composer himself was unable to master. His concern was to retrace Beethoven's creative methods and to illuminate the work in question. An edition of the Artaria Sketchbook provided ideal material for this purpose.[1] Combining his three professions of pianist, composer, and teacher, he arrived at an unusual and creative analytical approach to Beethoven's sonatas, "completing" the sketches as a means to an end, a creative vehicle, and a performable research report.[2]

Wyttenbach, born in Berne and resident in Basel, laid the foundations for this approach by studying the sonatas for decades. As a pianist, Beethoven's music has always held a place of honor on his music stand; even before his lecture-recitals on the late sonatas, beginning in 2005, he had demonstrated his deep engagement with Beethoven to a broad public by issuing a recording of the "Hammerklavier" Sonata in 1988.[3] Just how far back this engagement actually extends was recently revealed by a student assignment dating from 1959, in which he provided a descriptive analysis of this same group of works,[4] thereby showing their longstanding importance to him over a period of nearly fifty years.

Wyttenbach the composer approached Beethoven via a roundabout path. His "scenic collage" *Beethoven: Sacré? – Sacré Beethoven!* was written in 1977 for a Beethoven Week at the Basel Academy of Music, where he taught both piano and the performance of contemporary music from 1967 to 2001. As we can see from the verbal score, *Beethoven: Sacré?* combines excerpts from Beethoven's conversation books with quotations and recordings to create thirteen often grotesque scenes of music theater in the broadest sense of the term.[5] The loose-limbed form was designed to involve a maximum number of students. This educational component was, however, decisively broadened by incorporating historical contexts:

"Originally my collages are a sort of teaching device, for I find that whenever one wants to portray a composer – whether Mozart, Beethoven, Satie, Ives, or Stravinsky – the picture becomes fully rounded only when one shows and presents not only the pieces of music but also the ideas behind them, especially when the composers express themselves with sharpness, clarity and wit. Then it becomes truly instructive for audience and students alike."[6]

Wyttenbach then went on to develop two sections of *Beethoven: Sacré?* separately. The results were a "tango-collage after Beethoven," entitled *Noch weisst du nicht, wess' Kind du bist* (from the background music to Scene 9 of *Beethoven: Sacré?*),[7] and "Öde 'Ode' … oder 'Freunde, nicht diese Töne'" (Scene 6 from *Beethoven: Sacré?*), which he elaborated into "D'(h)ommage, oder 'Freu(n)de, nicht …': Spielzüge für einen Posaunisten" (1984–85), a virtuoso piece of instrumental theater for Vinko Globokar.[8]

After retiring from his teaching position, Wyttenbach deepened his study of Beethoven's late piano sonatas and presented them in several public

1 Wyttenbach drew on the facsimile edition *Artaria 195: Beethoven's Sketchbook for the Missa solemnis and the Piano Sonata in E Major, Opus 109*, ed. William Kinderman (Urbana: University of Illinois Press, 2003).

2 The completions are published in Jürg Wyttenbach, *Skizzen zu Ludwig van Beethovens Klaviersonate op. 109*, ed. Michael Kunkel (Saarbrücken: Pfau, 2011), in three volumes and two CDs. See Michael Kunkel's article "'Die Wahrheit gibt es nicht in der Kunst': Jürg Wyttenbachs Beethoven," in the commentary volume of this edition, 13–30.

3 The "Hammerklavier" Sonata (op. 106) was released along with a piano duet version of the *Grosse Fuge* (op. 134), recorded in a duo with Janka Wyttenbach in 1987 (CD Accord 200512).

4 Jürg Wyttenbach, "Ludwig van Beethovens letzte Klaviersonaten," carbon copy with handwritten music examples, dated Berne, 14 October 1959 (Jürg Wyttenbach Collection, PSS). See idem, "Meine gE (r) fahr ungen mit Beethoven," notes in the program leaflet "Die späten Sonaten von Ludwig van Beethoven," Basel Academy of Music, 3 March 2005 (Jürg Wyttenbach Collection, PSS); and Kurt von Fischer, "Einige Daten zu Jürg Wyttenbach – aus der Erinnerung spontan niedergeschrieben," in Jürg Wyttenbach: *Ein Portrait im Spiegel eigener und fremder Texte*, ed. Sigfried Schibli (Zurich: Pro Helvetia; Berne: Zytglogge, 1994), 94–95.

5 Jürg Wyttenbach, "Beethoven: Sacré? – Sacré Beethoven! Szenische Collage aus Texten, Musik, Aktionen, Film für Musiker, Sprecher u. a. Komponiert für ein Akademie-Konzert der Musik-Akademie Basel. Aufgeführt am 22. April 1977," in *Beethoven '77: Beiträge der Beethoven-Woche 1977*, ed. Friedhelm Döhl (Zurich: Amadeus, 1979), 135–63.

6 "Ursprünglich sind meine Collagen eine Art pädagogisches Mittel, denn ich finde, wenn man ein Porträt eines Komponisten machen will – sei es nun Mozart, Beethoven, Satie, Ives oder Strawinsky –, gibt das erst ein umfassendes Bild, wenn man nicht nur die Musikstücke zeigt und vorstellt, sondern auch ihre Gedanken, vor allem bei solchen Komponisten, die sich sehr pointiert, klar und witzig geäussert haben. Das ist für das Publikum und für die Studenten wirklich lehrreich." Jürg Wyttenbach, quotation taken from Sigfried Schibli, "'Ich bin ja noch nicht fertig!': Ein Gespräch mit Jürg Wyttenbach," in *Wyttenbach: Ein Portrait* (see note 4), 96–105, at 96–97. The composers Wyttenbach mentions relate to his other homage-collages, most of which are unpublished; see *L'histoire de Strawinsky / Die Geschichte vom Strawinsky* (Zurich: Tudor, 1984), LP Tudor 73045, and *Harlekinade: Mozarts "Musik zu einer Faschingspantomime,"* newly composed and adapted for the stage by Jürg Wyttenbach, 1988–91,

lecture-recitals at conservatories throughout Switzerland (2005–09). He owes the special position of the Sonata in E major, op. 109, in this cycle to one of his students, who drew his attention to the facsimile of the Artaria 195 sketchbook.[9] His study of the sketchbook persuaded (or seduced) him to expand several Beethoven sketches into short movements, which he then included in his recital on op. 109.[10] As the sketchbook contains nothing for the first movement, he initially focused on Beethoven's many attempts at the second movement, two of which he extracted and completed.[11]

Wyttenbach, however, devoted by far the greatest part of his attention to the sketches for the set of variations in movement 3, limiting himself entirely to rejected elements in order to create six new variations of his own. His sixteen-bar Variation 1, for example, emerged from a sketch of barely two bars (Artaria, p. 53). He elaborated it in the manner of a nocturne, adopting the character of Beethoven's definitive Variation 1. His Variation 2, though related as an *Allegro* to Beethoven's Variation 3, derives from a rejected *Allegro* sketch (Artaria, p. 61). The new Variation 3 emerges from a contrapuntal fragment (Artaria, p. 57) to produce a movement with playfully flowing strings of sixteenth notes. Another *Allegro* sketch (Artaria, p. 66) led to the Handelian Variation 4.

Wyttenbach based his Variation 5 on "one of Beethoven's most original sketches," a "witty, rhythmically buoyant *all'ungherese*" (Artaria, p. 62).[12] Being a complete eight-bar period, the original material was already formally coherent, and he completed it by adding a second eight-bar period (SEE PLATE 1). The flowing rhythm of the first part was confounded by a bar-by-bar shift of accents, and the voice-leading was varied with small-scale contrary motion. As the new Variation 5a seemed too short, despite repeats, he expanded it with a newly composed Variation 5b, a *double,* in which, he claimed, "the tonal material of the right and left hands is interchanged."[13] Not content to leave it at that, he playfully broadened it with changes of register and rhythmic subdivisions. He also introduced a reference to the main theme of movement 1 in the form of lilting pairs of ascending and descending eighth and sixteenth notes. With Variation 6, he ended his completions by combining an elaborately sketched Beethoven melody (Artaria, pp. 54–55) with a fragment marked "Ende" in the sketches (Artaria, p. 71) to create a coda.

In all modesty, Wyttenbach went on record saying that Beethoven would probably have fleshed out the completions "more courageously," if not "more bizarrely."[14] Yet he cannot be accused of lacking courage, for in many passages, especially the rapid roulades in Variation 3 and the *double* of Variation 5, we clearly see flashes of his own creative persona. Even so, he never elbowed his way into the foreground with virtuoso aplomb, but always kept his sights on the material, exploring its possibilities. However modest or pragmatic this may be, it is in any case enjoyable, and reveals Wyttenbach's versatile personality as a masterly composer, intelligent performer, and informative communicator. The final words in his lecture applied to Beethoven: "Maybe he would've liked it. I don't know, I can only hope so."[15]

Matthias Kassel

rev. 2003, available as rental material (Mainz: Schott).

7 Jürg Wyttenbach, *"Noch weisst du nicht, wess' Kind du bist": Tango-Collage nach Beethoven* for piano, violin, and voice ad lib [1977] (Winterthur: Amadeus, 1979).

8 This piece remains unpublished; manuscript preserved in the Jürg Wyttenbach Collection (PSS).

9 See note 1. See also the beginning of the radio broadcast "Jürg Wyttenbach über Beethovens op. 109 und seine Arbeit an den Artaria-Skizzen: Gespräch mit Roland Wächter," broadcast on DRS 2, *Parlando,* 9 and 17 December 2008; CD supplement to idem, *Skizzen zu Ludwig van Beethovens Klaviersonate op. 109* (see note 2).

10 See Jürg Wyttenbach, "'Rauschende Freude treibt mich oft gewalthätig wieder in mich selbst zurück': Meine Arbeit an den Artaria-Skizzen zu Beethovens Klaviersonate op. 109," in idem, *Skizzen zu Ludwig van Beethovens Klaviersonate op. 109* (see note 2), commentary vol., 5–12, esp. 5–6.

11 See the music section of Wyttenbach's edition *Skizzen zu Ludwig van Beethovens Klaviersonate op. 109* (see note 2), [2–3], where the completions are preceded by the relevant pages of sketches from the Artaria Sketchbook (see note 1), in this case Artaria, p. 35. See also the music section [4–7] and Artaria pp. 41–42.

12 Jürg Wyttenbach, "'Rauschende Freude'" (see note 10), 12.

13 Ibid.

14 Radio broadcast "Wyttenbach über Beethovens op. 109" (see note 9) at approx. 55'.

15 "Vielleicht hätte er Freude gehabt daran. Ich weiß es nicht – ich kann nur hoffen." Ibid.

PLATE 1
Jürg Wyttenbach, Completion of *Skizzen zur Klaviersonate op. 109 (Artaria 195)* (2005–06), Variations 5a and 5b. Printed edition, ed. Michael Kunkel (Saarbrücken: Pfau, 2011). Beethoven's sketches are printed in red, Wyttenbach's completions appear in black.
(JÜRG WYTTENBACH COLLECTION, PSS)
BY KIND PERMISSION OF PFAU VERLAG

Heinz Holliger
75th Variation
(2010)

Heinz Holliger (b. 1939) often proceeds from paramusical or extra-musical associations in order to stimulate his creative imagination. The little piano piece discussed here, written for the 75th birthday of his friend Jürg Wyttenbach, toys with a combination of such factors. Here he expresses his admiration for Wyttenbach as a performer of Beethoven, and as the composer who completed the Artaria sketches for the Piano Sonata in E major, op. 109 (see the commentary on Wyttenbach, 127–29); and he uses that admiration as a point of departure for an amusing homage in which a multitude of relations coincide. Initially he took his material from Variations 5a and 5b of Wyttenbach's edition, which draws on a sketch ultimately omitted from the final version of movement 3 of Beethoven's op. 109. Wyttenbach considered this sketched variation to be one of the most original of them all, and he expanded it with a newly composed *double* to lend it more weight. He derived the tonal material and the rhythmic scaffolding of his Variation 5b from Variation 5a and interchanged the right and left hands. He also sharpened the syncopated rhythm of the original and guided the harmony with a dissonant *sforzato* to a surprisingly gentle ending (the sketch of Variation 5a is incompletely harmonized). The manner in which he did this is sufficient by itself to illuminate the "subversive affirmation" of his completion.[1] Wyttenbach also detected a "witty, rhythmically buoyant *all'ungherese*" in the eight bars of Beethoven's rejected sketch and adopted its "*csárdás* character" for his completion,[2] no doubt surreptitiously confirming Holliger's sense of affinity among the composition students of Sándor Veress.

Holliger's *75th Variation on Variations 5a and 5b by Ludwytt Beetenbach* comprises eight highly allusive miniature variations, each of which does no more than gently expand the eight-bar periodic structure of Beethoven's theme.[3] The first and second sections of the piece employ a fifteen-note row – first in its prime form, then in inversion – containing the encrypted name of the dedicatee and couched in the rhythm of the second eight-bar phrase of Wyttenbach's Variation 5a (mm. 1–20). In contrast, the figuration added in the second voice is a chromatically compressed derivative of the runs in Variation 3 of op. 109 (SEE PLATE 1). This element, borrowed directly from Beethoven, is immediately given an ironic twist in section 4, first by being distributed between the two hands in étude-like contrary motion, and second by being set at a leisurely tempo with the expression mark *con molto sentimento* (mm. 30–40). The variation in section 3 (mm. 21–29), with its simple parallel thirds and the avoidance of flavorful harmonies, seems equally like a trivialization of Beethoven's original sketch of Variation 5a, albeit contrapuntally offset by the mirror-reflected stretto of the *csárdás* rhythm and a grimacing dissonant final chord.

The heart of this dedicatory piece is a serenade from a slightly modified and worded version of Wyttenbach's *double*. Here two *ad libitum* voice parts (e.g. the pianist and the page turner) present not only birthday greetings for the dedicatee, but a compliment from the highest authority of all for his brilliant achievement:

1 Michael Kunkel, "'Die Wahrheit gibt es nicht in der Kunst': Jürg Wyttenbachs Beethoven," in Jürg Wyttenbach, *Skizzen zu Ludwig van Beethovens Klaviersonate op. 109*, ed. Michael Kunkel (Saarbrücken: Pfau, 2011), with three volumes and two CDs, commentary vol., 13–30, at 21.

2 Jürg Wyttenbach, "'Rauschende Freude treibt mich oft gewalthätig wieder in mich selbst zurück': Meine Arbeit an den Artaria-Skizzen zu Beethovens Klaviersonate op. 109," in idem, *Skizzen zu Ludwig van Beethovens Klaviersonate op. 109* (see note 1), commentary vol., 5–12, at 12.

3 Published in Holliger's anthology *Albumblätter: 16 Klavierstücke* (Mainz: Schott, 2019), 26–29.

PLATE 1
Heinz Holliger, *75th Variation on Variations 5a and 5b by Ludwytt Beetenbach* for piano (2010). Sketch, p. [3]
(HEINZ HOLLIGER COLLECTION, PSS)

PLATE 2
Heinz Holliger, *75th Variation on Variations 5a and 5b by Ludwytt Beetenbach* for piano (2010). 1st fair copy, p. [3]
(HEINZ HOLLIGER COLLECTION, PSS)

> Yes, even Ludwig, the man from Bonn, sends warm greetings,
> and adds that your black notes
> will get along splendidly with his red ones.[4]

True, Wyttenbach's edition, with its red and black notes, did not appear in print until early 2011 (SEE PLATE 1 IN THE COMMENTARY ON WYTTENBACH, P. 129). But Holliger had been given the proofs several months earlier and was thus able to refer to them when conceiving his dedicatory piece. This is shown by the (photo-reduced) black-and-white copy of a proof sheet with crop marks on which he jotted down his initial ideas in November 2010.[5] Section 6, following the birthday serenade (mm. 58–66), then takes the "black notes" of Variation 5a as its theme, in an ironic note-for-note retrograde, and turns the Allegro with its halting retrograde time into an "Allegro indeciso." In compensation, he then puts the *csárdás* theme through its paces all the more rigorously in a tightly constructed four-voice mirror canon (SEE PLATE 2).

Although Holliger has engaged with Beethoven's music time and time again as a performer, he has rarely felt creatively challenged by his way of composition.[6] By taking the edition of the op. 109 sketches as an opportunity to expunge most of the Beethoven passages and pay tribute to his friend's completions, this humoresque becomes what might be called a Beethoven arrangement at one remove: it looks at the great composer through Wyttenbach's ingeniously tinted glasses and culminates in the conflation of the composers' names in its title: "Ludwytt Beetenbach."

Heidy Zimmermann

4 "Ja, auch der Ludwig, der aus Bonn, lässt herzlich grüssen, / und meint, dass sich deine schwarzen Noten / trefflich mit den seinen, roten, vertragen werden."

5 Heinz Holliger, *Albumblätter* folder, sketch for *75th Variation on Variations 5a and 5b by Ludwytt Beetenbach* (Heinz Holliger Collection, PSS).

6 See Philippe Albèra, "Entretien avec Heinz Holliger," in Heinz Holliger, *Entretiens, textes, écrits sur son œuvre,* enlarged new edn. (Geneva: Contrechamps, 2007), 17–61, esp. 50–51.

Kaija Saariaho
Chimera
(2019)

With an eye to the Beethoven Jubilee in 2020, the European Broadcasting Union (EBU) commissioned a short piece from Kaija Saariaho (b. 1952), asking her to compose an "audio sting" to announce Jubilee broadcasts on all of its member stations. The sting, they said, should not only be entirely in line with her own music, but suitable for recalling the great composer himself. The ninety-second miniature was premièred and recorded on 6 November 2019 by the BBC Symphony Orchestra under the Finnish conductor Sakari Oramo, and has since become available online.[1] From the very beginning, as Saariaho told BBC moderator Petroc Trelawny in an interview, she had decided that she was "not going to fake Beethoven."[2] Instead, she sought points of contact between her music and Beethoven's while making them stand out in contrast. She gave the little piece the title *Chimera,* alluding to the monster from Greek mythology consisting of a lion, a goat, and a dragon. It is, she said, "a new kind of strange animal"[3] of the sort that occurs in biology when two genetically different cells give rise to a new organism.

The pre-formed material for this hybrid composition, or what might be called its genetic material, is taken from the outer movements of Beethoven's Second Symphony, op. 36, and Saariaho's *Orion,* her first extensive work for symphony orchestra (composed in 2002). This heterogeneous material was subjected to a transformation as subtle as it is effective, and arranged for an orchestra midway between those of the two original compositions, the classical forces now being augmented with the characteristic sounds of two harps, piano, and a multi-hued percussion section.

A glimpse into the piece's underlying elements and ideas is provided by a diagrammatic sketch that outlines the continuity of this "trailer" in its temporal proportions (SEE PLATE 1). The five sections, symmetrically arranged and originally conceived to last sixty seconds, are subdivided by vertical strokes, with a corresponding timeline in seconds placed horizontally above it. The letter "B" marks the entrance of Beethoven elements, as might be expected, while "KS" stands for the composer, immediately overwriting a previously notated "B" at the beginning. In other words, the piece was originally intended to start with "Beethoven," but begins in its final form with a "KS" incipit. The sketch, headed "Beethoven jingle," also has cues for tempo progressions, dynamics, structuring chords, and textures – cues that Saariaho, as usual, has written in her native Finnish. This clearly indicates that the form, rather than resulting from filling in predefined structures, emerges from the contents of the material and the harmonic spaces.[4]

It is interesting to note in detail how the contrasting sonic elements are interwoven. The very opening bars of *Chimera* show how smoothly Saariaho transfers her own textures into the bold opening gesture of Beethoven's Second. The first two bars are developed from the opening of *Orion,* whose first section, headed "Memento mori," begins with rising eighth-note motifs in the woodwinds above a microtonally inflected B sonority, resulting in a *misterioso* texture at a tranquil pace. In *Chimera,* these two opening bars are now subtly transformed in such a way that they lead precisely to the unison D

1 Accessible under "Audio Sting" at www.ebu.ch/beethoven-2020 (accessed 16 April 2020).

2 Kaija Saariaho, interview with Petroc Trelawny, 18 December 2019, in ibid.

3 Ibid.

4 See the fundamental essay "Timbre et harmonie" (1987), in Kaija Saariaho, *Le Passage des frontières: Écrits sur la musique,* ed. Stéphane Roth (Paris: Éditions MF, 2013), 84–135, esp. 85.

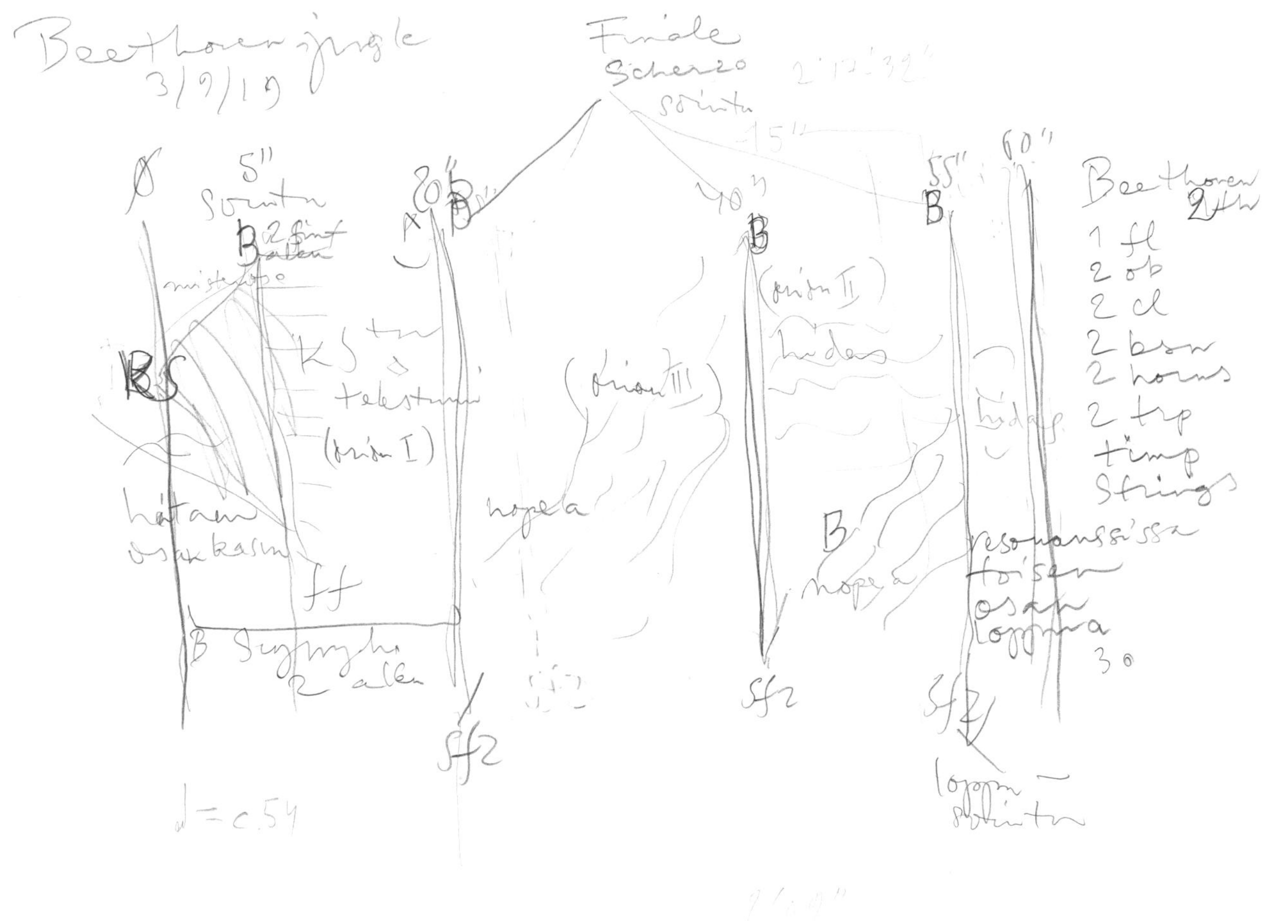

PLATE 1
Kaija Saariaho, *Chimera* for orchestra (2019). Sketch
(KAIJA SAARIAHO COLLECTION, PSS)

CHIMERA

Kaija Saariaho

EXAMPLE 1 (OPPOSITE)
Kaija Saariaho, *Chimera* for orchestra (2019), mm. 1–6. Beethoven sections highlighted in yellow.

of Beethoven's *adagio* introduction (SEE EXAMPLE 1). The harmonic bass in the double basses moves with a glissando from B to A, creating a dominant effect in combination with the seventh in the vibraphone and second harp. The melodic eighth-note motion, rising to C♯, reinforces the dominant sonority; it is also shifted from the clarinets to the oboes, so that it passes seamlessly into the wind melody of Beethoven's original introduction (m. 3). In bars 3 to 6, the *piano* cantilena in the woodwinds is superposed by the sustained texture from *Orion*, causing the Beethoven sonority and Saariaho's spectralist atmosphere to hover in a shimmering limbo.

Following a section of pure Saariaho, drawn from the propulsive third movement of *Orion* (mm. 7–24), for nearly twenty bars we hear equally pure Beethoven, namely, the closing bars from the finale of the Second Symphony (mm. 25–42), superposed only by decaying vibraphone and piano sounds and harp glissandos. The coda of this sonata-rondo movement, in which the capricious ritornello is heard one last time, provides a bold, almost tempestuous corroboration of the instant of recognition merely intimated at the beginning of the piece. It may seem surprising that Saariaho chose precisely this somewhat bizarre rondo finale as the quarry for her composition. She forthrightly states her reason in the above-mentioned interview: "I don't like rondos," she says, while admitting that Beethoven's rondos are invariably interesting and surprising.[5] The theme she selected, with its rhythmic energy and heavy "drive," doubtless serves the function of contrast; it is taken from one of his lesser-known symphonies but immediately signals his authorship. And after the *fortissimo* of Beethoven's percussive ending, the glittering hues of the final chord are especially striking (m. 43). In a mirror inversion of the opening, the D-based sonority, chromatically enriched and played *subito lentissimo* and *piano,* leads to the "resonance" of a contemplative excerpt from *Orion* (SEE PLATE 1, P. 135). As in a sudden metamorphosis, the final progressions of its second movement, "Winter Sky" (mm. 127–28), flow out of the pivot chord. The rotating eighth-note figure in the right hand of the piano is transposed upward by a major third so that it writhes organically out of the D. The motion comes to a stop via "timbred" string sonorities and harp glissandos in a descending semitone, after which it remains suspended in mid-air.

As befits its function, *Chimera,* this sophisticated piece of *Gebrauchsmusik,* can and should also be played live in concert by symphony orchestras. This has been rendered practically impossible by the worldwide corona pandemic, which brought public cultural life to a complete standstill in the first half of the Jubilee year. At the moment, we can only hope that the jingle will find use in reality, and not remain entirely chimerical in virtual space.

Heidy Zimmermann

5 Kaija Saariaho, interview with Petroc Trelawny (see note 2).

4

DISTORTION – DISMANTLEMENT

Esteban Buch

Beethoven at 200 + 50

The Changing Meaning of Commemorations

A first version of this essay was written in Paris in January 2020, a few weeks before the brutal disruption of everyday life caused by the coronavirus pandemic. This is how it began:

Like most commemorations of long-dead composers, the two-hundred-fiftieth anniversary of the birth of Ludwig van Beethoven in 2020 will entail massive amounts of repetition. All his symphonies, all his piano sonatas, all his concertos, all his string quartets: in any genre you care to name, myriad venues all over the world will perform Beethoven's music over and over again. By the same token, audio and visual recordings of earlier performances will also be heard, thus turning earlier repetitions of this music into new objects of perception. Similar pronouncements on this cultural hero will be uttered by musicians, organizers, journalists, politicians, and audiences, including pronouncements which for two centuries have raised the hermeneutic issue of "Beethoven and Us" in ever new historical situations. To say this is not to suggest that things could or should be otherwise. Indeed, this essay is also about the issue of "Beethoven and Us," and also intends to propose some new answers to it.

Predictions are always risky, be they grounded on science, on belief, or on tradition. They are especially risky for historians, who are supposed to be experts on the past, or rather, on a small part of it. On the other hand, the future tense in these opening sentences did not indicate an exercise in prophecy or in phenomenological protention, but a trivial reality of cultural life, namely, the fact that a commemoration of this kind always follows a long pre-established program.

For humanity, the sudden cancellation of Beethoven concerts, exhibitions, and conferences looks insignificant compared to so many catastrophes. Yet it is as good a spot as any to take the pulse of the random and dangerous reformatting of historicity in which humans are presently engaged. As the present second version of this essay is being written, in May 2020, some scholarly events are going virtual, and most concerts are being rescheduled. If this pattern holds, the disruption might eventually boil down to a chronological anomaly, with 2021 doubling for 2020. But who knows where things will stand at the end of the year on Beethoven's actual anniversary day, an event whose precise location in time was in any case always uncertain (only his baptism is documented, on 17 December). Indeed, this new version of the essay, too, is likely to be outdated by the time it reaches its readers. But one thing, at least, can be safely assumed as of today: the two-hundred-fiftieth anniversary of the birth of Ludwig van Beethoven in 2020 will *not* be like any previous commemoration of a long-dead composer.

This novelty is mostly negative, since social distancing rules forbid physically coming together to play music and/or to listen to it. The formidable diffusion of droplets from a brass section playing the opening chord of the last movement of Beethoven's Ninth might give new meaning to the name famously assigned to it by Richard Wagner: *Schreckensfanfare*. And even if the actual limit of the potential spread of the virus is still controversial, it is enough to upend the normal functioning of orchestras and choruses – including, of course, as they play and sing the same work's most joyful sections.[1]

Yet there are also signs of new ways of socializing Beethoven's music, as part of a resilient strategy in the face of the pandemic. Daniel Barenboim's playing of the *Diabelli Variations* on 10 April 2020 in a completely deserted Berlin Philharmonie, for listeners riveted to their computers in lockdown all over the world, was a powerful reminder of the radical solitude and silence that listening to classical music has always entailed.[2] Also, the jigsaw screens of YouTube clips with musicians performing Beethoven chamber music in different "chambers" – i.e. their homes – might prompt new inquiries into what playing together really means, and even into the ontology of music itself, given the difficulty of saying *where* it was actually happening.[3] From a different perspective, a pop version of the "Ode to Joy," sung by a young woman from a lonely balcony in Stuttgart as a homage to health workers and people employed at supermarkets and other essential places, updated the tune's pedigree of humanitarian resignifications.[4] Others, alarmed by the lack of supranational solidarity, joined forces in a virtual choir of pop singers to activate the same melody's political resonance as the European Anthem.[5]

All these examples are directly related to the coronavirus crisis, yet they all elaborate on existing hermeneutical traditions. Music is probably the art form that makes the greatest use of repetition, be it at the level of motifs and sonic objects, genres and canons, or the pleasure of aesthetic experience.[6] Recordings of Beethoven's music contribute to fill the void of cancelled performances of the same works, forming part of the long shadow of Walter Benjamin's era of mechanical reproduction.[7] Recent technological devices make it possible to produce more and more copies of the same thing while allowing for unheard-of technical and

1 See Claudia Spahn and Bernhard Richter, "Risikoeinschätzung einer Coronavirus-Infektion im Bereich Musik," www.kirchturm-verlag.de/media/Institut MusikermedizinFR_Risikoeinschaetzung-Freiburg.pdf (accessed 13 May 2020); Stefan N. Willich et al., "Stellungnahme zum Spielbetrieb der Orchester während der COVID-19 Pandemie," https://epidemiologie.charite.de/fileadmin/user_upload/microsites/m_cc01/epidemiologie/downloads/Stellungnahme_Spielbetrieb_Orchester.pdf (accessed on 13 May 2020); and "Aerosolausstoßtest: Geringes Infektionsrisiko durch die Verbreitung von Atemluft von Musikern," www.wienerphilhar moniker.at/orchester/philharmonisches-tagebuch/year/2020/month/4/blogitemid/1423/page/1/pagesize/20 (accessed 13 May 2020).

2 See "Concert: Daniel Barenboim interprète Variations Diabelli de Beethoven: Récital de piano à Boulez Saal," www.medici.tv/fr/concerts/daniel-barenboim-plays-beethoven/ (accessed 13 May 2020).

3 See "Quarantine Performance No. 1 – Beethoven's Trio (Minuet & Trio)," www.youtube.com/watch?v=cAk1397ulWk (accessed 13 May 2020).

4 See "'Ode an die Freude' Beethoven. Flashmob von Emily," www.youtube.com/watch?v=YTfK4_DlTjg (accessed 13 May 2020).

5 See "All together for European solidarity: 'United in Diversity' / Step 2," www.youtube.com/watch?v=0BYWf_CYw-E (accessed 13 May 2020).

6 See Elizabeth Hellmuth Margulis, *On Repeat: How Music Plays the Mind* (New York: Oxford University Press, 2014); and Robert Fink, *Repeating Ourselves: American Minimal Music as Cultural Practice* (Berkeley: University of California Press, 2005).

7 See *Musical Listening in the Age of Technological Reproduction*, ed. Gianmario Borio (Farnham: Ashgate, 2015).

aesthetic configurations. Beethovenian variation form, which stretches to the limit the very notion of variation, exemplifies the evolution both of his artworks and of his commemorations.

Now, this essay intends to show that the 2020 Beethoven Jubilee differs from previous commemorations not only because of the dramatic contingency of the pandemic, but also because the composer's oeuvre and image had already changed profoundly in significance over the last fifty years. Indeed, it makes the case that they have changed faster than in the many more years that passed between their initial impact on Western culture, during his lifetime, and the fateful *Beethoven-Jahr* of 1970.

Beethoven at 200

The 1970 bicentenary of Beethoven's birth was a world event, much in the way that the centenary of his death had been in 1927.[8] His music was the very core of the classical repertoire, widely understood as the sole truly legitimate and moral expression of sonic art. In many countries, especially in Europe, the coupling of society and the state resulted from official pronouncements and private utterances hailing Beethoven as the musical messenger of universal progress and world peace. This shared cultural heritage was meant to reach all human beings asymptotically, thanks to voluntarist politics on behalf of the democratization of art.

In both situations, the world and the universe were but names for an ethnocentric vision of culture which, in fact, privileged Western high art as a moral paradigm for colonial and neo-colonial thought and policies. Between the two commemorations, World War II and the Holocaust dramatically showed that Beethoven's music could also be claimed for the very opposite of joy and freedom. This inspired some questions about the nature of collective admiration. Most were answered by pinning the blame on the Nazis' "misuse" of Beethoven, but without essentially changing the belief in his music's moral content.

The cosmopolitan atmosphere of 1970 and 1927 differed from the 1870 centenary, when nationalist claims on Beethoven were favored by the Franco-Prussian War. But even in that situation, most discussions praised the composer's universality, which cultural nationalists saw as intrinsic to German art in the first place. On the other hand, the geography of the "civilized world," which some saw embodied in his music, was at that time much smaller, as institutions of classical music in the Americas, Asia, and elsewhere could not compete with Europe's soft power.

Still earlier in history, the festival held in Bonn in 1845 for the inauguration of Ernst Julius Hähnel's Beethoven monument turned the tension between nationalism and internationalism into a noisy collective performance. This resulted from the presence of royalty, including the King of Prussia and the Queen of the United Kingdom, and a cosmopolitan elite of musicians led by Franz Liszt, who, for all their transnational credentials, were prone to split along patriotic lines. On that occasion, the performance of Liszt's first Beethoven Cantata – to be followed in 1870 by a second, equally "sublime" one – set a pattern of composing special works

8 See Esteban Buch, *Beethoven's Ninth: A Political History*, trans. Richard Miller (Chicago: University of Chicago Press, 2003), esp. 178–200 and 220–42.

in homage to the great composer. This monumental music[9] was meant to incarnate in sound, through the balancing of humble obeisance and daring creativity, the historical dialectics of past and present.

In some respects the 1970 bicentenary was, of course, different from the commemorations in the nineteenth and early twentieth centuries. For one thing, it was a Cold War event. On both sides of the Iron Curtain, Beethoven was reclaimed as evidence of the moral superiority of each political system. One sign of this was the vehement objection of the German Democratic Republic to the adoption of the "Ode to Joy" as the European Anthem during a meeting held by the Council of Europe in 1971 in, of all places, West Berlin. As a result, the director of the Berlin Philharmonic, Herbert von Karajan, wrote an official arrangement, which was in fact a cut-and-paste collage of three excerpts from the Ninth. Another Cold War symptom was that musicians aligned with the New German Left showed reverence to Beethoven by being flagrantly irreverent.[10] Further, according to Elaine Kelly, "artists in East Germany, like their counterparts in the Federal Republic, began to explore aspects of the composer that were incongruous with the heroic model, focusing in particular on the late Beethoven."[11]

Aesthetic irony had roots in older times, as witness the *Marche funèbre composée pour les funérailles d'un grand homme sourd* (Funeral March for the Obsequies of a Great Deaf Man), a work composed by Alphonse Allais in 1897 and consisting of a twenty-four-bar empty score.[12] Another example, on the eve of the Great War, is Erik Satie's jokes on Beethoven's imaginary tenth symphony: "He liked the decimal system: 'I have ten fingers' he explained."[13] Before and after World War II, an anti-Beethovenian ethos was fashionable in avant-garde musical circles, where many felt estranged from his technical landscape. Still, in the aftermath of the student movements of May 1968, the anti-authoritarian atmosphere gave irony and irreverence an unexpected political relevance that actually went beyond revolutionaries and *artistes engagés*. Take the poem *Tell me*, written by the politically and aesthetically moderate Pierre Boulez, first published in a German newspaper in 1970:

> Everything Beethoven represents,
> this great era in our history,
> is making place for another that is only just beginning,
> in which Europe – and those affiliated with Europe –
> will no longer enjoy
> exclusive (almost) privileges.
> Is this not the moment to celebrate,
> not an individual birth,
> but a collective death?[14]

While Boulez's contribution to the 1970 bicentenary was not a piece of music, other composers wrote ironic pieces to criticize the Beethoven cult. A case in point is Louis Andriessen's *De negen symfonieën van Beethoven voor promenade-orkest en ijscobel* (The Nine Symphonies of Beethoven for Promenade Orchestra and Ice-Cream Vendor's Bell), premièred at the Amsterdam Concertgebouw in 1970, to huge success. This cheerful piece was basically a collage of bits of Beethoven scores.

9 See Alexander Rehding, *Music and Monumentality: Commemoration and Wonderment in Nineteenth-Century Germany* (New York: Oxford University Press, 2009).

10 See Beate Kutschke, "The Celebration of Beethoven's Bicentennial in 1970: The Anti-authoritarian Movement and Its Impact on Radical Avant-garde and Postmodern Music in West Germany," *The Musical Quarterly* 93, nos. 3–4 (2010): 560–615.

11 Elaine Kelly, *Composing the Canon in the German Democratic Republic: Narratives of Nineteenth-Century Music* (New York: Oxford University Press, 2014), 103.

12 Alphonse Allais, *Album primo-avrilesque* (Paris: Paul Ollendorff, [1897]), n.p.

13 Erik Satie, "Perfect Entourage," in idem, *The Mammal's Notebook: Collected Writings of Erik Satie*, ed. Ornella Volta, trans. Antony Melville (London: Atlas, 1996), 101–02, at 102.

14 Pierre Boulez, "Beethoven: Tell Me," in idem, *Orientations: Collected Writings*, ed. Jean-Jacques Nattiez, trans. Martin Cooper (Cambridge, MA: Harvard University Press, 1990), 205–11, at 210.

In keeping with Luciano Berio's handling of Mahler materials in *Sinfonia* (1968), and later with Pierre Henry's *La dixième symphonie: Hommage à Beethoven* (1979), it also implied that collage could be made politically significant through the vehicle of humor. According to the Bergsonian definition,[15] humor stems from the interference of two independent series of events – here the Beethoven corpus and the pop music idiom, plus the Dadaist-Duchampian addendum of an ice-cream vendor's bell to the classical orchestra.

Andriessen's technique was, however, far more complex than pure cut-and-paste. It included unprepared polytonal chords, sudden rhythmical asymmetries, *non sequitur* phrasing, ungrammatical silences stretching beyond predictable Beethovenian surprises, heterogeneous notational codes, orchestral arrangements of piano fragments, vocalizations by male instrumentalists, micro-alteration of emblematic motifs such as the Fifth's ta-ta-ta-taaa, short improvisatory sections, and an out-of-the blue quotation of *L'Internationale*. Last but not least, it featured the ice-cream vendor's bell noisily interfering with solemn excerpts of the *Eroica*, the Fifth, and the *Pathétique* Sonata.

On the other hand, the piece's ending, with euphoric variations on the "Ode to Joy," repeated the very structure of the Ninth and ran close to such deadly serious "homages" as Miguel Ríos's *Himno a la alegría (A Song of Joy)*, a commercial pop success. Andriessen's work arguably expressed some of the 1970s cultural tensions through the very mismatch of its alleged subversive intention and its actual social effect. Indeed, the composer himself acknowledged as much. According to Stephen Loy, "[t]hat the effectiveness of the postmodern critique of cultural orchestral practice through works such as *The Nine Symphonies of Beethoven* relied on the very institutions against which Andriessen had campaigned, prompted him to re-evaluate his own cultural compositional practice."[16] The composer eventually declared that his work was but "a truly disgusting, commercialized, weird mess with all sorts of gags and jokes. *Für Elise*, the "Moonlight Sonata" – nothing was beyond my reach in that piece," he said, confessing that its success triggered a year-long reflection during which he stayed "at home, sitting on the sofa, thinking about the meaning of composition."[17]

Mauricio Kagel's film *Ludwig van*, produced by West German Radio (WDR), did not project the same ambiguities, if one is to judge by its hostile reviews in both West and East Germany. The most influential was Hilde Spiel's attack on an "Anti-Beethoven-Film" in the *Frankfurter Allgemeine Zeitung*.[18] Yet *Ludwig van* was less about Beethoven than about the Beethoven cult and the obsessive repetition of his music and image this entailed. The composer stressed this very point in his initial outline of 1967, with the deaf composer observing his own bicentenary from a ship on the Rhine:

"Amazingly, Beethoven is played everywhere: his songs resound over the ship's public address system; medleys and arrangements of the symphonies for coffeehouse orchestra are heard in the Rhine terraces; boy scouts and groups in folk costume play overtures on recorders; military bands march to the Ninth Symphony; male and female choruses sing unisono; chamber music echoes from half-timbered houses."[19]

15 See Henri Bergson, *Laughter: An Essay on the Meaning of the Comic* (Mineola: Dover, 2005).

16 Stephen Loy, "Music, Activism and Tradition: Louis Andriessen's *Nine Symphonies of Beethoven*," *Context* 34 (2009): 15–34, at 31. See also Matthias Kassel's essay in this volume, 168–71.

17 Robert Adlington, *Composing Dissent: Avant-Garde Music in 1960s Amsterdam* (New York: Oxford University Press, 2013), 268.

18 Hilde Spiel, "Kagels Anti-Beethoven-Film in Wien uraufgeführt," *Frankfurter Allgemeine Zeitung*, reproduced together with reviews by Joachim Kaiser (*Süddeutsche Zeitung*) and Gerhard Brunner (*Die Welt*) in "Kagel und der 200. Geburtstag Beethovens," *Melos* 37, no. 9 (1970): 365–68, at 366–67. See also Buch, *Beethoven's Ninth* (see note 8), 229–31, and Matthias Kassel's essay in this volume, 161–67.

19 "Erstaunlicherweise wird überall Beethoven gespielt: aus dem Schiffslautsprecher erklingen seine Lieder, in den Rheinterrassen werden Potpourris und Arrangements der Symphonien für Caféhausorchester dargeboten, Pfadfinder und Trachtengruppen spielen Ouvertüren auf Blockflöten, Militärkapellen defilieren zur 9. Symphonie, Männer- und Frauenchöre singen unisono, aus Fachwerkhäusern tönt Kammermusik." Mauricio Kagel, *Das filmische Werk I, 1965–1985*, ed. Werner Klüppelholz and Lothar Prox (Cologne: DuMont, 1985), 89.

This outline set the tone for the work to come. As in the Andriessen piece, sonic collage was the structural principle of Kagel's film: "The music for this film is assembled entirely from motifs from Beethoven's oeuvre."[20] This is central in the *Musikzimmer* scene, where musicians randomly read bits of a physical collage of scores affixed to the walls and furniture of the room. The piece resulting from the unheard-of sonorities of Kagel's arrangements received the literally subversive name *Homage von Beethoven.*

Ludwig van begins with a Romantic tale, the composer's return to his birthplace two centuries later, to discover its 1845 monument and people listening to his music through telephone-like earphones. Also, the sequence of would-be rooms of the Beethoven-Haus, in fact a series of installations/performances by Joseph Beuys, Robert Filliou, Dieter Roth, Ursula Burghardt, and others, could still amount to a classical formal articulation. Yet the film's overall temporal structure radically departed from Beethoven's middle-period "integration" and teleological processes, displaying instead a late-style constellation of fragments. The collective production mode, with Kagel getting by with a little help from his friends, also contributed to this anti-heroic stance. And even if the final scene did feature bits of the Ninth, as if it were the *telos* of every possible Beethoven narrative, these were but sonic ruins of a collapsed statue. Still fun, though.

Now the critical edge of *Ludwig van* was multiple and rather serious, despite many hilarious passages. The final section, where bits of the "Seid umschlungen" passage of the Ninth are heard over images of animals in a zoo – including one caught in the act of producing authentic *Elefantenscheisse* – was as irreverent as it was unsettling. It might indeed inspire reflection on interspecies ethics and the limits of the concept of humanity as synonymous with universality, especially when beasts in cages echo the Prisoners' Chorus from *Fidelio.*

Kagel also suggested that the Beethoven cult was a matter of (very) old people. "All twelve announcers should be at least sixty-five years old and have wrinkled faces (truly elderly people preferred)," says the *Drehbuch,* which describes a sequence of clichés and nonsense statements to be shot at the WDR. In the film, this gives way to a venerable old man solemnly declaiming Beethoven's words: "From the heart – may it return to the heart."[21]

The main political point of Kagel's movie, associated with this generational issue, was the scandalous connection of Beethoven's legacy with the Nazis, summed up in the Beethoven-Haus *Führer's* physical resemblance to Hitler (SEE PLATE 1). A closet full of *"entartete Musik"* by Schoenberg and potential forerunners such as Liszt shared space with a *Konzert* by Karl Marx. In the *Drehbuch,* Kagel himself is on the list, whereas Marx is not; this shows a rhapsodic approach to ideological creativity. The spectral presence of pianist Elly Ney, a creepy figure obsessively playing the "Waldstein" Sonata's opening chord, also suggested that Beethoven's moral relevance for the present was polluted by ghosts of the Nazi era.

Still another scene mimicked a TV talk show on Beethoven's historical significance. Featuring Kagel and critic Hans-Klaus Metzger, among others, it was a parody of the WDR's *Internationale Frühschoppen* by Werner Höfer, who played his own role. There, Herbert von Karajan was targeted by Metzger as the

20 "Die Musik zu diesem Film wird ausschließlich mit Motiven aus Beethovens Schaffen zusammenmontiert." Ibid.

21 "Alle 12 Ansager und Ansagerinnen sollen mindestens 65 Jahre alt sein und faltenreiche Gesichter haben (wahre Greise sind als ideale Besetzung erwünscht)." "Von Herzen – Möge es wieder zu Herzen gehn." Mauricio Kagel, "Ludwig van. Drehbuch," typescript with annotations, 21 (Mauricio Kagel Collection, PSS).

PLATE 1
Günther Böhmert as *Fremdenführer* (tour guide) in the "Living Room" of the "Beethoven House" (designed by Ursula Burghardt) during the filming of *Ludwig van* (1969). Photograph by Brigitte Dannehl (MAURICIO KAGEL COLLECTION, PSS) © 2020, PROLITTERIS, ZURICH

symbol of an establishment devoted to a market-friendly, reactionary Beethoven cult. This was all but inconsequential. Somebody reportedly shouted "I am going to report this to Herr von Karajan" during the first screening in Vienna.[22] On the other hand, neither Höfer's nor Karajan's Nazi past was publicly known at the time, a fact that might count as a missing link between the anti-capitalist and the anti-Nazi stances of Kagel's critical discourse.

This connection was indeed familiar to readers of critical theory. Its musical hero, Theodor W. Adorno, had passed away just a year before, thus being spared both completing his book on Beethoven and living through the euphoric ambivalence of the 1970 Beethoven year. Adorno's scorn at people listening to actual Beethoven symphonies as if they were potpourris of Beethoven themes found an aesthetic reply in critical variations on potpourri form, such as Andriessen's or Kagel's. "Ever since Beethoven's last works those artists who pushed integration to an extreme have mobilized disintegration," says his posthumous *Aesthetic Theory*.[23]

22 Nikolaos Stavlas, "Reconstructing Beethoven: Mauricio Kagel's *Ludwig van*" (Ph.D., diss., Goldsmiths College, University of London, 2012), 87. The interjection is reported in the review by Joachim Kaiser; see "Kagel und der 200. Geburtstag Beethovens" (see note 18), 365.

23 Theodor W. Adorno, *Aesthetic Theory*, ed. Gretel Adorno and Rolf Tiedemann, trans. Robert Hullot-Kentor (London: Athlone, 1997), 45.

Beethoven in (Slow) Motion Across the Millennium

In 1970, Hans Heinrich Eggebrecht delivered a lecture on the history of Beethoven reception as a contribution to the bicentenary of his birth. In 1977, on the occasion of the one-hundred-fiftieth anniversary of Beethoven's death, he completed it with a historiographical essay.[24] There he made a case for the permanence of an invariable "nucleus" (*Kern*) of meaning, summarized by Beethoven's motto "Joy through suffering" (*durch Leiden Freude*), and he declared changing modes of reception to be but its contingent "envelope" (*Hülle*).[25] In 1955 Brigitte and Jean Massin had addressed a similar issue in quite different terms: "One of the great problems faced by any study of Beethoven is that whenever one sets down a judgment that appears to apply very exactly to the precise case of Beethoven, one also has the impression that one has written something that is grossly banal."[26]

In Eggebrecht's conservative and anti-historical view, as in the Massins' more critical assessment, the repetition of clichés was equivalent to truth, and difference tantamount to illusion. At a theoretical level, this idealist view was radically opposed to Gilles Deleuze's case for the ontological preeminence of difference over repetition.[27] At an empirical level, it was perhaps a reaction to signs that actual changes in Beethoven's reception were already underway in 1970.

Take the growing importance of women in Beethoven scholarship. Unsurprisingly, if one leaves aside Bettina Brentano's letters and contributions by Marie Lipsius (La Mara) in the 1920s, the exegesis of his life and work had been an overwhelmingly male affair. The bicentenary, though, inspired the Massins to produce a follow-up to their standard biography, namely the book *Recherche de Beethoven,* the first part of which was signed by Brigitte alone.[28] Her essay dealt with the composer's relationship to his "unique beloved" Josephine Brunsvik, also seen as the probable addressee of the 1812 "Immortal Beloved" letter. This conjectural solution to the historiographical riddle, already proposed by La Mara, was to be reaffirmed in the 2000s by Rita Steblin, after decades dominated by Maynard Solomon's theory on Antonie Brentano.[29] Steblin mentions La Mara's work, and wonders about the reasons for its dismissal: "Because a woman did the research?"[30]

Brigitte Massin explored the psychological background of Josephine's romantic liaison with the composer, namely a "feeling of liberation" after her husband's death, and her "desire to live now her younger years stolen by a premature marriage."[31] This empowerment of a female figure was unusual in narratives on the composer's life, commonly dominated instead by his homosocial friendships and his feud over his nephew Karl with the diabolical figure of his sister-in-law Johanna. Massin also suggested a musical thread of everlasting love, uniting the 1803–04 *Andante favori* (dedicated to Josephine and her sister Therese) with the 1816 *Ferne Geliebte* cycle and the 1823–24 *Bagatelles,* op. 126.

Josephine's story, however, did not challenge established Beethoven historiography, as Susan McClary certainly did by writing in 1987 that "[t]he point of recapitulation in the first movement of the Ninth is one of the most horrifying moments in music, as the carefully prepared cadence is frustrated, damming up energy which finally explodes in the throttling murderous rage of a rapist incapable of

24 Hans Heinrich Eggebrecht, "Zur Wirkungsgeschichte der Musik Beethovens: Theorie der ästhetischen Identifikation" (1977), in idem, *Zur Geschichte der Beethoven-Rezeption* (Laaber: Laaber, 1994), 113–33.

25 Ibid., 120–31.

26 Jean and Brigitte Massin, *Ludwig van Beethoven* (Paris: Fayard, 1967), 802. The book was first published in 1955.

27 See Gilles Deleuze, *Difference and Repetition,* trans. Paul Patton (New York: Columbia University Press, 1994); the French original, *Différence et répétition,* was published in 1968 by Presses Universitaires de France.

28 Brigitte Massin, "L'unique bien-aimée' de Beethoven: Joséphine von Brunsvik," in Jean and Brigitte Massin, *Recherche de Beethoven* (Paris: Fayard 1970), 11–140.

29 Maynard Solomon, *Beethoven* (New York: Schirmer 1977).

30 "Weil eine Frau die Recherchen machte?" Rita Steblin, "Beethovens 'Unsterbliche Geliebte': Des Rätsels Lösung," *Österreichische Musikzeitschrift* 64, no. 2 (2009): 4–17, at 5.

31 Massin, *Recherche de Beethoven* (see note 28), 37.

attaining release."[32] This single sentence, inspired by feminist poet Adrienne Rich and repeated in attenuated form in the 1991 book *Feminine Endings*,[33] was arguably the most important exegetic novelty in Beethoven reception over the last fifty years – witness the fierce and lasting controversy it unleashed. Beethoven's canonic status fueled a radical critique of classical music, as allegedly modeled on male sexuality. Eggebrecht would have had trouble dismissing it as part of the *Hülle*, given McClary's targeting the very *Kern* of the masculinist "Beethoven Hero."[34]

An early vehement reaction came from Pieter van den Toorn: "Analogous to Marxism, in which man is reduced to 'economic forces' [...], McClary's feminism reduces him to his sexual needs." He attributed to her a "personal animosity" towards Beethoven which he explained by nothing less than "an aversion for male sexuality."[35] Ruth Solie replied that van den Toorn's "musical formalism" amounted to "providing certain works with immunity to certain sorts of interpretation," and commented "A reader might be tempted to seek refuge in amusement at the exactitude with which his rhetoric enacts the very rage and aggression he says he's unfairly accused of. But there is no such refuge: on this side of the curtain it's not an academic exercise. A female is raped every six minutes in this country [the US]."[36] More than thirty years after its first publication, the passions unleashed by McClary's "horrifying" sentence on the Ninth have yet to abate.

Of course, the erosion of cultural hierarchies was not only the result of gender issues. The critique of "the great divide" between high and low art – a critique that had already begun to undermine the prestige of classical music in the 1960s – became more frequent through the 1970s, and beyond.[37] Yet even Pierre Bourdieu's influential book *La Distinction* of 1979, which portrayed high art as symbolic violence by the upper classes, made classical music the only empirical referent for the general category of "music."[38] In the long run, Beethoven's iconic role in controversies over canon and culture appears as a paradoxical sign of his enduring legacy. A recent example of his capacity to embody contentious views on the politics of culture is this ad for a social program of youth orchestras, displayed in the streets of Paris in the first days of 2020 (SEE PLATE 2, P. 152).

The critique of cultural hierarchies coincided with the oft-lamented aging and downsizing of classical music audiences across the world. Global figures seem not to exist, but sociological inquiries at the national level all point in the same direction, namely downwards. In 2018 only 6 per cent of French people declared having attended a concert of classical music in the last twelve months, and this number was only 2 per cent for people aged 28 or younger.[39] In the US, the surveys conducted since 1982 by the National Endowment for the Arts (NEA) "record a distinct decline in the public's overall participation in classical music."[40] The consumption of recorded music followed a similar curve: while classical music represented 3.5 per cent of record sales in the US in 1988 and 2.8 per cent in 1997,[41] a 2014 survey found this to be 1.4 per cent.[42]

Official figures in France and the US suggest not only the aging of concertgoers whose tastes are reputedly stable during their lifetimes, but also a tendency by some of them to progressively stop listening to classical music altogether. 17.8 per cent of French people born between 1949 and 1958 declared classical music

32 Susan McClary, "Getting Down Off the Beanstalk: The Presence of a Woman's Voice in Janika Vandervelde's *Genesis II*," *Minnesota Composers Forum Newsletter* 1 (January 1987): 4–7, at 7.

33 Susan McClary, *Feminine Endings: Music, Gender and Sexuality* (Minneapolis: University of Minnesota Press, 1991), 128.

34 See Scott G. Burnham, *Beethoven Hero* (Princeton: Princeton University Press, 1995).

35 Pieter C. van den Toorn, "Politics, Feminism, and Contemporary Music Theory," *The Journal of Musicology* 9, no. 3 (1991): 275–99, at 292f.

36 Ruth A. Solie, "What Do Feminists Want? A Reply to Pieter van den Toorn," *The Journal of Musicology* 9, no. 4 (1991): 399–410, at 401, 400, and 409.

37 See Herbert J. Gans, *Popular Culture and High Culture: An Analysis and Evaluation of Taste* (New York: Basic Books, 1974); Andreas Huyssen, *After the Great Divide: Modernism, Mass Culture, Postmodernism* (Bloomington: Indiana University Press, 1986).

38 Pierre Bourdieu, *La Distinction: Critique sociale du jugement* (Paris: Minuit, 1979); in English as *Distinction: A Social Critique of the Judgement of Taste*, trans. Richard Nice (Cambridge, MA: Harvard University Press, 1984).

39 Philippe Lombardo and Loup Wolff, "Cinquante ans de pratiques culturelles en France," Paris, Ministère de la Culture et de la Communication, www.culture.gouv.fr/Sites-thematiques/Etudes-et-statistiques/Publications/Collections-de-synthese/Culture-etudes-2007-2020/Cinquante-ans-de-pratiques-culturelles-en-France-CE-2020-2 (accessed 12 August 2020). See also Stéphane Dorin, "Introduction. Les publics de la musique classique aux avant-postes des transformations de la participation culturelle à l'ère numérique," in *Déchiffrer les publics de la musique classique: Perspectives comparatives, historiques et sociologiques / Unraveling Classical Music Audiences: Historical, Sociological and Comparative Perspectives*, ed. Stéphane Dorin (Paris: Editions des archives contemporaines, 2018), i–xvii.

40 Robert J. Flanagan, "The Search for Symphony Audiences," in *Déchiffrer les publics de la musique classique* (see note 39), 47–66, at 48. See National Endowment for the Arts, "A Decade of Arts Engagement: Findings From the Survey of Public Participation in the Arts, 2002–2012," www.arts.gov/sites/default/files/2012-sppa-feb2015.pdf, 7 (accessed 3 March 2020).

41 Ger Tillekens, "Trends and shifts in U.S. music sales (1997–1998)," www.icce.rug.nl/~soundscapes/VOLUME02/Trends_and_shifts_in_music_sales.shtml (accessed 3 March 2020).

42 "2014 Nielsen Music U.S. Report," www.nielsen.com/wp-content/uploads/sites/3/2019/04/nielsen-2014-year-end-music-report-us-1.pdf (accessed 3 March 2020).

PLATE 2
"Don't let culture become a private club." Advertisement for a social program of youth orchestras, Paris, January 2020. Photograph by Esteban Buch

to be one of their favorite genres in 1973; only 9.4 said so in 2013.[43] In the US, the average number of public classical concerts per year and per person decreased from 3.1 to 2.6 between 2002 and 2012. Nor are these trends likely to be reversed: a recent survey among French teenagers showed only 0.7 per cent spontaneously answering "classical music" to the question, "What is your favorite style of music?"[44]

As this data relates to genres, not composers, it does not identify Beethoven's position in this development. In the 1970s, Mahler's symphonies started challenging Beethoven's as the most frequently performed;[45] today, records of Johann Sebastian Bach's music are more popular than Beethoven's in UK charts of classical music, which are dominated by Andrea Bocelli, André Rieu, and Ludovico Einaudi.[46] On the other hand, in the last six years Beethoven has regularly been either the first or the second most frequently performed composer in classical concerts worldwide, with the Fifth and the *Eroica* towering over the repertoire, as in the good old days of "Beethoven Hero."[47] Beethoven's central position in the classical canon remains sound in 2020, as in 1970, 1927, 1870, and 1845. On the other hand, the hegemonic legitimacy and broad social impact of classical music as a whole – and the music of its most iconic composer – are becoming increasingly a thing of the past.

43 Hervé Glevarec, *La différenciation: Goûts, savoirs et expériences culturelles* (Lormont: Le bord de l'eau, 2019), 243.
44 Esteban Buch, "La musique classique est-elle un genre? Quelques remarques sur les pratiques de catégorisation à l'ère numérique," in *Déchiffrer les publics de la musique classique* (see note 39), 3–14, at 3.
45 See Carl Dahlhaus, *Foundations of Music History*, trans. J. Bradford Robinson (Cambridge: Cambridge University Press, 1983), 157.
46 See "Best Sellers in Classical," www.officialcharts.com; and www.amazon.com/Best-Sellers-Music-Classical/zgbs/music/85 (accessed 19 December 2019).
47 "La musique classique en 2019" and other yearly statistics, https://bachtrack.com (accessed 3 March 2020).

The present Beethoven commemoration is also unprecedented in that the technological mutations, from LPs to CDs to mp3s to streaming, have weakened the stability and preeminence of the musical work (*opus*) as the basic unit for listening to recorded music. The historical construct Lydia Goehr aptly named the "Beethoven Paradigm"[48] might well be slowly coming to an end, at least as the hegemonic Western musical practice. If you searched for "Beethoven" in Spotify the day after his two-hundred-and forty-ninth birthday, the first five answers were the opening movement of the "Moonlight" Sonata, performed by Paul Lewis; *Für Elise,* by Nelly Kokinos; again the opening of the "Moonlight" Sonata, by Louis Lortie; the Allegretto from the Seventh Symphony, conducted by Terry Davies; and the Cavatina from String Quartet, op. 130, by the Danish String Quartet. Except for *Für Elise,* all these pieces are movements from longer works, and they last between three minutes (*Für Elise*) and less than eight minutes (Cavatina), close to the average time of a pop song. In both cases the "Moonlight" movement is, quite traditionally, taken from an album featuring Beethoven piano sonatas, and the Cavatina from an album including the whole of opus 130, together with works by Schnittke and Bach. *Für Elise,* however, is part of a "Beethoven Greatest Hits" album that includes no complete multi-movement work; and the second movement of the Seventh forms part of the soundtrack of the movie *The King's Speech* by Tom Hooper (2010), where, incidentally, it is titled "Speaking unto Nations." And, of course, the fact that some of these pieces belong to albums does not mean that the other pieces on the album are played – quite the contrary, as shown by this very search.

Now the two "Moonlight" adagios add up to more than 65 million hits; *Für Elise* has close to 40 million hits, and the Allegretto over 12 million. The number of versions of the same *Adagio sostenuto* on Spotify includes most historical and recent recordings by famous and less famous pianists, as well as countless easy listening collections entitled "Chill Classical," "Calm Study Music for Studying," "Serenity Time," "Beautiful Classical Music," and so on. Under these and similar guises, Beethoven's music is arguably undergoing a process of partial de-classicization that conflates it with non-classical repertoires in ambient music playlists and other mood management devices – at the cost of being drastically reduced, more than it already was, to a handful of "greatest hits."

In short, "Beethoven" is not likely to disappear from the brains of twenty-first century people – far from it. Yet between 1970 and 2020 the sonic referent of this iconic name has arguably changed. Even if the classical concert still replicates what it was back in the nineteenth century, when Beethoven rose to unanimous acclaim in restricted social circles, nowadays the dominant phenomenology of his music, viewed at a transgenerational and transnational level, has quite different temporal shapes, emotional contents, listening locations, technical channels of dissemination, and arenas for verbal commentary. Thus, Beethoven-the-composer-of-musical-works is being progressively replaced by a globalized audiovisual Beethoven-flux.

48 Lydia Goehr, *The Imaginary Museum of Musical Works: An Essay in the Philosophy of Music* (Oxford: Clarendon Press, 1992), 205–42.

Beethoven at 250

The actual geography of Beethoven admiration is in transition. It might well be that "the future of classical music is in China," since, it is claimed, "[t]o like Beethoven, as everyone is assured, is considered in the large Chinese cities to be modern, and part of a western lifestyle to be imitated."[49] But sources are scarce, beyond Hong Kong and a few other spots,[50] and wishful thinking on this cannot be ruled out.

In 2020, at an international level, governments are not as engaged in the commemoration as they were in 1927, when Vienna became a social theater of high diplomatic significance. Still, some states do promote the Beethoven symbol, starting with the two countries where the composer lived and died. Over the centuries, Austria and Germany have honored "their" great composer, while occasionally claiming that "Beethoven belongs to everyone."[51]

In November 2019, Vienna's mayor Michael Ludwig launched the Beethoven year by declaring that "Ludwig van Beethoven, although born in Bonn, lived among us here for so long, and created so much, that we are perfectly justified in claiming him for ourselves." And also: "Vienna, as a world capital of music, is barely conceivable without Beethoven!"[52] The city of Bonn has also programmed special activities under the banner of "BTHVN2020" – a logo designed after Beethoven's idiosyncratic signature and standing for Bürger (citizen), *Tonkünstler* (composer), Humanist, Visionary, and Nature. The press invited "Beethoven pilgrims" to attend.[53] Things have changed since 1845, when visitors to the Beethoven-Haus chopped off actual bits of stairs and furniture with their own hands as "relics." But the modeling of secular cultural festivities on religious traditions has not disappeared, if only as rhetorical language for cultural tourism. On the other hand, the Beethoven-Haus has given strong impetus to historical research, as witness, among other activities, the exhibition presented in this volume. It is no consolation to think that the crisis of music tourism unleashed by the pandemic might in turn become an object of scholarly research.

The German Federal Minister of Culture, Monika Grütters, declared in November 2019, at the opening of the commemoration: "Ludwig van Beethoven's music touches, inspires, and connects people all over the world. With unparalleled radicality, he revolutionized music and burst the musical boundaries of his age. Today we again stand in need of the visionary power with which he took his stance, both politically and especially in art. His music is a symbol on behalf of the democratic achievements of a united Europe, and against the growing populist cries for isolation and exclusion."[54]

This is a good example of old ideas being recirculated as new. The alleged capacity of Beethoven's music to unite people from all over the world is an allusion to the Ninth Symphony, entrenched in its text and early exegesis. The emphasis on radicalism and revolutionary potential belongs to a later, liberal line of thought that underlined the composer's early interest in the French Revolution. The mention of democratic Europe and the threat of populism address a contemporary situation with roots in the darkest hours of the 1930s.

This, of course, is not only a governmental issue. In recent years, citizens have sung the "Ode to Joy" as spontaneous statements on behalf of democratic

49 "Beloved Worldwide," www.lvbeethoven.de/en/composer-wordlwide/worldwide (accessed 3 March 2020).

50 "South China city to launch celebrations for Beethoven's 250th birthday in 2020," *Global Times*, 18 December 2019, www.globaltimes.cn/content/1173970.shtml (accessed 3 March 2020).

51 See, for instance, the Beethoven 2020 website by the Vienna Symphony Orchestra, www.wienersymphoniker.at/en/news/2019/11/beethoven-2020 (accessed 3 March 2020).

52 "Ludwig van Beethoven ist zwar in Bonn geboren, hat aber hier bei uns so lange gelebt und so viel geschaffen, dass wir ihn gut und gerne für uns vereinnahmen dürfen." "Wien als Welthauptstadt der Musik ist ohne Beethoven schwer vorstellbar!" "Stadt Wien: Start für Beethoven 2020," APA-OTS, 7 November 2019, www.ots.at/presseaussendung/OTS_20191107_OTS0085/stadt-wien-start-fuer-beethoven-2020 (accessed 3 March 2020).

53 Rick Fulker, "A new attraction for Beethoven pilgrims planned in Bonn," *Deutsche Welle*, 27 February 2018, www.dw.com/en/a-new-attraction-for-beethoven-pilgrims-planned-in-bonn/a-42760090 (accessed 3 March 2020).

54 "Ludwig van Beethovens Musik berührt, begeistert und verbindet Menschen überall auf der Welt. Beethoven hat mit unerhörter Radikalität die Musik revolutioniert und die musikalischen Grenzen seiner Zeit ge-sprengt. Wir brauchen auch heute wieder die visionäre Kraft, mit der Beethoven politisch und vor allem künstlerisch Position bezog. Sein Werk ist ein Zeichen für die demokratischen Errungenschaften eines geeinten Europas und gegen das Erstarken populistischer Rufe nach Abschottung und Ausgrenzung." "Kultur-staatsministerin Monika Grütters und Ministerpräsident Armin Laschet stellen Höhepunkte des Beethoven-Jahres 2020 vor," press release 400, 29 November 2019, Die Bundesregierung, www.bundesregierung.de/breg-de/suche/kulturstaatsministerin-monika-gruetters-und-ministerpraesident-armin-laschet-stellen-hoehepunkte-des-beethoven-jahres-2020-vor-1700356 (accessed 3 March 2020).

values, in places like Ukraine during the Maidan revolt (2013), in Mainz to protest xenophobic reactions to the arrival of refugees (2015), and in Paris during the *Nuit Debout* movement (2016). This symbolic potential on behalf of democracy is probably not exhausted, even if it is unpredictable by its very nature. On the other hand, as Grütters implied in another statement, it has a stable rationale in the "Ode to Joy's" status as the European anthem: "Beethoven's entire output stands for values that are understood and shared all over the world. The final movement of his Ninth Symphony has become the European anthem."[55]

By 2022 the people of Europe will have spent fifty years paying royalties to private individuals, including a former Nazi party member and his heirs, in order to collectively celebrate a democratic Europe with Beethoven's music.[56] The revision of this paradoxical situation could be an appropriate "symbol on behalf of the democratic achievements of a united Europe," provided one is willing to go beyond fulsome verbiage. Indeed, the years that separate the two-hundred-fiftieth anniversary of Beethoven's birth from the two-hundredth anniversary of his death, in 2027, look like an appropriate historical moment to break away from this lasting ghost of the Nazi era, a ghost similar to those Mauricio Kagel exorcised fifty years ago in *Ludwig van*.

This would be timely, whether the impact of the 2020 pandemic ends up fueling nationalism, racism, and authoritarianism, or, on the contrary, further unveils their long-term incompatibility with humanity's survival. For the time being, were it not for the coincidence that all this is happening during "his" Jubilee, Beethoven is only one virtual player among many in the bizarre landscape of coronavirus music practices. On the other hand, one might make a case for an analogy between this year's global lockdowns and Beethoven's decades-long experience with deafness. In both cases, though in obviously different ways, sonic interaction appears separated from bodily interaction, and in one way or another, solitude lies at their heart.

Indeed, the painful obligation of social distancing in the everyday life of the composer whose iconic trace is the Heiligenstadt Testament is a key element of his myth, culminating in the notion that his detachment from worldly sounds allowed him to conceive sounds from another world. Even if the precise impact of his hearing impairment on his creativity will likely never be elucidated, this might well be more than a Romantic legend. His canonic status, derived from both the superlative quality of his music and the historical precedence of his cult, had in his deafness a paradoxical core. As a social construct, Beethoven is the canon of all musical canons, and – together with, say, Leonardo or Shakespeare – a lasting model for artistic and literary canons per se. This construct implies simultaneously that he was better than others, as a *primus inter pares,* and different from others, as in the Promethean narrative grounded in his physical singularity. Now that humanity struggles with both the aggravation of old social ailments and the exceptionality of the new public health situation, his "to joy through adversity" motto has an uncanny potential relevance, provided that social conditions allow it to "return to the heart."

But Beethoven affords much more than narratives on resilience. Beyond the heroic style, and beyond the anti-heroic late style, his music offers a broad spectrum of sensorial and intellectual pleasures. And these include the pleasure

55 "Beethovens Gesamtwerk steht für Werte, die auf der ganzen Welt verstanden und geteilt werden. Der letzte Satz aus Beethovens 9. Sinfonie ist zur Europa-Hymne geworden." "250 Jahre Beethoven – Jubiläumsjahr 2020," SWR2, 21 January 2020, www.swr.de/swr2/musik-klassik/Musik-250-Jahre-Beethoven-Jubilaeumsjahr-2020,beethovenjahr-2020-100.html (accessed 3 March 2020).

56 See Esteban Buch, "Beethoven in the Shadows of Berlin: Karajan's European Anthem," *Dissent* 56, no. 4 (2009): 14–17.

of compulsive repetition – even if Freud saw this as leading "beyond the pleasure principle," thus revealing the death drive in every living being.[57] Indeed, critics have sometimes taken issue with the morbid aspect of commemorations, forcing admirers to reply that, in some mysterious, transcendental way, Beethoven is (still) alive. The continuity of life actually plays a role, as canonic works are ritually played not only for audiences already familiar with them, but also for young people for whom they are presumably unknown. That means, by definition, to hand down the old as new. Now, given their average birthdates, many Beethoven lovers are especially vulnerable. If Beethoven after 250 is to remain a cultural figure of the twenty-first century, rather than a name in a mood management playlist, transmitting his full legacy is more urgent than ever.

57 Sigmund Freud, *Beyond the Pleasure Principle* (London and Vienna: The International Psycho-Analytical Press, 1922).

Igor Stravinsky
Souvenir d'une marche boche (1915)

Léon Bakst hadn't exaggerated: when he sent a card to Igor Stravinsky on 17 August 1915, urging him to contribute a piece to an anthology by Edith Wharton (she had sent Stravinsky a similar request five days earlier), he exclaimed "On est dans une bonne compagnie."[1] Indeed, Wharton's anthology, published in 1916,[2] assembled an impressive number of illustrious names among its contributors, from writers of the caliber of Jean Cocteau, Joseph Conrad, Henry James, Maurice Maeterlinck, and William Butler Yeats to visual artists such as Claude Monet, Auguste Renoir, and Auguste Rodin. There were also two composers: Vincent d'Indy and Stravinsky. But there was something special about *The Book of the Homeless:* Wharton, who later won a Pulitzer Prize, compiled her anthology for humanitarian reasons, and the proceeds from the sales went to two aid organizations that she herself had founded for Belgian war orphans and refugees.[3] And just as her book arose from a specific event – the invasion, bombardment, and occupation of neutral Belgium by the German Reich – Stravinsky's contribution, the piano piece *Souvenir d'une marche boche* (dated 1 September 1915), bears witness to the situation at the time (SEE PLATE 1, P. 158).

The piece is little known, probably because it was never published officially during Stravinsky's lifetime (its proper publication had to wait until 1997[4]). Nor did he once mention it in his writings or conversations. When discussed at all, it has generally been dismissed as a superficial *pièce d'occasion* "of small importance."[5] Indeed, at first glance it appears perfectly trivial: it employs only the two simplest harmonic functions (I and V), and even then it is largely dominated by pseudo-harmony, being written in parallel octaves for large stretches at a time (mm. 1–13 and 24–34). It makes do with nothing more than seven rhythmic snippets (and only one in the trio, apart from m. 48), further emphasizing its blatant march rhythm. Its melody, if the term is warranted at all, consists mainly of brief scales and broken triads, all of them perfectly diatonic. And apart from a few accents, there is only one dynamic level: *sempre f.*

However, the essence of the piece is not to be found on its structural surface but in the principle of that surface: its ostentatious triteness. In other words, the trivial nature of the piece can be understood as staged triviality, for it highlights its own reductionism with glaring clarity. Compounding this effect is its restriction to the low register and simplistic accompaniment phrases in the A section, conveying the impression that it is the low *secondo* part of a march originally written for piano four hands, but whose *primo* part has gone missing. In this sense, it is logical to view the piece as a caricature that exposes the typical features of a march by subjecting them to broad-brushed exaggeration. But another essential element of the piece's theatricality is the "framing" of its title, according to which it is not a march *per se* but the memory of a German march,[6] with the national attribution pejoratively couched in the term *boche*. Granted, the *Souvenir* is an occasional piece, and it bears the impress of current political events. Yet any criticism of its artlessness would be wrong, for it would misconstrue the piece as a *marche boche,* mistaking the means for the end, the caricature for what is being caricatured.

1 Léon Bakst, letter card of 17 August 1915 to Igor Stravinsky (Igor Stravinsky Collection, PSS). Edith Wharton's letter of 12 August 1915 to Stravinsky is preserved in the same collection.

2 *The Book of the Homeless (Le Livre des Sans-Foyer)*, ed. Edith Wharton (New York: Charles Scribner's Son, 1916).

3 Wharton's anthology, which was also published in a parallel edition for the British market by Macmillan in London, belongs to a series of similar humanitarian publications issued during the First World War. See Hazel Hutchison, *The War That Used Up Words: American Writers and the First World War* (New Haven: Yale University Press, 2015), 118–60.

4 It appeared in the collection *Stravinsky for Piano: A Collection of Miniatures and Arrangements for Piano Solo and Duet* (London: Boosey & Hawkes, 1997), 2–3.

5 Eric Walter White, *Stravinsky: The Composer and his Works*, 2nd edn. (London: Faber & Faber, 1979), 238. Just how little attention White paid to the work is evident in the fact that his description of the A section refers to "[t]hirty-seven bars of a brash sort of march in C major," mistakenly counting the upbeat as a bar. A no less careless slip found its way into the print of the piece (see note 4): m. 41 gives a second inversion F major chord in the right hand instead of a C major seventh chord.

6 This was pointed out by Glenn Watkins, to whose discussion of this piece I am indebted for many particulars. Glenn Watkins, *Proof through the Night: Music and the Great War* (Berkeley: University of California Press, 2003), 140–45, esp. 140.

PLATE 1

Igor Stravinsky, *Souvenir d'une marche boche* for piano (1915). Facsimile print in *The Book of the Homeless (Le Livre des Sans-Foyer)*, ed. Edith Wharton (New York: Charles Scribner's Son, 1916), p. [52], mm. 14–28

(IGOR STRAVINSKY COLLECTION, PSS)

One of the devices that Stravinsky applies in his parody of crude German militarism is a Beethoven quotation that appears no less than three times: the motif that opens the coda to the last movement of the Fifth Symphony, op. 67 **(SEE EXAMPLE 1)**, occurring in bars 14, 19, and 22.[7] Yet Stravinsky distorts it by omitting the dotted rhythm (which he sets aside for the trio), transposing several notes to other registers (mm. 14 and 19), and turning the target note in bar 20 into an A–to–G suspension, an expressive cliché that adds to the piece's parodic aura. Other parallels to the finale can be discerned: both pieces begin with an ascending triad that halts on the top note and, following an upbeat, returns in stepwise motion to the starting note (albeit on the dominant in Stravinsky); and both reach their next section via a downward scale ending on C (m. 26 in Beethoven, m. 5 in Stravinsky). As for the quotation, Glenn Watkins stresses that Stravinsky did not so much take aim at Beethoven as mock the mindless appropriation of his music in those years.[8] Nonetheless, we might well ask what led him to choose precisely this motif from the finale of the Fifth.

EXAMPLE 1
Ludwig van Beethoven, Symphony No. 5 in C minor, op. 67, movt. 4, bassoon, mm. 320–21

The musical properties of the quoted motif – its fanfare-like triadic melody in C major and its marching rhythm – make it a perfect fit for the *Souvenir*. More than that, the coda of the finale is notorious for alternating between V and I for minutes on end. But most of all, the significance of the finale in the consciousness of French musical culture at that time must be taken into account. Unlike the *topos* of the 'Fate Symphony' that prevailed in the reception of the Fifth in the German-speaking lands – a *topos* drawn basically from the opening movement – in France this popular symphony "was by and large understood from the standpoint of its finale." Corroborative evidence for this can be found in the various nicknames bestowed upon it from the late 1820s: *marche gigantesque, marche colossale, chant de victoire, marche triomphale,* and *marche militaire* are only a few of the epithets that crop up.[9] That these terms were still circulating at the beginning of the twentieth century is shown by their appearance in Jacques-Gabriel Prod'homme's prizewinning and frequently reissued study *Les Symphonies de Beethoven*.[10]

In this light, Stravinsky's motivation for quoting the finale in his caricature is entirely logical. There were probably two reasons for this. For one thing, he bore a grudge against Germany, not only since the outset of the war, but certainly thereafter. Several statements along these lines have come down to us, such as a letter of September 1914 to Bakst in which he writes that his hatred of the Germans is increasing by the hour.[11] For another thing, throughout his life he had a fraught relationship with Beethoven. This was related to the fact that any form of programmatic exegesis or hypertrophic exaltation of music was anathema to his aesthetic way of thinking, particularly in what he considered its "German" variety. In his memoirs, and again in his Harvard lectures, he devoted several pages to this phenomenon and took Beethoven as an example. However, as early as 1913 he opined that Beethoven was, to be sure, a great figure, "but there is too much literary thought in his music."[12] These two grudges could find no better expression than in a letter he wrote to Maurice Delage in 1913 following a performance of Gustav Mahler's Eighth Symphony: "What can I say about the music of this German *'Kolossalwerk'*? [...] It's terrible, my friend! Fancy that for two hours you are made to understand that two times two is four, to the accompaniment of E-flat major performed FFFFF by 800 people. [...] It's gruesome – all this music, these Germans, that forte-fortissimo."[13]

7 Only since Richard Taruskin pointed out the quotation in 1996 has it found an echo among scholars. See Richard Taruskin, *Stravinsky and the Russian Traditions: A Biography of the Works Through* Mavra (Oxford: Oxford University Press, 1996), vol. 2, 1475. Yet Wolfgang Osthoff had already unveiled the quotation eight years earlier in "Symphonien beim Ende des Zweiten Weltkriegs: Strawinsky – Frommel – Schostakowitsch," *Acta Musicologica* 60 (1988): 62–104, esp. 89f.

8 Watkins, *Proof through the Night* (see note 6), 143.

9 Beate Angelika Kraus, *Beethoven-Rezeption in Frankreich: Von ihren Anfängen bis zum Untergang des Second Empire* (Bonn: Beethoven-Haus, 2001), 294 and 298.

10 See Jacques-Gabriel Prod'homme, *Les Symphonies de Beethoven (1800–1827)* (Paris: Delagrave, 1906), 201 and 219–23.

11 See Stephen Walsh, *Stravinsky: A Creative Spring, Russia and France, 1882–1934* (New York: Knopf, 1999), 244–45.

12 "Musical Revolutionary: M. Stravinsky on His Dislike of Opera," *The Daily Mail* (13 February 1913). See also Igor Stravinsky, *Chroniques de ma vie*, vol. 2 (Paris: Denoël et Steele, 1935), 63–68, and idem, *Poetics of Music: In the Form of Six Lessons* (Cambridge, MA: Harvard University Press, 1982), 106–05.

13 "Que dirai-je de la musique de ce 'Kolossalwerk' allemand? [...] C'est terrible mon vieux! Songez que pendant 2 heures on vous fait comprendre que 2 fois 2 font 4 et tout cela accompagner [sic] par un FFFFF de mi b majeur exécuté par 800 personnes. [...] Cet [*sic*] effroyable – tout cela cette musique, ces allemands, ce forte-fortissimo." Igor Stravinsky, letter of 15 December 1913 to Maurice Delage, reproduced in *L'Année 1913: Les formes esthétiques de l'œuvre d'art à la veille de la première guerre mondiale*, ed. Liliane Brion-Guerry, vol. 3, *Manifestes et témoignages* (Paris: Klincksieck, 1973), 329f. See also Walsh, *Stravinsky: A Creative Spring* (see note 11), 223.

In Wharton's anthology, the English man of letters Edmund Gosse reports an incident with German soldiers that he had experienced during a journey through the Reich in 1911, but which was kept secret by everyone involved. An acquaintance offered him a confidential explanation: "We never criticize the Army!" This prompted Gosse to remark that he could only recognize in such conduct the "arrogance and servility" of military rule.[14] Stravinsky probably shared this attitude, and his *Souvenir,* one might say, was a reply to Gosse: if Germans lack all critical awareness of their militarism, it is all the more deserving of mockery and derision. Beethoven served this end perfectly well.

Simon Obert

14 Edmund Gosse, "The Arrogance and Servility of Germany," in *The Book of the Homeless* (see note 2), 101–04, esp. 103–04.

Mauricio Kagel *Ludwig van* (1969–70)

Spiegel: Herr Kagel, your satirical film *Ludwig van* has been, for the most part, misunderstood as an anti-Beethoven film. Instead, you recently let it be known that it's a declaration of love to the composer. What does Beethoven's music mean to you?
Kagel: It means so much to me that I decided to make *Ludwig van* and risk the misunderstandings.[1]

By the time Mauricio Kagel made this statement, his film *Ludwig van* had already been premièred at the Vienna Festival, in May 1970, and televised for the first time by West German Radio (WDR).[2] A short while later, the music periodical *Melos* assembled a selection of West German reviews of the Vienna première.[3] The reactions were mixed. On the one hand, as was to be expected, there were outraged viewers who vented their anger at the predominantly grotesque scenes to such an extent that Kagel was suspected of having instigated the reviews himself. On the other hand, on closer inspection, the film could not simply be read as a bitter exposé of Beethoven marketing strategies run amok, still less as an ornate *héroiade* for a musical forebear. Kagel's musical art-film was far too multi-layered for this, with opportunities for misunderstandings at every turn.

That said, it cannot be assumed that the commission was naïvely given to the wrong man. When the WDR asked Kagel for a contribution to the 1970 Beethoven Bicentennial, the responsible producers must have known not to expect anything conventional. In the mere decade that he had been living in Cologne, Kagel had acquired a reputation as an indomitable free spirit on the contemporary music scene. His previous compositions and films stood out not only for their high-quality craftsmanship, but equally for their experimental, often amusingly critical, and always non-dogmatic approaches. It was presumably not the commission's intention to lure Kagel from this path, particularly as the world of music did not uniformly welcome the Bicentennial with open arms. Kagel met expectations to a tee: in *Ludwig van* he delivered a magnum opus, a manifesto of ambivalent Beethoven veneration that has retained its validity to the present day. It is a skillful tribute and a merry dismantlement all rolled into one.

Strictly speaking, *Ludwig van* is a three-part complex of works, including not only the film but two related works derived from it and bearing the same title: a printed score consisting of photographic reproductions of the film's "Music Room" along with detailed performance instructions, and an LP recording devised and produced by Kagel himself in the spirit of this performance concept.[4] The rich body of sources for *Ludwig van* in the Mauricio Kagel Collection captures in great detail the various stages in the gestation of all three parts: verbal sketches for underlying thematic ideas and procedures, documents on the choice of source material, a synopsis, several copies of the script and other production materials for the film, a great many notes for the recording, and documents on the performance score, augmented with all manner of photographs and audio material.[5] But the main focus of Kagel's

1 "Spiegel: Herr Kagel, Ihr satirischer Film 'Ludwig van' ist größtenteils als Anti-Beethoven-Film mißverstanden worden, aber er ist vielmehr eine Liebeserklärung an den Komponisten, wie Sie neuerlich zu verstehen gegeben haben. Was bedeutet Ihnen das Werk Beethovens? / Kagel: Es bedeutet mir so viel, daß ich beschloß, 'Ludwig van' zu drehen und die Mißverständnisse in Kauf zu nehmen." Mauricio Kagel, "Beethovens Erbe ist die moralische Aufrüstung: Ein Spiegel-Gespräch," *Der Spiegel*, no. 37 (7 September 1970): 195–98, at 195. This interview with Felix Schmidt was reprinted in Mauricio Kagel, *Tamtam: Monologe und Dialoge zur Musik*, ed. Felix Schmidt (Munich: Piper, 1975), 77–86, at 77.

2 The film was given its first public screening in the Vienna Künstlerhauskino on 28 May 1970 as part of the Vienna Festival's "Arena 70" studio program. The initial broadcast on WDR took place four days later, on 1 June 1970.

3 "Kagel und der 200. Geburtstag Beethovens," with reviews by Joachim Kaiser (*Süddeutsche Zeitung*), Hilde Spiel (*Frankfurter Allgemeine Zeitung*), and Gerhard Brunner (*Die Welt*), *Melos* 37, no. 9 (1970): 365–68. See also Beate Kutschke, "The Celebration of Beethoven's Bicentennial in 1970: The Antiauthoritarian Movement and Its Impact on Radical Avant-garde and Postmodern Music in West Germany," *The Musical Quarterly* 93, nos. 3–4 (2010): 560–615; and Michelle Ziegler, "Rettungsversuch im Jubiläumsjahr: Mauricio Kagels Aufarbeitung der Beethoven-Rezeption in der *Ludwig van*-Werkgruppe (1970)," in *Rund um Beethoven: Interpretationsforschung heute*, ed. Thomas Gartmann and Daniel Allenbach (Schliengen: Argus, 2019), 465–75.

4 Mauricio Kagel, *Ludwig van:* film (Cologne: WDR, 1969–70); score (London: Universal Edition, 1970; UE 14931); recording (Hamburg: Deutsche Grammophon Gesellschaft, 1970; DGG 2530 014).

5 For an initial overview, see the provisional description of *Ludwig van* sources preserved in the Mauricio Kagel Collection (PSS) in Knut Holtsträter, *Mauricio Kagels musikalisches Werk: Der Komponist als Erzähler, Medienarrangeur und Sammler* (Cologne: Böhlau, 2010), 131–41.

engagement with Beethoven was undoubtedly the film – not the first, but surely the most significant example of his consummate mastery of what, for a composer, is an unusual métier.[6]

The film's overall form cannot be retraced in Kagel's script, where the scenes and shots are arranged, not in the chronological order of the film, but according to extrinsic production conditions and participants. This probably explains why he wrote down the "Reihenfolge" (sequence of scenes) in a two-page manuscript as a table of contents, though minor departures in Part II of the finished film imply the existence of a draft before the final cut (SEE PLATES AND TABLES, PP. 164–67). The pages reveal a division into six "acts," each represented technically by two reels of film. In addition, the little slash at the end of Act 3 marks the bipartite subdivision of the film's contents. Part I is preceded by a prologue, the "Statement Wewerka." Here the visual artist Stefan Wewerka, dressed in a bathrobe and shaving, mumbles about the impending "Beethoven anniversary business ... this Beethoven bum-bum-bum-business ... this Beethoven bumsis, every 2000 years this bumsis [*Bumserei* – an indelicate German slang word for fornication]." This is followed by an initial television announcement: "From the heart, may it go to the heart." Now comes Part I of the film (Acts 1–3), assembled from a frame story (Beethoven revisiting the town of his birth, Bonn, and the local Beethoven House) together with the artistically reworked rooms and situations he encounters in the course of his visit. Rather than a historicizing setting, the scenes were time-shifted, with Bonn appearing as it was in 1969, the year the film was shot. Nor is Beethoven visible from the outside, but only in the eye of the beholder; occasional pans reveal such historical emblems as buckle shoes, velvet knee breeches, and lace oversleeves, all worn by the cameraman Rudolf Körösi. The gaze of the historical figure is thus identified with the subjective camera.

This frame story is discarded in Part II (Acts 4–6). Now the action is interspersed with sporadic television announcements, largely delivered by elderly, no longer telegenic male and female announcers, with sometimes more, sometimes less relevance to the surrounding scenes. This invariably invokes associations with "television," likewise establishing a sort of frame. In between, we are shown (to maintain the metaphor) all manner of "broadcasts" related to Beethoven or his historical impact (SEE TABLE, P. 165).

Structurally, Part II thus resembles Part I, where the freely designed scenic waystations are likewise set apart from the frame story by various degrees of abstraction and association. In Part I, these waystations are the rooms of a surreal Beethoven House, preceded by the quasi-documentary scenes "Arrival Train," "Bonn Marketplace," the "Electrola" pressing plant, and customers sampling records in the "Record Shop" (Act 1, Reel 1). The rooms conjure up worlds of artistic association, followed by a return to purported "Reality" with the more poetic scenes in the park and on the Rhine steamship (Act 3, Reels 5 and 6). However, in the tour of the Beethoven House, the frame story is tightly linked with the interior scenes, in that the perspective of the subjective camera is repeatedly revealed to be that of Beethoven the visitor, led into the picture either by hand gestures and eye contact from the museum guide, or by reflections and intrusions of costumed hands or legs. While the reception in the Beethoven House by the museum guide was filmed at the original location, the following rooms were arranged elsewhere by the participating artists in accordance with their personal aesthetic (SEE TABLE, P. 167).

The alienation procedures Kagel employed for the film's soundtrack are reflected to some extent by the wallpaper in the Music Room: the point of departure for both the musical arrangement and the visible wallpaper collage

6 On this and Kagel's other films see Mauricio Kagel, *Das filmische Werk I*, ed. Werner Klüppelholz and Lothar Prox (Cologne: DuMont, 1985), with special reference to *Ludwig van* on 87–98. Still photographs can also be found in Dieter Schnebel, *Mauricio Kagel: Musik, Theater, Film* (Cologne: DuMont, 1970), 285–88, and Werner Klüppelholz, *Mauricio Kagel: 1970–1980* (Cologne: DuMont, 1981), 81–83.

is always Beethoven's music, dissected, reassembled, disfigured, and warped. The choice of compositions – mainly familiar piano sonatas or excerpts from the Ninth Symphony, the *Leonore* Overture No. 3, and other pieces – deliberately toys with recognition and alienation. Many of the extracted and fragmented motifs, passages, or snippets were reorchestrated for a special ad hoc "Gesamtdeutsches Kammerorchester" (a sort of salon orchestra), prerecorded, and precisely edited by Kagel to match the action in the film. This approach finds its visual correlative in the Music Room, where at first isolated notes, chords, and motivic fragments are both seen and heard simultaneously until sound and image go separate ways and become increasingly asynchronous.

In later scenes, the film montages and musical montages less obviously coincide. Yet even here, at deeper structural levels, music-based editing procedures remain in force. They follow different modes of synchronicity, from audio-visual congruence to various degrees of shifts and delays to contradictions and, finally, to a complete disconnect between visible image and audible music.[7] The result is disconcerting, often amusing, and in some scenes highly provocative. In the "Elly Ney Recital," for example, the opening of the "Waldstein" Sonata, op. 53, is buried after a few bars beneath the recklessly off-key ensemble arrangement of the same passage until, in the end, all that remains are the chords of the opening bars, endlessly repeated. The grotesquely exaggerated film figure initially displays her exalted pianism; later we see her smoking a cigarette, then drinking milk through a straw, while her gray hair spills over the instrument. Much the same happens in the coda-like final scene, where, to the unbroken repetition of the same opening chords of opus 53, we see pictures of zoo animals, gradually permeated visually and overlaid acoustically by the Prisoners' Chorus from *Fidelio* and the inevitable "Ode to Joy".

With these clearly provocative final sections in mind, it comes as no surprise in retrospect that *Ludwig van* kindled extremely defensive reactions from sections of the public. However, the film was not intended exclusively to provoke; it also ran through many possible ways of commemorating Beethoven, some of them quite quotidian, with multi-layered commentary and sometimes a high artistic impulse. True, the visual surface usually forces the grotesque into the foreground; but the broad range of themes, the aesthetic transformations, and the sophisticated techniques of editing, montage, and synchronization between picture track and soundtrack prevent the film from being considered a simple spoof. Beneath the surface, the seeming nonsense proves to be a thorough dissection of the world of reception as it really exists, in all its media and touristic manifestations. Once we accept Kagel's invitation to view the sets empathetically with the eyes of the time-travelling Beethoven, we take an active, personified part in the grotesqueries, where what is shown invariably *seems* but never *is* real. In this game of alienated reality, the participating artists – including Joseph Beuys, Robert Filliou, and Dieter Roth – were chosen not so as to enhance the film's prestige, but to involve leading figures from the then current artistic movements of object art, happening, and fluxus, and thereby to incorporate their approaches. These movements likewise sought new ways of examining the relation between everyday life, everyday objects, and everyday events in and by means of art. This type of art, too, interrogates contexts of meaning, using the resources of the prevailing or revealed "non-sense." Since it does so within its own métier, it undermines that very métier, and thus, in the final analysis, itself. Kagel, too, was especially fond of walking just this sort of tightrope.

Matthias Kassel

7 See Knut Holtsträter, "Kompositionsweisen in Mauricio Kagels filmischer Arbeit zu *Ludwig van*, dargestellt an der *Handschuhsequenz* und dem *Musikzimmer*," in *"Alte" Musik und "neue" Medien*, ed. Jürgen Arndt and Werner Keil (Hildesheim: Olms, 2003), 56–103, esp. 87–94. See also Kagel's description of the procedures in conversation with Karl Faust, the producer of the DGG recording, first published on the sleeve of the recording (see note 4); reprinted in the preface to the Universal Edition score (see note 4), 5–6, and as "Zu 'Ludwig van'," in *Beethoven '70* (Frankfurt am Main: Fischer, 1972), 56–61.

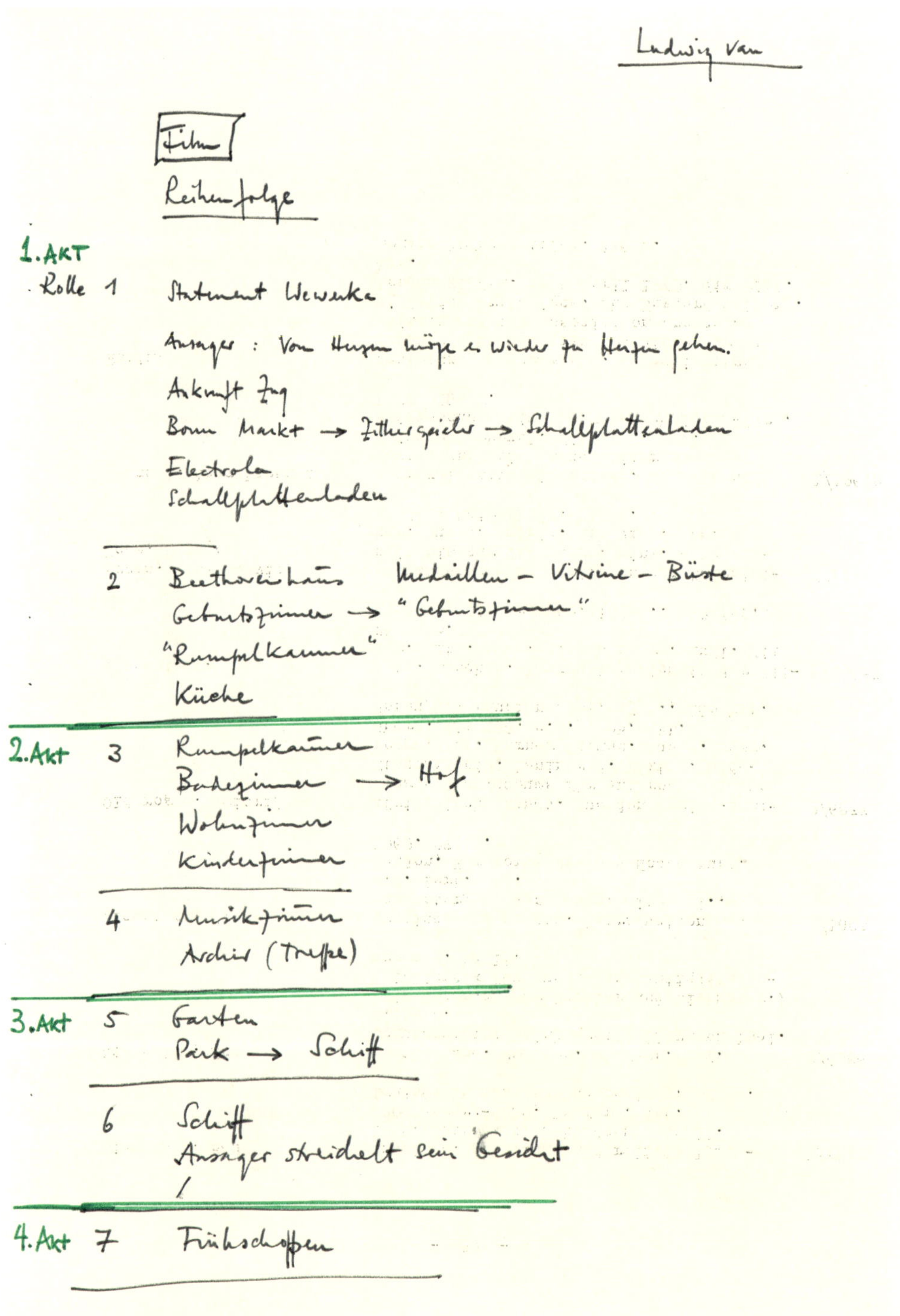
Ludwig van

Film

Reihenfolge

1. AKT

Rolle 1 Statement Wewerka

Ansager: Von Herzen möge es wieder zu Herzen gehen.

Ankunft Zug

Bonn Markt → Zitherspieler → Schallplattenladen

Electrola

Schallplattenladen

2 Beethovenhaus Medaillen – Vitrine – Büste

Geburtszimmer → "Geburtszimmer"

"Rumpelkammer"

Küche

2. Akt 3 Rumpelkammer

Badezimmer → Hof

Wohnzimmer

Kinderzimmer

4 Musikzimmer

Archiv (Treppe)

3. Akt 5 Garten

Park → Schiff

6 Schiff

Ansager streichelt sein Gesicht

/

4. Akt 7 Frühschoppen

PLATE 1
Mauricio Kagel, *Ludwig van: Ein Bericht*, film (1969–70). Sequence ("Reihenfolge") of scenes, fair copy, p. 1
(MAURICIO KAGEL COLLECTION, PSS)

Approx. timeline Start of scene	Transcription Sections (Kagel)	Transcription Scene titles (Kagel)	Notes on contents of scenes
00:00:00	Act 1, Reel 1	Statement Wewerka	Actor: Stefan Wewerka
00:00:53		Announcer: "From the heart, may it go to the heart"	
00:01:02		Arrival Train	"Bonn" station
00:02:33		Bonn Marketplace → Zither Player → Record Shop	Tour of Bonn
00:05:36		Electrola	LP production
00:07:45		Record Shop	Listening booths with customers
00:08:10	[Act 1, Reel] 2	Beethoven House Medals – Showcase – Bust	Path to Beethoven House
00:11:20		Birth Room → "Birth Room"	Beethoven House
00:11:54		"Storage Room"	Beethoven House
00:13:00 00:13:49		Kitchen	Designer and actor: Joseph Beuys Pseudo Beethoven House; insertion: title sequence
00:16:28	Act 2, [Reel] 3	Storage Room	Pseudo Beethoven House
00:16:33		Bathroom → Courtyard	Designer and actor: Dieter Roth (aka Diter Rot) Pseudo Beethoven House
00:22:04		Living Room	Design: Ursula Burghardt Pseudo Beethoven House
00:24:30		Children's Room	Design: Stefan Wewerka Pseudo Beethoven House
00:25:13	[Act 2, Reel] 4	Music Room	Design: Mauricio Kagel after an idea by Jiří Kolář Pseudo Beethoven House
00:32:18		Archive (staircase)	Design: Robert Filliou Pseudo Beethoven House
00:34:12	Act 3, [Reel] 5	Garden	Design: Ursula Burghardt after an idea by Bazon Brock Pseudo Beethoven House
00:36:50		Park → Ship	Path to Rhine
00:38:02	[Act 3, Reel] 6	Ship	Rhine steamship "Cecilie"
00:44:24		Announcer caresses his face	Mute announcer
		/	
00:45:29	Act 4, [Reel] 7	Pre-Lunch Gathering	Werner Höfer, Mauricio Kagel, Heinz-Klaus Metzger, José Montes, Victor Staub, Otto Tomek

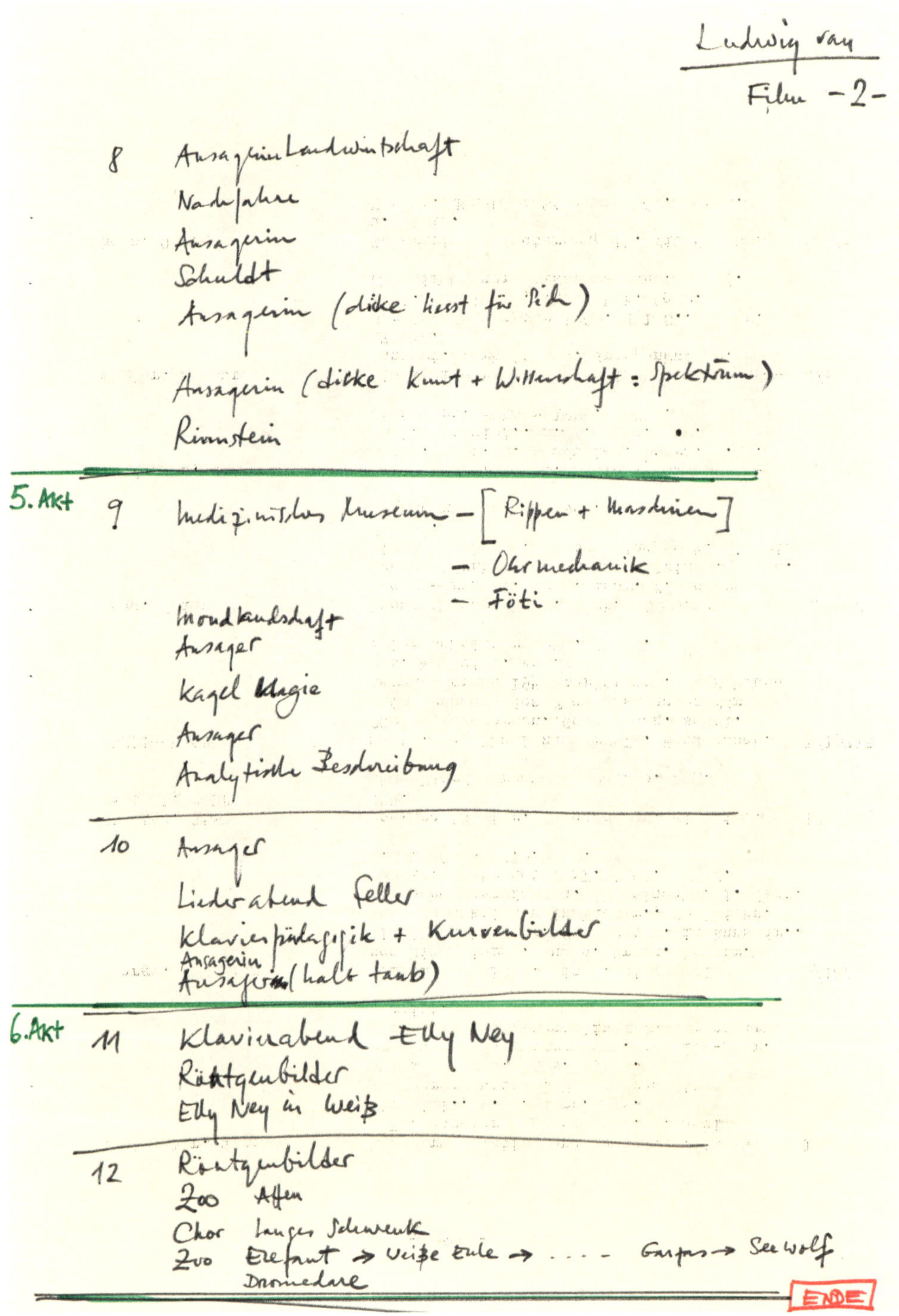

PLATE 2
Mauricio Kagel, *Ludwig van: Ein Bericht*, film (1969–70). Sequence ("Reihenfolge") of scenes, fair copy, p. 2
(MAURICIO KAGEL COLLECTION, PSS)

00:55:20	[Act 4, Reel] 8	Female Announcer Agriculture	recte: male announcer, back announcement of pre-lunch gathering
00:55:43		Descendent	Descendent in the field
00:58:48		Female Announcer	"ignoble frailty ..."
00:59:04		Schuldt	Actor and speech: Herbert Schuldt
01:00:29		[Glove Sequence]	[Object actions; not in Kagel's "sequence of scenes"]
01:01:58		Female Announcer (fat lady reading to herself)	Announcer reads silently
01:02:15		[Continuation of Glove Sequence]	[Object actons; not in Kagel's "sequence of scenes"]
01:02:30		Female Announcer (fat lady art + science = spectrum)	Announcer now synchronous
01:02:37		Gutter	Cigarette butts washed into gutter

01:02:59	Act 5, [Reel] 9	Medical Museum - [ribs + machines] - ear mechanism - foetuses	Model actions
01:04:35		Lunar Landscape	Model action: moon with German federal eagle
		Announcer	[not in film]
		Kagel Magic	[not in film]
		Announcer	[not in film]
		Analytic Description	[not in film]

01:04:47	[Act 5, Reel] 10	Announcer	"The world has lost its innocence ..."
01:04:52		Feller Song Recital	Carlos Feller sings "In questa tomba oscura ..."
01:06:57		Piano Teaching + Graphs	"Laboratory" action with wired pianist (Klaus Lindemann)
01:12:20		Female Announcer	"and with this, German Television ends this evening's broadcasts..."
01:12:34		[Prop Sequence]	[Object actions; not in Kagel's "sequence of scenes"]
01:13:58		Female Announcer (half deaf)	recte: male announcer with hearing aid, "From the heart, may it go to the heart ..."

01:14:14	Act 6, [Reel] 11	Elly Ney Piano Recital	Performance by "Elly Ney" (Klaus Lindemann)
01:18:41		X-Ray Photographs	Series of x-ray photographs
01:20:12		Elly Ney in White	Continuation of "Elly Ney"

	[Act 6, Reel] 12	X-Ray Photographs	[not in film; see Reel 11]
01:22:16		Zoo Monkeys	Chorus, "Seid umschlungen, Millionen ...", with scenes at zoo
01:24:08		Chorus, long pan	Chorus in studio
01:24:40		Zoo Elephant → White Owl → ... Garzas [Span. heron] → Wolffish Dromedaries	Scenes at zoo
01:28:56	[END]		Abrupt ending, final credits

Louis Andriessen
De negen symfonieën van Beethoven (1970)

With *De negen symfonieën van Beethoven,* scored for "promenade orchestra and ice-cream vendor's bell," the Dutch composer Louis Andriessen (b. 1939) was not intent on paying obeisance to the great master. Woven into his barely ten-minute conflation of the nine Beethoven symphonies is a series of quotations, usually verbatim, interspersed with snippets from other music, including the *Internationale,* the Dutch national anthem, and passages in the jazz, pop, and rock idioms, marked at several junctures by the urgent clinging of an ice-cream vendor's bell.[1] The work is full of humor while standing in close rapport with Andriessen's aesthetic background at the time.

After studying at the Royal Conservatory of The Hague, Andriessen spent two important periods of study with Luciano Berio between 1962 and 1965. One basic attitude that he developed then would remain valid for the whole of his subsequent career: precise craftsmanship combined with non-dogmatic stylistic open-mindedness. This attitude found expression particularly in *Anachrony I* for orchestra (1965–66), a collage of quotations and stylistic allusions from Bach to Stravinsky and salon music.[2] Unlike Berio's *Sinfonia* (1968–69), where Mahler's Second Symphony forms a frame of reference for interpolated material from other composers, *Anachrony I,* a work manifestly dedicated to Charles Ives, combines quotations and allusions without reference and grants free rein to changes of style. According to the composer himself, this was crucial in order to depict the heterogeneity of the many-layered music of the time. The piece contains "too many styles to have a style of its own. That is not, however, the purpose of *Anachrony I*. It is much more a mirror, in which the musical reality of today is reflected."[3]

Viewed in this light, *De negen symfonieën* is more than just a musical prank: it continues this de-hierarchization in the form of a tribute. As Stephen Loy has shown, Andriessen, after first testing the collage with a tape compilation of available LP recordings, proceeded several times using the same principle: the quotations, which appear in the chronological order of Beethoven's originals, are first imperceptibly manipulated, then increasingly distorted and combined with unexpected quotations.[4] For example, in the introductory passages, taken from the opening movement of the First Symphony, the harmonies are first tinged with dissonances, then followed by longer excerpts from the original, minimally displaced. The alterations intensify with the material from the third movement of the Second Symphony (rehearsal no. 4, m. 47),[5] which is rhythmically redefined, expanded with dissonances, and followed by material from the opening movement of the *Eroica* (rehearsal no. 6, m. 88), leading to a jazzy passage in 4/4 time derived from it (rehearsal no. 7, m. 102). The next *Eroica* quotation is interrupted by the first ringing of the ice-cream vendor's bell, after which the section from the First Symphony reappears in the manner of a recapitulation (rehearsal no. 8, m. 133), unexpectedly followed by the iconic opening motif of the Fifth (before rehearsal no. 9, m. 124). The appearance of this motif again activates the bell – evidently a "warning signal" announcing that the chronological order of the Beethoven quotations has been violated (SEE PLATE 1, P. 171). Similar procedures occur with the manipulation of

1 The structure of the collage is decoded in Stephen Loy, "Music, Activism and Tradition: Louis Andriessen's *Nine Symphonies of Beethoven*," *Context* 34 (2009): 15–34.

2 See Yayoi Uno Everett, *The Music of Louis Andriessen* (Cambridge: Cambridge University Press, 2006), 46–49.

3 Louis Andriessen, "*Anachrony I* and Charles Ives," in *An Ives Celebration*, ed. H. Wiley Hitchcock and Vivian Perlis (Urbana: University of Illinois Press, 1977), 227. Available with different wording as an introduction to the work on the Boosey & Hawkes website at www.boosey.com/cr/music/Louis-Andriessen-Anachronie-I/5163 (accessed 13 March 2020).

4 See Loy, "Music, Activism and Tradition" (see note 1), 20–23. The descriptions below can also be retraced in Loy. I wish to thank Evert de Cock (Amsterdam), the custodian of Andriessen's sound archive, for providing a copy of the tape collage.

5 References relate to the printed edition: Louis Andriessen, *De negen symfonieën van Beethoven voor promenade-orkest en ijscobel* (Amsterdam: Donemus, 1970, new edn. 2020, D 03407).

the Fourth and Fifth Symphonies, transmuted in combination with the *Internationale* and the national anthem. Materials from the Sixth and Seventh lead to popular song forms, and the Eighth is followed by the Overture to Rossini's *Barber of Seville* (rehearsal no. 25, m. 340). Finally, in the madcap ending, Andriessen recasts the "Ode to Joy" melody from Beethoven's Ninth into a driving rock passage, even repeating it a half-step higher in typical pop fashion. The piece then comes to a striking close with several tutti chords.

Written for the final concert of the Holland Festival, *De negen symfonieën* was premièred at the Amsterdam Concertgebouw on 9 July 1970 by an ad hoc "promenade orchestra" under the baton of Gijsbert Nieuwland. Also featured on the remarkably diverse program were classical lieder, chamber music, "organ pop," South American folk music, ragas, and much else.[6] As Andriessen's expertly crafted collage not only convinced music connoisseurs but attained a high level of fun, its success was assured, and the composer was amply celebrated after the performance. But his own opinion went along different emotional tracks: the success, he said, was a sign "that I was completely on the wrong way, and that made me sit on the couch for about a year, rethinking the sense of composing."[7]

To understand his reaction, we need to look at the cultural-political situation in Amsterdam at the time. The colorful final concert of the Holland Festival was not simply a merry get-together of motley musicians, but the expression of a cultural movement that for years had demanded the opening of cultural life to less well-established currents. As in many European cities, Amsterdam was in turmoil in 1968; several protest actions by the student movement took the form of interdisciplinary happenings with a large element of fun, and were, at root, directed against the establishment and its outdated institutions.[8] In the realm of music, their target was the Concertgebouw and its orchestra, representing élite bourgeois culture as a whole. The object of the critique was, first, its conservative programming, and second, the institution of the orchestra itself, which, with its authoritarian hierarchical structure, seemed out of tune with the times. Accordingly, efforts had begun in the music scene to replace the "conductor-centric" hierarchy with more democratic interacting structures and to loosen the programming policy by including pop genres, jazz, and improvisation, thereby dissolving the sharp distinction between "high-brow" and "low-brow" culture.

In the process, a group of composers came to the fore who were later known as "The Five" *(de vijf)*: Andriessen, Reinbert de Leeuw, Misha Mengelberg, Peter Schat, and Jan van Vlijmen. They had met while studying at the Royal Conservatory of The Hague and reconvened in Amsterdam in the mid-1960s. The Five, either singly or collectively, took part in various actions with the aim of renewing musical life. Their efforts were not merely abstract: for example, they demanded that Bruno Maderna, a conductor deeply committed to contemporary music, be installed at the Concertgebouw Orchestra alongside Bernard Haitink. In the end, their lobbying work failed to penetrate this solid institution, and in November 1969 they vented their frustration by obstructing a Concertgebouw concert – an event known as the *Notenkrakersactie*.[9] Shortly thereafter they organized "inclusive concerts" that presented, free of charge, a very wide range of musical genres in informal settings. That the cultural-political stances of these concerts also coincided with the aesthetic leanings of all five composers can be seen in their collective composition *Reconstructie*, a large-scale musico-theatrical action mounted in the same year and combining Che Guevara, Mozart, jazz and pop, improvisation, dance, and other stage activities.[10]

6 See Ernst Vermeulen, "Holland Festival 1970 en de Notenkrakers," *Ons Erfdeel* 14 (1970–71): 143–45, available online at www.dbnl.org/tekst/_ons003197101_01/_ons003197101_01_0038.php#38 (accessed 20 March 2020).

7 Louis Andriessen, quoted from Loy, "Music, Activism and Tradition" (see note 1), 31. See also Robert Adlington, *Louis Andriessen:* De Staat (Aldershot: Ashgate, 2004), 22.

8 See Robert Adlington, *Composing Dissent: Avant-garde Music in 1960s Amsterdam* (New York: Oxford University Press, 2013), 5–7, and idem, *Louis Andriessen:* De Staat (see note 7), 10–20.

9 The term *Notenkraker* is a double pun on the Dutch word for "nutcracker," which can also mean "note cracker" or "note squatter." On the *Notenkrakersactie* see Louis Andriessen, *The Art of Stealing Time*, ed. Mirjam Zegers (Todmorden, Lancs.: Arc Music, 2002), 36–37, and Rudy Koopmans, "On Music and Politics: Activism of Five Dutch Composers," *Key Notes* 4 (1976): 19–31.

10 See Adlington, *Louis Andriessen:* De Staat (see note 7), 16–20, and idem, "'A sort of *guerrilla*': Che at the Opera," *Cambridge Opera Journal* 19, no. 2 (2007): 167–93.

As a collage, Andriessen's *De negen symfonieën* thus coincided with the aim of de-hierarchizing the levels of music. On the other hand, in its form of presentation, it was the work of a single composer to be played by an orchestra rigorously in accordance with the written page, and thus fell short of the claim to democratize the production of music. In this respect, Andriessen and his comrades-in-arms in *Reconstructie* had already gone one step further, and the rousing applause that greeted *De negen symfonieën* seemed to him like a bad omen. The conclusions he drew led him, on the one hand, to take up socio-political topics (e.g. in *De Staat*, 1972–76), and, on the other, to strike out on new paths of collective music-making with his grassroots ensemble De Volharding and the like-named composition of 1972. *De negen symfonieën* marked the turning point. Beethoven himself, however, was not to blame:

"So it was [...] certainly a kind of criticism, not toward Beethoven himself, because from the first to the last minute of my life, I admired the composer. Almost nothing wrong with the guy, except that I worry about his sense of humour [...]. [T]he piece was not criticizing Beethoven, but was criticizing the bourgeois concertgoer or concert. The whole situation of the normal symphony orchestra concert. And that was very evident in all the things I did at that time."[11]

Nevertheless, for a very long time thereafter, Andriessen avoided the symphony orchestra as a medium for his music.

Matthias Kassel

PLATE 1 (OPPOSITE)
Louis Andriessen, *De negen symfonieën van Beethoven voor promenade-orkest en ijscobel* (1970). Draft score, p. 5
(LOUIS ANDRIESSEN COLLECTION, PSS)

11 Louis Andriessen, quoted from Loy, "Music, Activism and Tradition" (see note 1), 34.

pec: yscobel
lunga
inzet
G.P. 2
5e symfonie
1e maat
2e maat
dimi-nuendo teken toevoegen
12
inzet
IVe Symfonie (pag 5)
Allegro
G.P. 2
lunga
13 alles verder als Beethoven
crescendo poco a poco
1e violen
2e violen
(3e maat pag 8)
4e maat
(3e maat)
4e maat (etc)
maat 3
maat 4
1e V
2e V
m 3
4
maat 5
maat 6
maat 7
als Beethoven
BEHALVE:
molto cresc
trombones a3
hoorns a4
trompetten 2 a3
flatterzunge
molto cresc.
attacca volgende pag.
-5-

Luciano Berio "Amores" (early 1970s)

In the early 1970s Luciano Berio (1925–2003) made plans for a music theater project, "Amores," in which he envisaged a personification of Beethoven.[1] However, this latter was to be decontextualized and reduced to an "object": in the setting of an amusement park, where culture and its symbols are treated as merchandise, Berio sketched a stylized icon of a vulgar person offering "burps for sale" who must be impersonated by an "actor who looks like Beethoven or Wagner" (SEE PLATE 1). Does Beethoven, then, become a theatrical symbol to be desecrated, or an icon of a supposed cultural community to denounce in an extreme way an unstoppable process of the commercialization of art? The few extant traces of this unfinished project do not allow for the provision of an unambiguous answer. Nevertheless, some thoughts can be advanced by observing, in a broader context, the various footprints Beethoven and his music left on Berio's path.

On the terrain of composition, nothing allows us to speak of forms of "anxiety": on the musical horizon, or rather, Berio's existential horizon, Beethoven was simply a permanent presence. All the reasons for this "unconditional presence" are listed in a text on Beethoven written in 1998:

"… because his spirit is always within us, even when we can no longer discern (recognize, know, see) it or when it is transformed in its opposite or in something completely different and new … because he was the first to experiment (try, explore, apply, venture into) the dialectics of development through conflict … because his music needs nothing, not even memory, it is eternally (always) there, hidden in every fold of our musical experience (being) … because the broadness of his vision, the novelty of his thought, the highness of his ideas have placed in our hands a unique tool of intellectual awareness … because his spirit has generated forms, forms that are the creative process, not its mere container, forms born out of structure, forms overpowered (overwhelmed) by structure, forms inexistent as such … because with him the (friendly) dialogue between polyphony and harmony was interrupted forever, giving birth to other modes of speech where all is transformed and new dignity is acquired … because Beethoven was deaf to the superfluous … because."[2]

Among the many reasons given by Berio, however, one wonders whether the real answer to the ineffable question "why Beethoven?" may be hidden not in the spoken, but rather in the unspoken, that is, in each of those ellipses which, like a "refrain of the inexpressible," emerge between one answer and another. Composers' statements must always be interpreted in a contrary light and recalling the invitation "à la prudence" suggested by Gérard Genette:[3] prudence that, in the case of Berio, must be multiplied, given the almost total absence of Beethovenian "footsteps" in his compositional endeavors. Rather, Beethoven's presence can be seen in Berio's intense activity of analyzing and studying works by and about Beethoven.[4] And it is found in his essays and lectures and not least in the radio and television broadcasts he conceived. Of special interest among the latter is the series *C'è musica & musica* (RAI, 1972),[5] which may be considered to be one of the most successful music broadcasting projects in the history of Italian television, and which originated around the same time as "Amores."

1 "Amores" is an unfinished project undertaken jointly by Berio and Edoardo Sanguinetti (text) and was commissioned by the Holland Festival. For more information on "Amores" see Ute Brüdermann, *Das Musiktheater von Luciano Berio* (Frankfurt am Main: Lang, 2007), 135–43.

2 Luciano Berio, "Beethoven," original in English (electronic Word file), signed and saved on 28 July 1998. A printout of the text, then apparently unpublished, is now at the PSS. Published in Italian translation in Luciano Berio, *Scritti sulla musica*, ed. Angela Ida De Benedictis (Turin: Einaudi, 2013), 351 (with notes at 532).

3 Gérard Genette, *Seuils* (Paris: Édition du Seuil, 1987), 354.

4 In Berio's library, maintained at the Radicondoli residence, approximately thirty volumes on Beethoven are conserved, as well as almost the entire *opera omnia*.

5 The entire series (12 episodes) is now available in the box set *C'è musica & musica*, 2 DVDs with the supplementary volume *Una polifonia di suoni e immagini*, ed. Angela Ida De Benedictis (Milan: Feltrinelli, 2013).

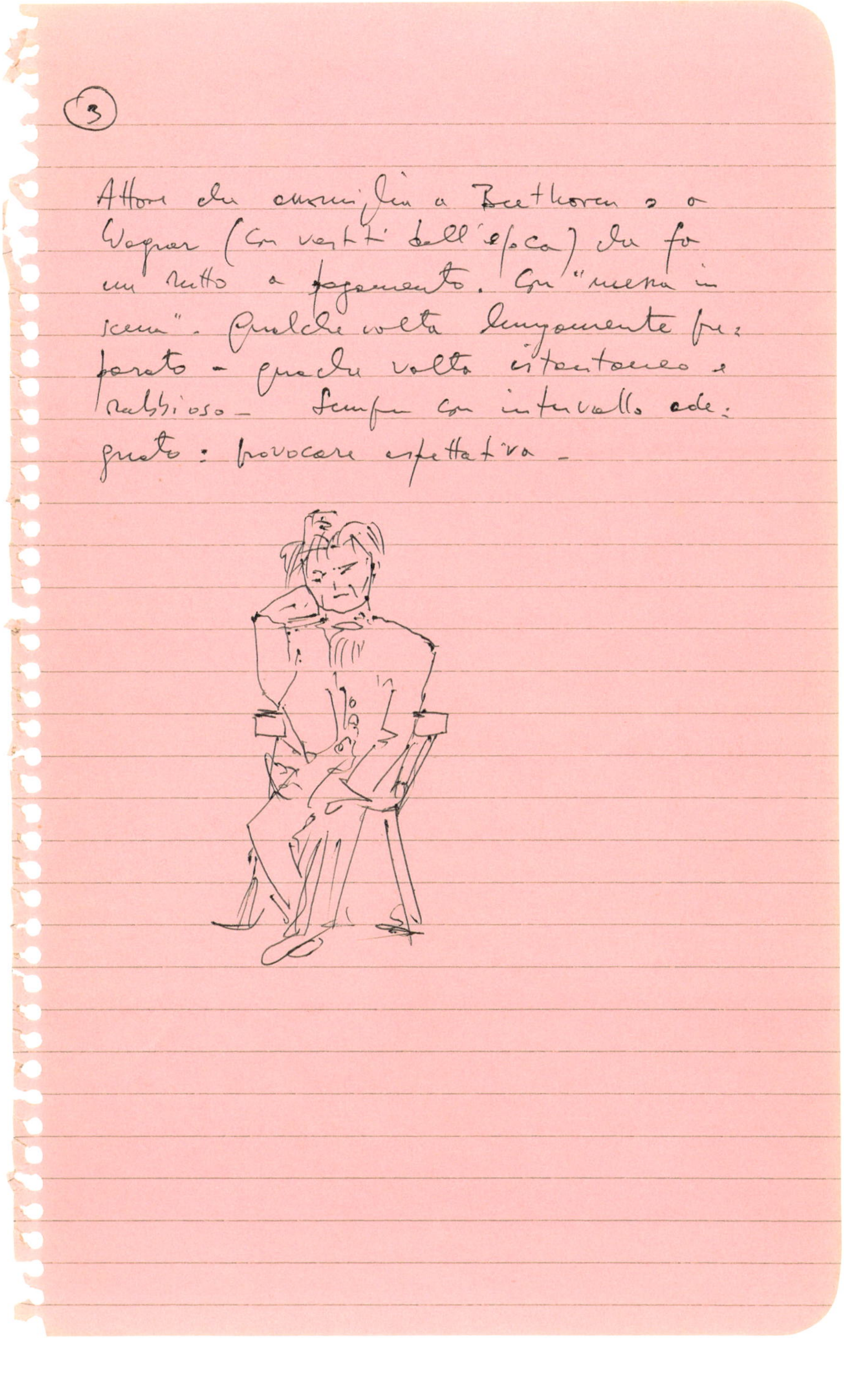

PLATE 1
Luciano Berio, "Amores" (unfinished music theater project from the early 1970s). Handwritten notes, p. 3
(LUCIANO BERIO COLLECTION, PSS)

TRANSCRIPTION
Attore che assomiglia a Beethoven o a Wagner (con vestiti dell'epoca) che fa un rutto a pagamento. Con "messa in scena". Qualche volta lungamente preparato – qualche volta istantaneo e rabbioso – Sempre con intervallo adeguato: provocare aspettativa –

TRANSLATION
An actor who looks like Beethoven or Wagner (in period clothes) who offers burps for sale. With "staging." Sometimes carefully prepared – sometimes instantaneous and rabid – Always with adequate intervals: to provoke expectations –

Following these trails, we can all the more clearly see the "dialogue" with Beethoven in which Berio engaged. Beethoven is the composer of the past mentioned most often by him after Bach, Mozart, Mahler, Debussy, and Stravinsky. It was the last three movements of his String Quartet in C-sharp minor, op. 131, that Berio initially thought of as the *fil rouge* on which to erect the sound framework of the third movement of *Sinfonia* (ultimately built on the Scherzo of Mahler's Second Symphony).[6] It is to Beethoven's music, and specifically to the Piano Trio in C Minor, op. 1, no. 3, that Berio links (almost symbolically) a childhood *souvenir,* the "emotive baptism" at the piano that occurred during the chamber music sessions organized by his father Ernesto in the house at Oneglia.[7] It is Beethoven, through the pages of *Jean-Christophe* by Romain Rolland, that marks one of his early memories as a reader.[8] As a student, Beethoven became the object of orchestration tasks conducted in Giorgio Federico Ghedini's composition class at the Milan Conservatory.[9] And Beethoven, together with Monteverdi, represented for him the epitome of a composer so rooted in tradition and his present as to be able to project his work beyond the boundaries of time.[10]

For Berio, Beethoven is an architect of music who manages to erect "edifices of sound" in which everything speaks of logic, functionality, totality, balance, change, and innovation, from the smallest internal space to the largest external element:

"Think of the most famous example, the *Eroica,* surely one of the most impressive organic creative events in music. He takes you by the hand in exploring this miraculous thing in which the smallest element is connected to the largest. That connectedness for me is one of the most beautiful aspects of communication."[11]

For Berio, it is precisely the *Eroica* that becomes the work that allows him to express in public his love for the "probably greatest revolutionary in the history of music."[12] It is to this Symphony that he dedicates an entire episode, no. 7, of *C'è musica & musica* – the only case of a "deep dive" devoted to a single work by a single composer in this series. Thus, explaining the *Eroica* to a wide television audience becomes a way of packaging the most political and committed episode of *C'è musica & musica:* taken as a symbol of a precise historical period – filled with social changes still more than musical ones – the *Eroica* allows one to speak in a historical perspective (but implicitly projecting everything onto one's present) of the concepts of strength and hope, of a music that is capable of destabilizing conventions and certainties.[13]

The sounds of the *Eroica* and other Beethoven works also resonate in almost all other episodes of the series,[14] with diverse and at times subliminal functions and meanings. A special example may be seen in the relentless condemnation that is subtly directed towards the commercialization of art music in the sixth episode, "Non tanto per cantare" (Not just to sing). During discussions dedicated to songs and pop songs, the sounds of the *Leonore* Overture No. 3 unexpectedly sneak in. They precede a question posed by Berio in a seemingly neutral way: "Someone whistling a Beethoven motif in a bathroom, are they whistling a song or what?"[15] The answer is artfully insinuated by letting the music itself speak. Slowly, the sounds of the overture are overlaid with the honeyed voice of a well-known Italian singer who, using the melody of the *Ode an die Freude* of the Ninth Symphony, intones the insipid words "Lei non sapeva amare, ma era la più bella..." (She did not know how to love, but she was the most beautiful...). From a well-stocked basket of pop songs of the Italian Sanremo Festival, Berio selects one of the most fashionable commercial hits of the time, the *L'inno della gioia* by Johnny Dorelli, the result of

6 See, among others, Luciano Berio, *Two Interviews with Rossana Dalmonte and Bálint András Varga,* trans. and ed. David Osmond Smith (New York: Marion Boyars, 1985), 107–08.

7 Ibid., 46.

8 See, e.g., ibid., 47.

9 Some orchestrations made during his period of study with Ghedini are preserved in the Luciano Berio Collection (PSS).

10 See, for example, his statements in Chad Hardin, "An Interview with Luciano Berio," *Articles* 3, no. 1 (1987): 22–27, esp. 25.

11 Ibid.

12 Berio in Ramon Chao, "Musica y sociedad: Luciano Berio" (interview), *Triunfo* 29, no. 639 (1974): 49–51, at 50 ("el mayor revolucionario, quizá, de la historia de la música").

13 See also in this regard the transcription of the episode in *Una polifonia di suoni e immagini* (see note 5), 84–93.

14 The only exception is the fifth episode, "Mille e una voce," devoted to Cathy Berberian.

15 "Qualcuno che fischietta in una stanza da bagno un motivo di Beethoven, fischietta una canzone o che cosa?" *Una polifonia di suoni e immagini* (see note 5), 81.

a recording made in the wake of the success of Miguel Ríos' *Song of Joy*. Once the sounds of Dorelli-Beethoven have faded away, the camera focuses in with a close-up of Bruno Maderna, who states: "I was really shocked by the *Song of Joy* [...]; it seems to me that this is just slinging mud at any notion of high ideals."[16]

In these words, and in the television montage assembled by Berio, one seems to be able to make out an answer, albeit a veiled one, to the question posed with regard to the Beethoven character outlined in the sketch of "Amores" (which, we remember, was made around the same time as *C'è musica & musica*). And so, another "because" is added as answer to the many elicited by that unspoken "why," one that goes beyond Beethoven himself and his music.

For Beethoven is, to Berio, neither totem nor taboo in terms of "musical language," but in the realm of commercialized music he is made to become both of these things. Thus Berio came to say, in 1981, that "all aspects of the creative process, even the most insignificant ones, have begun to acquire a price: the composer's manuscripts, the composer's glasses [...], the composer's bed, his school report, his house, his chair, his habits, and, naturally, his interviews."[17] The actor disguised as Beethoven in "Amores" adds something more to this list: some vulgar burps for sale.

In a manner absolutely consistent with the implicit denunciation of the commercialization and spectacularization of art characteristic of *Esposizione* (1962–63),[18] the stylized character sheds all his seemingly ironic or iconoclastic significance and is finally seen for what he is: a personified denunciation of commercialism which reveals the most committed face of the composer Luciano Berio.

Angela Ida De Benedictis

16 "[S]ono rimasto veramente *choqué* dalla *Song of Joy* [...]; mi sembra che sia proprio gettare fango in cima a degli ideali." Ibid., 82.

17 Berio, *Two Interviews* (see note 6), 19.

18 In this regard, and for a more general picture of other works that reveal Berio's political commitment, see Angela Ida De Benedictis, "From 'Esposizione' to 'Laborintus II': Transitions and Mutations of a 'Desire for Theatre'," in *Le théâtre musical de Luciano Berio*, ed. Giordano Ferrari (Paris: L'Harmattan, 2016), vol. 1, 177–246.

Cathy Berberian
Trennung von dem Geliebten
(1970s and 80s)

The French philosopher Henri Bergson noted that comedy produces its full effect only where it appeals "to intelligence, pure and simple."[1] Interpreted within this simple theoretical assumption, many of the artistic practices of the twentieth century, though usually branded as secondary, or as recycled art, reveal instead that the boundary line between kitsch and culture is not as nearly marked as some would like to believe. And this is especially so when the figure entering the sphere of the ridiculous, bursting through the main entrance of the stage, is an artist of such remarkable culture as Cathy Berberian (1925–1983). Much may have been written about her, but not enough to completely capture the acuity of those of her performances in which she was able, as a great connoisseur of the "art of bad taste,"[2] to use to maximum effect the tool of "humor" as a subtle means to her ends.

Let's imagine, then, a platinum blonde, her chubby figure – awkwardly disguised – exhibited in satin dresses and dropped into an unlikely *fin de siècle* scene. Complementing on stage the silvery-white of her garments and feathers is the black of a large grand piano and the slender figure of a pianist who, with great devotion, begins one of the most famous Beethoven sonatas: the first movement of the so-called "Moonlight" Sonata (op. 27, no. 2). The audience is captivated by those well-known sounds: in the dramaturgy of the show, they are a doorway towards "mass recognizability" in a context usually reserved for an élite. The sonata continues, but gradually the listeners are disturbed by increasingly obvious gestures of impatience from the singer, tired of remaining in the background of sounds that, judging by her grimaces, she is finding decidedly boring. Gradually, the listener's expectations are directed no longer towards what is actually happening, but rather towards the decidedly unorthodox "something" that is about to occur on stage:

"In the Moonlight Sonata, there is a by-play between the prima donna and her accompanist. She is convinced that the public is interested only in her singing and that the piano prelude, interlude and postlude are best hurried through. The accompanist is determined to reveal the mysteries of pianistic Romanticism and it becomes an open struggle for supremacy ... over his tempi. Needless to say, he wins the first round."[3]

But the final battle is won by the singer who, having overcome the encumbrance of the introduction, wrests the sublime melody from the pianist's right hand, intoning it to the words of the arrangement *Trennung von dem Geliebten* (Separation from the Beloved), created in the mid-nineteenth century by Friedrich Konrad Griepenkerl (SEE PLATES 1, OPPOSITE, AND 2, P. 178). A victory highlighted proudly by the exclamation: "How lucky we are that in this way we have a song that is not wasted merely as a piece for piano!"[4]

Even today, and to the most elitist audience, listening to Cathy Berberian perform this vocal paraphrase of the "Moonlight" Sonata may smack of sacrilege or raise a supercilious smile: in the end, what do we have here other than the "anti-Callas" of the twentieth century who is going so far as to mock, with hedonistic nonchalance, the genius of Bonn – and is doing so without fear of making a mockery of herself? And yet, if we look beyond the veil of

1 Henri Bergson, *Laughter: An Essay on the Meaning of the Comic* [1900], trans. Cloudesley Brereton and Fred Rothwell (New York: Macmillan, 1914), 5.

2 Among the various volumes on the comic and bad taste available in Berberian's library (held only in part at the PSS) those of Gillo Dorfles stand out; among them: *Il Kitsch. Antologia del cattivo gusto* (Milan: Mazzotta, 1968), or *Artificio e natura* (Turin: Einaudi, 1968).

3 Cathy Berberian, introductory text to LP *Cathy Berberian's Second Hand Songs*, live recording of a concert on 17 and 19 October 1980 at the Theater am Turm (Frankfurt am Main) with Cathy Berberian (voice) and Harold Leister (piano) (Frankfurt am Main: Theater Am Tum Edition, 1981, PHL 8104).

4 Berberian in the recital "Second-Hand Songs," recorded by Radiotelevisione della Svizzera Italiana on 9 and 10 January 1975 and broadcast on 3 and 10 February of the same year (video tape recording in the archive of RSI, Lugano, a copy of it in the Cathy Berberian Collection, PSS).

PLATE 1
Friedrich Konrad Griepenkerl, *Trennung von dem Geliebten* for alto and piano, arranged from Ludwig van Beethoven's Piano Sonata in C-sharp minor, op. 27, no. 2 ("Moonlight"), movt. 1. Printed edition (Brunswick: Eduard Leibrock, [1841]), p. 5, photocopy
(CATHY BERBERIAN COLLECTION, PSS)

PLATE 2
Cathy Berberian and Bruno Canino during a performance of the recital "Second-Hand Songs." Film still from the recording of Radiotelevisione della Svizzera Italiana on 9 and 10 January 1975

the smile, and reflect on certain aspects related to both the source chosen for this performance and its position in recitals that Berberian created during the last fifteen years of her career, the meaning of the operation proves to be far sharper than one might imagine.

Trennung von dem Geliebten numbers among the many arrangements for voice and piano from Beethoven's instrumental works.[5] Published in 1841 (together with the Andante of the Piano Sonata, op. 26),[6] this vocal arrangement was not the only one that attracted Berberian's attention. Her archives also contain those of Friedrich Silcher,[7] as well as at least two other Beethovenian *trouvailles:* a choral arrangement by Julia W. Bingham of the first theme of the Violin Concerto, op. 61, entitled *Challenge of Youth;* and a vocal arrangement of the theme of the second movement of the Piano Concerto No. 5, op. 73, adapted for synagogue use: *Yèchaddèsheihu* (*before New Moon*).

Among all these, however, the piece most universally known to a wide audience was indeed the "Moonlight" Sonata, introduced by Berberian into her repertoire around 1971,[8] the inaugural year of one of her best-known recitals: "À la recherche de la musique perdue." Along with perhaps her most famous recital, "Da Monteverdi ai Beatles," "À la recherche" marks a crucial stage in the artist's biography. Conceived of at the turn of the 1960s and 70s, these shows can be understood as true declarations of an earned independence: from being an (ancillary) "instrument" of the New Music, Berberian now used her voice to stage independent ideas, permitting her to construct her own repertoire and her own character. This shift was marked by a thorough research for scores, with the aim of combining music of the past and present. And it was accompanied by an almost manic attention to all aspects of performance: from costumes to stage furnishings, from the choice of titles to the overall "dramaturgy", from lights to colors to props, to the study of her facial mimicry and physical gestures.

From the "reservoir" of music collected for "À la recherche," Berberian then modeled two more recitals during the 1970s. One of these is "Second-Hand Songs," introduced in Paris at the 1973 Festival d'Automne, which was

5 See Helmut Loos, "Zur Textierung Beethovenscher Instrumentalwerke: Ein Kapitel der Beethoven-Deutung," in *Beethoven und die Nachwelt: Materialien zur Wirkungsgeschichte Beethovens*, ed. Helmut Loos (Bonn: Beethoven-Haus, 1986), 117–37. A list can also be found in George Grove, *Beethoven und seine neun Symphonien*, German edn. by Max Hehemann (London: Novello, 1906), 30–32.

6 The date ("September 1841") is taken from the *Hofmeister XIX* online catalog (www.hofmeister.rhul.ac.uk; accessed 8 August 2020).

7 For example, the *Melodien aus Beethovens Sonaten und Sinfonien zu Liedern für eine Singstimme eingerichtet von Fr. Silcher* (Stuttgart: Zumsteeg [c. 1840]), 3 vols.

8 The date is derived from the program of a concert in Berlin on 25 September 1971 (Berliner Festwochen), where Berberian jotted down "Adagio: Sonata Cis Moll (Moonlight)" (Cathy Berberian Collection, PSS). The handwritten note, however, does not reveal whether the piece was actually performed on that occasion or, rather, whether this is merely a note for an extension of the program in future performances. But certainly, this is the first occurrence of the title in Berberian's papers.

dedicated almost entirely to a "degré second" of music.[9] In moving from a *milieu* of "lost" songs to a *mélange* of "second-hand music" (in the sense of "used", but perhaps abused as well), the arrangement of the "Moonlight" Sonata finally found its ideal place: reversing the order, the pseudo-Beethoven of *Trennung von dem Geliebten* moved from the end (in "À là recherche") to the beginning of a program made up exclusively of vocal arrangements of famous pieces, from Bach to Debussy and Ravel.[10] It is with Beethoven that the voice, in appropriating a purely instrumental repertoire, captured the audience's attention right from the opening bars of the concert, leading them on a journey of sound that, through irony, is meant to lay bare "certain vocal vices of the singers of the past" and, at the same time, lighten the mood of the contemporary concert stage by responding with a smile to that "insatiable need to bring amusement back to a musical performance."[11]

Within this *milieu,* the choice of *Trennung von dem Geliebten* represents a paradigmatic example of the singer's performative strategies. Berberian shows herself to be an acrobatic caricaturist, in the sense of one who, "[b]eneath the skin-deep harmony of form, [...] divines the deep-seated recalcitrance of matter."[12] Already in itself, this adaptation constitutes a heavy-handed attempt to dress up, with hollow and stodgy words, a piece of music by Beethoven. But Berberian not only seizes upon the conflict inherent in this material, but even strengthens its significance as kitsch, performing it in a way that pushes it closer to the threshold of overt parody. This is achieved not only with her *fin-de-siècle* stage costumes or her mimicry, but also by playing with the original linguistic context, that of Beethoven as well as Griepenkerl: on a rare occasion in her career, Berberian does not translate but instead sings in German, a language she disliked in performance contexts and almost always avoided, even where the chosen repertoire seemed not to leave other possibilities (just think of Schoenberg's *Pierrot lunaire,* which she sang in three languages with the exception of the original).[13] A mechanism of distortion and disguise is thus activated: one smiles at a German that is stunted and clearly not fluent even to a non-native listener, at times with invented words, and with phrasing broken up by breaths that contradict the musical and textual syntax. All this is seasoned by completely artificial poses and gestures and a farcical displacement of the performative context.

It is through this sophisticated creative comic mechanism that all of Berberian's intellectual and interpretive stature is revealed: the sounds of Beethoven pass from the sphere of the sublime to that of the harlequin in a progressive game of distorting mirrors that, step by step, will restore to the public only "distorted reflections of the original, exactly like the images in the mirrors at Luna Park."[14]

Ladies and gentlemen – Berberian seems to tell us – the moonlight is served, in a dish already used, and it is ready to be applauded. Like the upholstery on stage, so too those sounds are painted papier-mâché, ready to be dismantled at the end of the show, and used for the next concert...

Giovanni Cestino and Angela Ida De Benedictis

9 See the program in the press release of the *Journées de Musique Contemporaines* (Semaines Musicales Internationales de Paris): 18–28 October 1973 (https://www.festival-automne.com/uploads/Publish/archive_pdf/FAP_1973_MU_04_DDP.pdf; accessed 6 August 2020).

10 The recording of this recital (see note 4) inspired our description of Berberian's staging of her performance.

11 Cathy Berberian, remarks to "Second-Hand Songs," program, Rome, Teatro Eliseo, 14 February 1978 (Cathy Berberian Collection, PSS).

12 Bergson, *Laughter* (see note 1), 26.

13 See in this regard Angela Ida De Benedictis, "Arnold Schönberg. *Pierrot lunaire,* op. 21, Druckausgabe des Klavierauszugs mit eingetragenem italienischem Text von Cathy Berberian," in *"On revient toujours": Dokumente zur Schönberg-Rezeption aus der Paul Sacher Stiftung,* ed. Paul Sacher Stiftung (Mainz: Schott, 2016), 163–65.

14 Berberian, remarks to "Second-Hand Songs" (see note 11).

György Ligeti
Le Grand Macabre
(1974–77)

"Beethoven became a musical commodity, just like the pop song and almost everything lying between him and the pop song."[1] György Ligeti made this sober pronouncement in a radio lecture as early as 1959. And this same commodity quality attaches to a seminal Beethoven quotation prominently displayed in his "anti-anti-opera" *Le Grand Macabre,* a work written in the 1970s. Here the Hungarian composer, now teaching in Hamburg, arrived at a post-modern position all his own. In both its subject matter and its music, *Le Grand Macabre* is considered a quintessential piece of pop-art musical theater. Proceeding from Michel de Ghelderode's *La Balade du grand macabre* (1935), the plot, set in a fictitious "Breughelland," introduces a wholly disreputable society intimidated by its ruler Nekrotzar, menacingly posing as Death. In the end it discovers, to its relief, that the apocalypse was only a bluff and life will continue on its merry alcoholic way – for the time being. This grotesque "Dance of Death" takes the form of a stunning series of parodies and polystylistic collages resembling a musical comic strip, its spectrum ranging from Monteverdi to Stravinsky and popular music. Shrill exaggeration of all its elements is part of its raison d'être, as is the explicit reference to Pieter Breughel's painting, *The Triumph of Death.*

One of the most important scenes in the entire opera, also with respect to Ligeti's parody techniques, is undoubtedly Nekrotzar's Entrance in Scene 3, a three-minute *danse macabre* built upon a direct reference to Beethoven. Here an adaptation of the pizzicato theme from the finale of the *Eroica* Symphony becomes the load-bearing layer of a multitier collage (SEE EXAMPLE 1, P. 183). The leaf of sketches for this section shows how Ligeti "twisted" Beethoven's thirteen-note theme into a twelve-tone series while retaining its exact rhythmic shape. The isorhythmic superposition of these two building blocks (thirteen rhythmic pulses, twelve pitches) gives rise to the twelve iterations shown in the upper half of the sketch. Thanks to Ligeti's prescribed tempo, their duration is defined precisely as 1'36", or 3'12" for what eventually becomes twenty-four iterations (SEE PLATE 1, P. 182, AND EXAMPLE 2, P. 183). The E-flat major theme from the *Eroica* is readily recognizable in the unchanging rhythm and in the fact that its melodic contours are largely replicated by the motion of the intervals.[2]

To be sure, the *Eroica* theme, in its dodecaphonic disguise, loses any feeling of affirmation and is presented with fractured irony on many levels. Following a moment of complete silence, it is stated as a bass ostinato which, with limping orchestration, expands from *piano* to multiple *forte* while gradually vanishing beneath the tumultuous cacophony of superimposed layers. These layers are successively introduced and piled up with no apparent coordination. Once the ostinato has been established by three iterations in the low strings and timpani, the next layer appears: a quodlibet played by Nekrotzar's outlandish retinue. The quodlibet, displaying not only polymeter and polytonality but also polytempo, is dispatched into a loop. A solo violin then scratches a "Ragtime two-step" in dissonant *scordatura,* recalling the diabolical violin of Stravinsky's *Histoire du soldat.* This is followed by a syncopated whole-tone dance in the bassoon, a shrill E-flat clarinet with a pseudo-folk "Capriccio," and finally by the madcap twittering of a piccolo. Now a third layer appears, a

1 György Ligeti, "John Cage und die experimentelle Musik in Amerika" [1959], in idem, *Gesammelte Schriften*, ed. Monika Lichtenfeld (Mainz: Schott, 2007), vol. 1, 451–55, 451–55, at 453.

2 Further discussion in Peter von Seherr-Thoss, *György Ligetis Oper* Le Grand Macabre *(Erste Fassung): Entstehung und Deutung* (Eisenach: Wagner, 1998), 276–84. See also Peter Edwards, *György Ligeti's* Le Grand Macabre: *Postmodernism, Music-Dramatic Form and the Grotesque* (London: Routledge, 2017), 84–86.

fanfare-like intervention repeated at irregular intervals, but always unchanged. Theatrically positioned at the door of the auditorium, a Basel drum and a bass trumpet play a fanfare for Nekrotzar's entrance in the manner of a medieval *danse macabre*. The "brutal" drumroll is followed by a trumpet call whose intervallic and rhythmic outlines again recall the *Eroica* theme (**SEE PLATE 1, LOWER HALF, P. 182, AND EXAMPLE 3, P. 183**). That the score expressly calls for a Basel or parade drum at this point has an anecdotal background: during one of his visits to Basel in the 1970s Ligeti was impressed by the town's special form of Carnival, the *Fasnacht*. As he later told the journalist Bálint András Varga: "By chance I heard the Basel *Fasnacht* drums (terrifying! crowds of children drumming away). This experience had a direct (conscious) influence on Macabre."[3] In this way, the Carnival atmosphere and the *danse macabre* parody intersect in the ensemble of drums and winds. And as befits this ambiguity, the scene of Nekrotzar's Entrance, with its exaggerated menace, is announced by two sirens, abruptly followed by the Basel drum with a thirty-second drumroll marked "with great force; very fast roll, penetrating. Play as if insane" (rehearsal number 448).

While the entire opera is dominated by an aesthetic of stylistic parody and pastiche, Ligeti explicitly calls Nekrotzar's Entrance a "Collage" in the score (rehearsal numbers 451–75). Its musical material, and thus the *Eroica* theme, is proclaimed to be a historical commodity and placed in the associational purlieus of junk or random objects, of acoustical scraps from a submerged cultural heritage. Ligeti also viewed this as "a sort of homage to Charles Ives."[4] He only came to know Ives's work relatively late and was excited by his collage technique, which went beyond that of his model Mahler.[5] A note on Ives's prototypical collage pieces *Calcium Light Night*, Fourth Symphony, and *The Fourth of July* is already found in an early version of the *Macabre* libretto.[6] Indeed, there are striking similarities with these models. At the same time, it seems as if the collage, with its rigid ostinato bass and multiple verbatim repetitions of the trumpet fanfare, was also meant to parody the developmental procedures driven to a climax in the *Eroica*.

Still, for Ligeti, Beethoven's music was what might be called his "musical home turf." He gained his first musical experiences from recordings of the overtures and symphony movements, played on his parents' phonograph in the late 1920s. Among them were the opening movements of the *Eroica* and the Fifth, both of which held him spellbound (in those days there was no space on shellac discs for complete symphonies).[7] "In 1933," he recalled, "we already had improved radio sets," and he listened voraciously to live broadcasts of concerts from the metropolises of Bucharest and Budapest, where "there was Beethoven, Beethoven, and Beethoven to be heard."[8] Even then, he "somehow knew" that "a Beethoven symphony from Budapest, on radio, was of a completely different stature" from what he heard when "seated in a symphony concert in Cluj."[9] The standard classical-romantic literature was already "absolutely familiar" to him when he began taking piano lessons at the age of fourteen.[10] Music now arose in his head en route to his lessons: "There was a convenient bus line, but usually I preferred the forty-minute walk, for during that time I could imagine an exactly forty-minute symphony. They were invariably complete three- or four-movement symphonies in a passionately emotional style, as if a Schumann epigone were trying to imitate Beethoven's Fifth."[11] Beethoven also had pride of place when Ligeti was able to gather experience as a performing musician. At the age of sixteen, in an amateur orchestra, he played timpani in several symphonies, though the Third and the Fifth, each with three obligato horn parts, were not among them.[12]

3 György Ligeti, postcard of 3 January 1983 to Bálint András Varga, Archive of the Akademie der Künste, Berlin, Bálint András Varga Collection.

4 *György Ligeti in Conversation with Péter Várnai, Josef Häusler, Claude Samuel and Himself* (London: Eulenburg, 1983), 120.

5 György Ligeti, "Zur Collagetechnik bei Mahler und Ives" [1971], in *Gesammelte Schriften* (see note 1), vol. 1, 285–90.

6 György Ligeti, *Le Grand Macabre*, libretto (György Ligeti Collection, PSS).

7 György Ligeti, "Musikalische Erinnerungen aus Kindheit und Jugend" [1972], in *Gesammelte Schriften* (see note 1), vol. 2, 11–18, esp. 12.

8 Ibid., 14.

9 "'Ja, ich war ein utopischer Sozialist': György Ligeti im Gespräch mit Reinhard Oehlschlägel," *MusikTexte* 28–29 (March 1989): 85–102, at 87.

10 *Träumen Sie in Farbe? György Ligeti im Gespräch mit Eckhard Roelcke* (Vienna: Zsolnay, 2003), 31.

11 Ligeti, "Musikalische Erinnerungen" (see note 7), 16. Many passages copied from Beethoven during those years are found in Ligeti's sketchbooks [1]–[3] (1939–40) (György Ligeti Collection, PSS).

12 *Träumen Sie in Farbe?* (see note 10), 34.

♩= 100 Andante misurato

EXAMPLE 1
Ludwig van Beethoven, Symphony No. 3 in E-flat major, op. 55 (1802–03), movt. 4, mm. 12–19

EXAMPLE 2
György Ligeti, *Le Grand Macabre* (1974–77), rehearsal no. 451

EXAMPLE 3
György Ligeti, *Le Grand Macabre* (1974–77), 1 m. after rehearsal no. 457

PLATE 1 (OPPOSITE)
György Ligeti, *Le Grand Macabre,* opera in four scenes (1974–77). Sketch for Scene 3: Nekrotzar's Entrance (rehearsal nos. 451–75), p. 39
(GYÖRGY LIGETI COLLECTION, PSS)

Given that the score of *Le Grand Macabre* is saturated with parody and irony (both captured in a nutshell in the scene here on display), the question arises as to what meaning attaches to the portentous *Eroica* theme. The *Eroica* is heroic music par excellence, a symphony with both a semantic and an ideological burden, and its wide-ranging implications surely impinge upon the opera. And certainly the Prometheus myth reverberates within the work as a program for emancipatory humanism.[13] But equally inscribed in Beethoven's Third, with its "Marcia funebre," is the theme of death. This seems to be a key associational element. By incorporating the emblematic Beethoven theme in *Le Grand Macabre,* Ligeti takes aim at the *topos* of heroism *per se* and brings off a double ironic fracture: the sublimity of the heroic theme is seemingly shifted to the personification of Death, yet its distortion, and its embedment in the music and stage action, ensure that Death (alias Nekrotzar), for all the explosive bombast of his entrance, remains a fully-fledged anti-hero. In this way, his menacing gestures become an object of laughter, and the fear of death is dispelled. Mortal fear, death, the Last Judgment: these were central lodestars in Ligeti's artistic universe, not only since the *Requiem* (1963–65), for which, incidentally, he was awarded the Beethoven Prize of the City of Bonn in 1967.[14] In *Le Grand Macabre,* the theme is magnified into the grotesque, and death loses its sting.

Heidy Zimmermann

13 See Martin Geck and Peter Schleuning, *"Geschrieben auf Bonaparte": Beethovens* Eroica: *Revolution, Reaktion, Rezeption* (Reinbek bei Hamburg: Rowohlt, 1989).

14 The Beethoven Prize of the City of Bonn was awarded from 1961 to 1992. Ligeti was the third prizewinner after Heimo Erbse (1961) and Milko Kelemen (1963).

Exhibits

LEARNING AND TEACHING THROUGH BEETHOVEN

1 [Plate p. 28]
Henry Brant (1913–2008), String quartet arrangement of Ludwig van Beethoven's Piano Sonata in B-flat major, op. 106 ("Hammerklavier") (c. 1935). Full score fair copy, p. 1, 34.4 × 54.3 cm (open)
(Henry Brant Collection, PSS)

2 [Plate p. 29]
Henry Brant, Two-piano arrangement of Ludwig van Beethoven's *Grosse Fuge* in B-flat major for string quartet, op. 133 (c. 1933). Cover, 31.8 × 25.1 cm
(Henry Brant Collection, PSS)

3 [Plate p. 33]
Edgard Varèse (1883–1965), Lecture delivered on 14 September 1937 in the lecture series "Music as Living Matter," Arsuna Galleries, Santa Fe. Handwritten notes, p. 3, 27.9 × 21.6 cm
(Edgard Varèse Collection, PSS)

4 [Plate p. 34]
Robert Frank (1924–2019), Photograph of Edgard Varèse's desk in New York City (1962), 36.6 × 27.8 cm
(Edgard Varèse Collection, PSS)

5 [Plates pp. 36 and 39]
Bruno Maderna (1920–1973), Orchestration of Ludwig van Beethoven's Piano Sonata in E-flat major, op. 7, movt. 1 (c. 1937–38)
A: 1st full score with annotations by Alessandro Bustini, p. 1, 32.4 × 23.6 cm
B: 2nd full score, p. 1, 32.4 × 23.6 cm
(Bruno Maderna Collection, PSS)

6 [Plate p. 41]
Earle Brown (1926–2002), Analysis of Ludwig van Beethoven's Piano Sonata in E-flat major, op. 81a ("Les Adieux") (c. 1949). Manuscript, pp. 1 and 3, both 27.7 × 21.4 cm
(Earle Brown Collection, PSS)

7
Brochure of the Schillinger House School of Music, Boston (1949). Cover, 22.7 × 15.2 cm
(Earle Brown Collection, PSS)

8 [Plate p. 44]
György Ligeti (1923–2006), *A klasszikus harmóniarend: Összhangzattani példák a barokk és a bécsi klasszikus zeneirodalomból* [The System of Classical Harmony: Examples of Harmony in Music from the Baroque Era to Viennese Classicism] (1956)
A: Handwritten music example from the production showing the opening of Ludwig van Beethoven's Piano Concerto No. 4 in G major, op. 58, 29.8 × 22.2 cm
B: First edition (Budapest: Zeneműkiadó Vállalat, 1956), vol. 1, Cover, 22.7 × 15.8 cm
(György Ligeti Collection, PSS)

9
György Ligeti's faculty identification card for the Zeneművészeti Főiskola [College of Music], Budapest (1952–56), pp. 2–3, 8 × 24.8 cm
(György Ligeti Collection, PSS)

10 [Plate p. 48]
György Kurtág (b. 1926), Analysis of Ludwig van Beethoven's String Quartet in A minor, op. 132, movt. 1 (early 1960s)
A: Table of motifs, 35 × 25 cm
B: Fair copy, p. 1, 35.6 × 25.3 cm
(György Kurtág Collection, PSS)

IDEALIZATIONS

11 [Plate p. 67]
Anton Webern (1883–1945), Diary 1 (c. 1900–06). Entry of or after 6 November 1904, pp. 96–97, 19.4 × 25.4 cm
(Anton Webern Collection, PSS)

12 [Plate p. 68]
Photograph from an unidentified newspaper showing the Schwarzspanierhaus (House of the Black-Robed Spaniards), the building in which Beethoven died, scheduled for demolition (c. November 1903), 12.7 × 18.4 cm
(Anton Webern Collection, PSS)

13 [Plate p. 73]
Charles Ives (1874–1954), Piano Sonata No. 2 ("Concord, Mass., 1840–60") (c. 1915–19). First edition (Redding, CT: C.E. Ives, 1920), movt. 3 ("The Alcotts"), pp. 56–57, 31.3 × 47.7 cm
(Elliott Carter Collection, PSS)

14 [Plate p. 75]
Ivan Wyschnegradsky (1893–1979), "Zhizn' Betkhovena" (The Life of Beethoven) (1918). Handwritten notes: cover and p. 3, both 22 × 36.1 cm
(Ivan Wyschnegradsky Collection, PSS)

15 [Plate p. 78]
Richard Strauss (1864–1949), *Metamorphosen: Study for Twenty-Three Solo Strings* (1944–45). 2nd full score fair copy, with conductor's markings by Paul Sacher, p. 50, 33.5 × 54.4 cm (open)
(Paul Sacher Collection, PSS)

16
Richard Strauss and Paul Sacher in Zurich preparing the première of *Metamorphosen,* given on 25 January 1946 (Photographer: Peter Zimmermann), 12.8 × 16.3 cm
(Paul Sacher Collection, PSS)

17 [Plates pp. 81 and 82]
Rolf Liebermann (1910–1999), *Leonore 40/45,* opera semi-seria (1951–52)
A: Full score fair copy of version 1, prelude, p. 23, 34.1 × 25.7 cm
B: Printed edition of version 1 with handwritten corrections for version 2, Finale, p. 16, 33.8 × 25.2 cm
(Rolf Liebermann Collection, PSS)

18 [Plate p. 85]
George Rochberg (1918–2005), "Passions According to the Twentieth Century" for solo voices, chorus, jazz quintet, wind instruments, percussion, piano, and tape (1967). Draft score, pp. 14–15, both 26.9 × 35.7 cm
(George Rochberg Collection, PSS)

19 [Plates pp . 90 and 91]
Helmut Lachenmann (b. 1935), *Staub* for orchestra (1985–87). Sketches, 2 pp., 35.8 × 53.3 cm (open)
(Helmut Lachenmann Collection, PSS)

20
"Nicht mit Beethoven und nicht vor Späth": Helmut Lachenmann interviewed by Hans Brender, published in *Deutsche Volkszeitung/ die tat* (8 August 1986), p. 11, 25.3 × 36 cm (half-page)
(Helmut Lachenmann Collection, PSS)

STRATEGIES OF REFERENCE

21 [Plate pp. 112 and 114]
Béla Bartók (1881–1945), Piano Concerto No. 3, BB 127 (1945)
A: Sketches for movt. 2, p. 7, 34.2 × 27.3 cm
B: Full score fair copy, p. 22, 37.7 × 28 cm
(Béla Bartók Collection, PSS)

22 [Plate p. 118]
Cristóbal Halffter (b. 1930), String Quartet No. 2, *Mémoires 1970* (1970). Draft score, p. 1, 48.4 × 32.2 cm
(Cristóbal Halffter Collection, PSS)

23 [Plates pp. 121 and 122]
Dieter Schnebel (1930–2018), *Beethoven-Symphonie* for chamber ensemble (1985)
A: Sketch, 14.8 × 20.9 cm
B: Full score fair copy: title page and p. 1, both 34.1 × 26.7 cm
(Dieter Schnebel Collection, PSS)

24 [Plate p. 125]
Aribert Reimann (b. 1936), *Nahe Ferne: Moments to Ludwig van Beethoven's Piano Piece in B-flat major, WoO 60* for orchestra (2002–03). Full score fair copy, p. 16, 59.3 × 41.9 cm
(Aribert Reimann Collection, PSS)

25
Ludwig van Beethoven (1770–1827), Sketches for the Piano Sonata in E major, op. 109 (1820), from the "Artaria 195" sketchbook, p. 62. Facsimile print in *Skizzen zur Klaviersonate op. 109* (Artaria 195), completed by Jürg Wyttenbach, ed. Michael Kunkel (Saarbrücken: Pfau, 2011), 24.1 × 34.1 cm
(Jürg Wyttenbach Collection, PSS)

26 [Plate p. 129]
Jürg Wyttenbach (b. 1935), Completion of *Skizzen zur Klaviersonate op. 109* (Artaria 195) (2005–06), Variations 5a and 5b. Printed edition, ed. Michael Kunkel (Saarbrücken: Pfau, 2011), 24.1 × 34.1 cm
(Jürg Wyttenbach Collection, PSS)

27 [Plate p. 132]
Heinz Holliger (b. 1939), *75th Variation on Variations 5a and 5b by Ludwytt Beetenbach* for piano (2010). 1st fair copy, p. 2, 21 × 29.6 cm
(Heinz Holliger Collection, PSS)

28 [Plate p. 135]
Kaija Saariaho (b. 1952), *Chimera* for orchestra (2019)
A: Sketch, 21 × 29.7 cm
B: Full score fair copy (computer printout), p. 1, 42 × 29.7 cm
(Kaija Saariaho Collection, PSS)

DISTORTION – DISMANTLEMENT

29 [Plate p. 158]
Igor Stravinsky (1882–1971), *Souvenir d'une marche boche* for piano (1915). Facsimile print in *The Book of the Homeless (Le Livre des Sans-Foyer)*, ed. Edith Wharton (New York: Charles Scribner's Son, 1916), pp. [52–53], 33 × 52 cm
(Igor Stravinsky Collection, PSS)

30
Igor Stravinsky, *Chroniques de ma vie* (1934–35). First edition (Paris: Denoël et Steele, 1935), vol. 2, pp. 66–67, 19.2 × 26.7 cm
(Igor Stravinsky Collection, PSS)

31 [Plates pp. 164 and 166]
Mauricio Kagel (1931–2008), *Ludwig van: Ein Bericht,* film (1969–70). Sequence ("Reihenfolge") of scenes, fair copy, 2 pp., 29.1 × 20.7 cm
(Mauricio Kagel Collection, PSS)

32 [D: Plate p. 149]
Six photographs from the filming of *Ludwig van* (Photographer: Brigitte Dannehl), all 23.9 × 18.2 cm
A: Rudolf Körösi, Mauricio Kagel, and Wilhelm Bruck (left to right) filming of the "Music Room" in the "Beethoven House"
B: Beethoven busts made of fat and chocolate in the "Bath Room" of the "Beethoven House" (designed by Dieter Roth)
C: "Laboratory" action with wired pianist (Klaus Lindemann)
D: Günther Böhmert as tour guide in the "Living Room" of the "Beethoven House" (designed by Ursula Burghardt)
E: "Music Room" in the "Beethoven House" (designed by Mauricio Kagel)
F: Detail from the "Garden" of the "Beethoven House" (designed by Ursula Burghardt)
(Mauricio Kagel Collection, PSS)

33 [Plate p. 171]
Louis Andriessen (b. 1939), *De negen symfonieën van Beethoven* for promenade orchestra and ice-cream vendor's bell (1970). Draft score, p. 5, 32.2 × 49 cm
(Louis Andriessen Collection, PSS)

34
Program leaflet of the J. Pzn. Sweelinck Student Orchestra of Amsterdam, conducted by Roland Lieft, Amsterdam, 11 December 1970, 21.3 × 15.1 cm
(Louis Andriessen Collection, PSS)

35 [Plate p. 173]
Luciano Berio (1925–2003), "Amores" (unfinished music theater project from the early 1970s). Handwritten notes, 3 pp., all 23.9 × 15.2 cm
(Luciano Berio Collection, PSS)

36 [Plate p. 177]
Friedrich Konrad Griepenkerl (1782–1849), *Trennung von dem Geliebten* for alto and piano, arranged from Ludwig van Beethoven's Piano Sonata in C-sharp minor, op. 27, no. 2 ("Moonlight"), movt. 1. Printed edition (Brunswick: Eduard Leibrock, [1841]), p. 5, photocopy, 31.4 × 22.9 cm
(Cathy Berberian Collection, PSS)

37
Friedrich Konrad Griepenkerl, Text of *Trennung von dem Geliebten.* Handwritten copy by Cathy Berberian, 27.8 × 21.5 cm
(Cathy Berberian Collection, PSS)

38
Program booklet for Cathy Berberian's recital "À la recherche de la musique perdue" with Bruno Canino (piano). Berlin Festival, 25 September 1971, with Berberian's handwritten note on the arrangement of the "Moonlight" Sonata, 21.4 × 26 cm
(Cathy Berberian Collection, PSS)

39
Fan used as prop by Cathy Berberian in her recitals of the 1970s, 37 cm in diameter
(Cathy Berberian Collection, PSS)

40 [Plate p. 182]
György Ligeti (1923–2006), *Le Grand Macabre,* opera in four scenes (1974–77). Sketch for Scene 3: Entrance of Nekrotzar, p. 39, 34 × 27.1 cm
(György Ligeti Collection, PSS)

Contributors

ESTEBAN BUCH is professor of music history at the École des Hautes Études en Sciences Sociales in Paris. His special field of study is the relation between music and politics. Among his book publications are *La Neuvième de Beethoven: une histoire politique* (1999, Ger. trans. 2000, Eng. trans. 2003) and, most recently, *Trauermarsch: L'Orchestre de Paris dans l'Argentine de la dictature* (2016).

GIOVANNI CESTINO received his master's degree from the University of Pavia with a thesis on Cathy Berberian's performative approach (2014). In 2019 he took his PhD at the University of Milan with a cross-disciplinary dissertation on the relationship between performers and their notational artifacts. He is currently a collaborator at the Centro Studi Luciano Berio.

HERMANN DANUSER is an emeritus professor at the Humboldt University in Berlin and continues to coordinate research at the Paul Sacher Foundation. In 2017–18 he was a visiting professor at the Central Conservatory of Music in Beijing, where he lectured on "Musical Topics." He is currently preparing a book based on these lectures to follow upon *Weltanschauungsmusik* (2009) and *Metamusik* (2017).

ANGELA IDA DE BENEDICTIS is a scholarly staff member and curator at the Paul Sacher Foundation. Until 2013 she taught at various universities in Italy, where she received her *abilitazione* in 2019. Her research focuses on avant-garde music of the twentieth and twenty-first centuries. She has edited the complete writings of Nono (2001), Berio (2013), and Maderna (2020) and published a monograph on radio art (2004).

SIMONE HOHMAIER is a research associate at the State Institute for Music Research in Berlin. Among the subjects of her research and publications are Hungarian music and the Viennese School, including the book *"Ein zweiter Pfad der Tradition": Kompositorische Bartók-Rezeption* (2003) and the essay "Crossing the line: Musikalischer Transfer zwischen Neuer Musik und Popmusik" (2011).

MATTHIAS KASSEL has been a scholarly staff member and curator at the Paul Sacher Foundation since 1995. His research focuses on the composer collections preserved in the Foundation's archive (most recently the works of Mauricio Kagel) and on the digital materials of those collections. In 2018 he published the monograph *Das Auge hört mit: Mauricio Kagels Instrumententheater von "Der Schall" bis "Zwei-Mann-Orchester."*

FELIX MEYER has been the director of the Paul Sacher Foundation since 1999, having previously worked there as a curator. His scholarly interests apply particularly to twentieth-century classical modernism and American music. He has edited several books, most recently *Alberto Ginastera in Switzerland* (with Angela Ida De Benedictis, 2016) and a facsimile of Béla Bartók's *Sonata for Two Pianos and Percussion* (2018).

SIMON OBERT is a scholarly staff member and curator at the Paul Sacher Foundation. His main fields of interest are the contemporary and popular music of the twentieth and twenty-first centuries. Most recently he edited the volume *Re-Set: Rückgriffe und Fortschreibungen in der Musik seit 1900* (with Heidy Zimmermann, 2018). He is also a member of the directory of the Anton Webern Complete Edition.

WOLFGANG RATHERT is professor of musicology at Ludwig-Maximilians-Universität in Munich, with an emphasis on twentieth-century music. His main scholarly interests include the music of the United States, classical modernism, and piano music. His most recent publication is *Musik der USA: Kultur- und musikgeschichtliche Streifzüge* (with Berndt Ostendorf, 2018).

MATTHIAS SCHMIDT has been a full professor of musicology at the University of Basel since 2007. His research focuses primarily on music aesthetics and music history from the eighteenth to the twenty-first century. His most recent book publication is *Eingebildete Musik: Richard Wagner, das jüdische Wien und die Ästhetik der Moderne* (2019).

ANNE C. SHREFFLER has taught at Harvard University as the James Edward Ditson Professor of Music since 2003, having previously served as professor of musicology at the University of Basel. Her research interests include the musical avant-garde, with special emphasis on the political and ideological associations of new music. She has also published on historiography, composers in emigration, performance theory, and contemporary opera.

MICHELLE ZIEGLER is a research associate at the Paul Sacher Foundation, where she works in the D-A-CH research project "Writing Music." She received her PhD from the University of Berne in 2018 with a dissertation on the graphical working methods of the composer Hermann Meier. Her research interests and publications cover such subjects as Mauricio Kagel, Anton Webern, and the materiality of musical writing.

HEIDY ZIMMERMANN has been a scholarly staff member and curator at the Paul Sacher Foundation since 2002. She has published many articles on twentieth-century music and edited several books, such as *Mondrian-Musik: Die graphischen Welten des Komponisten Hermann Meier* (with Michelle Ziegler and Roman Brotbeck, 2017) and *Re-Set: Rückgriffe und Fortschreibungen in der Musik seit 1900* (with Simon Obert, 2018).

Index

This index includes the names of all persons and the titles of all musical works and writings, except for those names and titles cited in bibliographical and similar references. In the case of composers represented by works as well as writings, the works are listed first, followed by the writings. The index omits references to Beethoven's name but includes his compositions. Boldface page numbers indicate a textual commentary on an exhibit.